Edenbank

Edenbank

THE HISTORY OF A CANADIAN PIONEER FARM

OLIVER N. WELLS

EDITED BY

MARIE & RICHARD WEEDEN

Published by
Harbour Publishing Co. Ltd.
P.O. Box 219, Madeira Park, BC V0N 2H0
www.harbourpublishing.com

Cover and page design by Jan Perrier
Editing by Naomi Pauls, Paper Trail Publishing
Front cover photograph of Shelley Weeden in the Edenbank farmhouse ca. mid-1970s
Back cover photograph of David and Geoffrey Weeden in the farm lane ca. mid-1970s
by Norman Williams
Photograph facing title page of the farm home ca. 1940 by Oliver Wells

All photographs and archival material from the Wells archive maintained by Marie and Richard Weeden
unless otherwise credited.
All pen-and-ink drawings by Pat Erickson except: sketch of the big cattle barn ca. 1975 on the contents
page by Molly Pauls; valley view (page 11), root house (page 100), gulls following the plough (from a
photo by Oliver Wells, page 128) by Marie Weeden; interior of big barn (page 45) by Oliver Wells;
pheasants (page 145) from *Game Trails in Canada,* February–March 1940; Oliver Wells Slough (page
149) by Albert Hochbaum; golden eagle attacking Canada goose (page 151) by Allan Brooks.
Map of Cariboo trails on page 6 by Marie Weeden
Map of the Fraser Valley on pages 172–73 by Jan Perrier
Family tree pages 174–75 courtesy of Richard Weeden, Richard Wells, Allen Wells, Sarah Reay and
Barbara Nielsen.

Printed and bound in China through Colorcraft Ltd., Hong Kong

Harbour Publishing acknowledges the financial support from the Government of Canada through the
Book Publishing Industry Development Program (BPIDP) and the Canada Council for the Arts, and the
Province of British Columbia through the British Columbia Arts Council, for its publishing activities.

BRITISH
COLUMBIA
ARTS COUNCIL
Supported by the Province of British Columbia

THE CANADA COUNCIL | LE CONSEIL DES ARTS
FOR THE ARTS | DU CANADA
SINCE 1957 | DEPUIS 1957

National Library of Canada Cataloguing in Publication Data

Wells, Oliver, 1907–1970
  Edenbank : the history of a Canadian pioneer farm / Oliver N. Wells ;
edited by Marie & Richard Weeden.

  Includes bibliographical references and index.
  ISBN 1-55017-303-0

  1. Edenbank Farm (Chilliwack, B.C.)—History. 2. Wells, Oliver,
1907–1970. 3. Farm life—British Columbia—Chilliwack Region—History.
4. Dairy farming—British Columbia—Chilliwack Region—History.
5. Chilliwack Region (B.C.)—History. 6. Chilliwack Region
(B.C.)—Biography. 7. Wells family. I. Weeden, Marie. II. Weeden,
Richard. III. Title.
S451.5.B7W45 2003   630.'9711'37   C2003-910954-2

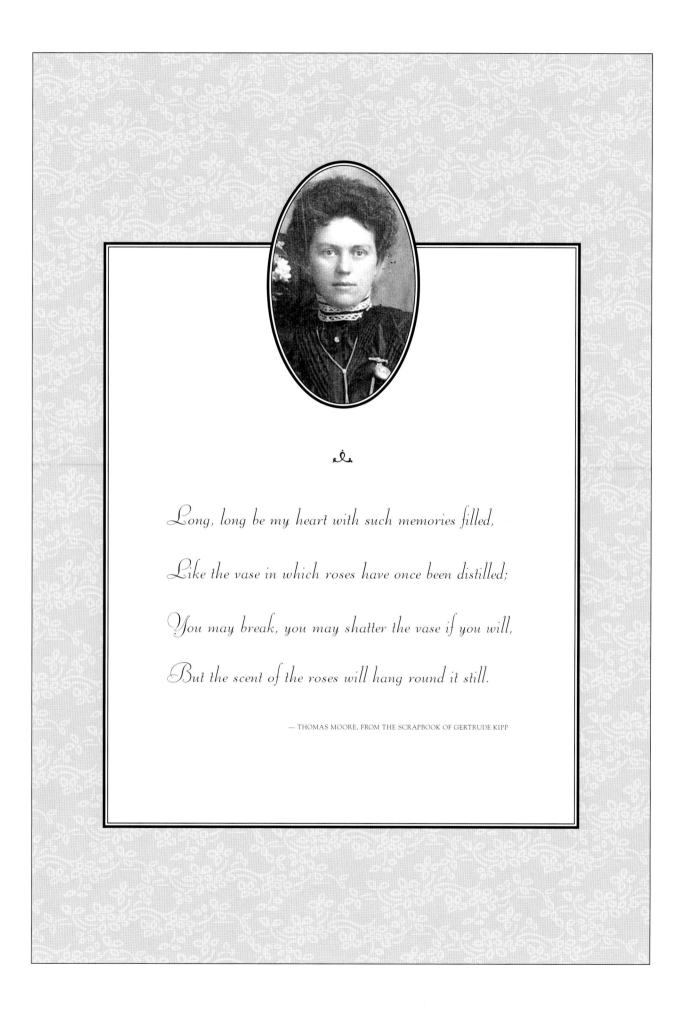

Long, long be my heart with such memories filled,

Like the vase in which roses have once been distilled;

You may break, you may shatter the vase if you will,

But the scent of the roses will hang round it still.

— THOMAS MOORE, FROM THE SCRAPBOOK OF GERTRUDE KIPP

To the pioneer spirit;

to Ron Wells,

the only living grandson

of Allen Wells;

and to our grandchildren,

Chantelle and Kyle Edwards

Contents

Allan Fotheringham as a child at Edenbank, ca. 1940. In the background is the former creamery, the hired man's house, where he and his family were living at the time.

Foreword

BY ALLAN FOTHERINGHAM

*P*icture this. It is 1940 and Edna Fotheringham, with her four young children, is leaving Hearne, Saskatchewan, population 36, getting on a train in Moose Jaw. Neither mother nor brats have ever been on a train. They roll across the broad sweep of the Prairies, through snow-capped mountains they have never seen. Days and nights go by.

Down beside the cascading waters of the Fraser Canyon, the Prairie kids, used only to gophers, are goggle-eyed at the physical roughness of what they see through the train windows. Finally, they arrive in Agassiz, B.C., early in the morning, and take a small ferry across the Fraser, aiming for a rendezvous that will change their lives.

Picture this. Captain Doug Fotheringham, newly assigned at the start of the war to the newly built Camp Chilliwack at Vedder Crossing, notices an ad in the *Chilliwack Progress* from a family – welcoming all the new troops flooding in – who would be pleased to house a "non-drinking, non-smoking" soldier seeking room and board.

His wife and children – I will remember it to this day – arrived on a Saturday morning at Edenbank. It was a lush September day, heavy with sunshine.

The prize-winning cattle were sloshing down in the Luckakuck. Huge Canada geese strutted about beneath the willow trees. Ripe apples and pears were dropping on the ground. I actually thought – I was eight – that we had landed in the Garden of Eden. Being from Hearne, I was stunned.

Oliver Wells was the first "Green." Long before the environmentalist movement was born, he conducted his life – and his career – that way. He, who had never travelled, corresponded with like-minded people around the globe who lived close to the land and loved it and wanted to preserve it. He bred prize cattle, loved birds, loved people of his ilk – I can hear his deep, hearty and throaty laugh to this moment. My brother, now Dr. John Fotheringham, used to snuggle down and sleep with his prize cows at the PNE in Vancouver.

His tragic death in Scotland, on his first and only trip abroad, was of course a major loss not only to his family, to Edenbank, to Sardis and to B.C., but to Canada as a whole. Because he set an example. Of how fine a man could be.

Century-old Edenbank Farm, including the bird sanctuary along Luckakuck Creek, was proposed and approved as a heritage site by B.C.'s Heritage Advisory Board in the 1970s, a designation refused by the provincial cabinet. COURTESY OF NORMAN WILLIAMS

Foreword

BY DOUG NICOL

*M*y earliest experience with Edenbank Farm dates from the late 1970s, when I came to Chilliwack to teach geography at Fraser Valley College. I entered the area for the first time by tracing the route of the Yale Wagon Road around the edge of Sumas Lake, along the route of the B.C. Electric Railway, then through Yarrow and Vedder Crossing. From the main road, I remember Edenbank as a remarkable landscape: a majestic farmhouse like no other I had yet seen in the lower Fraser Valley; a marvellous collection of historic barns and outbuildings; a wildlife sanctuary; a distinctive office building at the roadside; and rolling, verdant land along the Luckakuck.

As the first chairman of the then new Heritage Advisory Committee, I found Edenbank on our agenda immediately, and the history of the farm and its founding family became essential reading for my first summer in Sardis. It wasn't easily found reading; little had been written about the Wellses at that time, other than short passages in a small and undistinguished local history and some newspaper pieces from the past. But the Wellses themselves had been generous in their donations of documents to the local museum and archives. Poring over these, I came to know that the Wells family name was as much a part of the history of the area as the farm was part of the landscape. And when, a short time later, the farm was being touted as a heritage site of provincial if not national significance, I came to realize the appropriateness of such designations. Preparing for such a hoped-for eventuality sent me off reading the context in which Edenbank should be considered . . .

Although the native people of the West Coast were agriculturalists of a sort, the earliest farming in British Columbia is generally considered to be an immigrant experience. Established in 1867, the Wells farm was very much at the vanguard of dairying in the colony and represents some of our earliest farming activity, akin to the important ventures at Fort Langley and Fort Victoria a few decades before. Edenbank, like most dairy farms in B.C., began as a small family farm, but while it remained in the family for over a century, it grew in the early years to be larger than most. And it certainly represented those valley farms that confronted head-on a dairy industry that became more specialized, market oriented and capital intensive. Even before World War I, Edenbank was a large farm and a leading example of the industry in many respects. Though the farm was eclipsed in size in later years, its reputation in dairying remained well-known throughout its history.

This history of Edenbank Farm and of the Wells family portrays the interaction of early settlers with both the land and those who occupied it before them. And while all the Wellses were significant in some respects, Oliver Wells was arguably the most remarkable. Building on the oral traditions of the native people in the area, he became clearly the community's first local historian. His unending curiosity, compelling interest in a range of fields, and breadth of experiences set him apart from both his own family and from the bulk of agriculturalists in the valley. This was an exceptional man, and this book documents very effectively not only his life on the farm in Chilliwack, but his love for the land and his respect for those he interacted with over his lifetime.

Today, those who had any experience of the Edenbank landscape and the roles of the farm and its associated enterprises in the community, or of the Wells family so long associated with them, are only vaguely reminded of any of this by the modern signboard and glimpses of the elegant old farmhouse now almost completely hidden behind the walls and gates of an upscale residential complex on Vedder Road. Those who have never heard of the place and do not purposefully seek out its history will find little evidence in what is left today. For those, this book will be invaluable in reconstructing a place that was outstanding by many measures and that, without doubt, should have been saved as a heritage site. This would have been a rare example of a Canadian working dairy farm, dating from Confederation.

But this book is equally if not more important for what it says in other ways. It tells us much about the pioneer immigrant experience generally and gives us wonderfully detailed accounts of how that experience played out in the upper Fraser Valley. It documents the history of a United Empire Loyalist family from Ontario whose father – like many others – came for the gold rush, abandoned that myth, saw wider opportunities and pursued them with persistence, at times in the face of untold difficulties. It recalls the achievements accomplished at Edenbank over the century, the innovations it represents, and the way of life that was carved from the forests of the Fraser Valley and moulded by a truly remarkable family.

Sara and Oliver Wells enjoyed their mountain rides. They became engaged on top of Liumchen Mountain and subsequently married, in 1931. Oliver took over management of Edenbank Farm from his father, Edwin, in 1939. He witnessed and recorded many changes in the dairying industry during his lifetime.

Introduction

Two hundred years ago the eastern Fraser River valley was carpeted by a forest of towering Douglas fir and first-growth cedar. It lay unburdened by houses and washed over by clean, clear air. The Cheam Range of the Cascades rose above the surrounding hills. The fast-flowing Fraser and the smaller Chilliwack River surged through this quiet valley towards the sea. The valley was inhabited only by local native people, the Stó:lō, who had been living in its foothills for nearly as long as the river had flowed.

Passing through this valley in the mid-nineteenth century en route to the Cariboo goldfields, men like my great-grandfather Allen Wells observed a few lush natural meadows amongst the dark forests. Later these men came back to explore the rich valley land and to establish small homes for themselves and their families, eventually opening up fields and building barns for livestock. They drove cattle up from the Whatcom area of the United States over ancient trails, often struggling around deadfalls and through heavy underbrush and mud.

Allen felt fortunate to make his new home in this pristine valley. As the heavy burden of land clearing began, he forged a strong bond with this place. During the long workdays these pioneers single-handedly cleared woods into meadows and split trees into fence rails using simple tools – brush hooks, shovels, axes and saws. Young wives and new babies soon arrived, and a close-knit community of friends began to develop. By long days of labour working the fertile soil with worn and toughened hands, the work slowly progressed.

His son, Edwin, and my father, Oliver, inherited Allen's love of the land. Eventually Oliver began to write the story of our family's history and the development of a productive farm. I can recall my father sitting in front of a warm fire lit in the dining-room grate, perhaps with a woollen sweater draped over his shoulders, reading old records and diaries and, with pen in hand, composing the farm's story. As the weeks went by he talked with his usual infectious enthusiasm about his project.

He tried to recall in his writing the way things had been for the pioneers. He had a deep urge to tell how the land had changed and how farming in the valley had developed. He wished others to join in imagining Allen's journey from the quiet of the dark barn where the cattle were settled for the night at the end of a satisfying day. How, lantern in hand, he would make his way towards the lamp that Sarah had placed in the window in the kitchen, where supper would be simmering on their wood stove.

Through his research and because of his own friendship with his native neighbours, he knew personally the bond that existed between the two peoples. He respected the wisdom of the Stó:lō, who often accompanied Edwin and his boys into the hills and mountains and knew the valley so intimately. His summer trips into the Liumchen Mountain range with Chief Billy Sepass were among his fondest memories.

Oliver had grown up listening to tales of the old days. He knew it had been an exhausting and hard life. But he also knew that his grandfather and others had persevered while some had given up and returned to the east. He loved the old horse stories, the family legends, the precious memories of his mother, who died quite young, and as he himself worked the land he was a completely contented man. In his spare time he made notes, he wrote to former farm employees, he tape-recorded memories of some of the old-timers, and then he set about trying to write it all down.

In Canada's centennial year, 1967, he finally completed his story. It was also the hundredth anniversary of Edenbank Farm. By this time it was a green and productive landscape pasturing black Aberdeen Angus beef cattle and handsome North Country Cheviot sheep. Much of the foundation stock had been imported from Scotland, where Oliver believed some of the greatest livestock were still to be found. In his memory, he could still see his beloved Ayrshires munching those same pastures – those elegant and sleek red and white cattle he had nurtured and loved and helped develop into championship breeding stock but eventually parted with in 1962.

My father wanted to preserve in written form the success and legacy of Edenbank. He wanted, I believe, to show how one family, like so many other farm families at the time, strove so diligently to achieve the richness of life that comes from working intimately with the soil and with livestock. I feel he wished to portray, as he himself had underlined in his farm library book *Great Farmers,* how "a great constructive breeder of livestock . . . had a very definite ideal type clearly in mind . . . 'stuck' to his own notions with quiet but stubborn persistence, listening to other men's opinion, arguing rarely for his own, but going in the end, his own way." That quote personified my father – his agricultural career and his subsequent writings.

Always wisely looking to the future, Oliver decided in 1967 to encourage his family to share in planning and financing the operation of the farm. With monetary assistance from the family, my father was able to continue as general manager of the operation, and a new arrangement provided him freedom from worry. He and my mother, Sara, remained living and farming at Edenbank while he continued the breeding programs for the Black Angus and North Country Cheviots. Their home continued to be a centre of welcome to friends, neighbours, environmentalists and agriculturists. Oliver carried on with his research into local history and native language, spending many days and hours in this enjoyable pursuit.

Among other activities, he was instrumental in starting the Chilliwack Historical Society. He taped interviews with native friends and elders and recorded stories and legends they shared with him. Many of these conversations were subsequently transcribed and published as *The Chilliwacks and Their Neighbors* (Talonbooks, 1987). Oliver assisted the local native women in reviving their traditional Salish weaving. He was also able to devote more time to working in and improving the wildlife sanctuary he had established in the 1930s on the gravel bars adjacent to the Luckakuck, the stream in front of the farm.

Tragically, my father's final years were cut short. He died in a car accident in Scotland on November 1, 1970. My mother and I were with him. We had just visited a farm in Aberdeen, from where he had first imported his Angus cattle. It was a joy to see the respect and mutual understanding with which he and his friend Mr. McPherson discussed their cattle breeding programs. As he notes in this book, there was a great fraternity between stock breeders. We were heading farther north to visit with Alister and Margaret Clyne at Field of Noss in Wick, Caithness, to see their fine flock of North Countries grazing on the high Scottish plateau above the North Sea.

We did not make Wick. On that narrow, winding road north we were involved in an accident. Oliver lived for a few days afterwards – long enough to ask me to pass on his love to each of his grandchildren and to warmly hold my hand. His beloved Sara had no doubt of her place in his heart.

It is over thirty-two years now since that date, and I have now lived for four years longer than my father. Yet in my heart, as I write these sentences, it is yesterday again on that winding narrow road by the cold North Sea. And I remember so well the warmth in our automobile as we travelled that route together. The beech trees along the undulating stone fences beside us were massive yet elegant and their huge pewter-grey trunks like satin. Often their branches met above us.

After our sad return to the Chilliwack Valley and to Edenbank, our family, together with Dad's friends and neighbours, planted a hedge of beeches in Dad's memory along the angled western boundary of the farm. These trees are now a great height and have been nurtured by our good neighbours, the Friesens. They form a solid and living memorial to a strong and solid Canadian.

This manuscript, written so long ago, has been edited lovingly by both myself and my husband, Richard (Dick)Weeden. With great gratitude we acknowledge the support and assistance of many friends and professionals who have continuously encouraged us to complete this project when we became discouraged that it would ever be done. There is a special page of acknowledgements at the back of the book. The editing of the manuscript started some twenty or more years ago. We have had scholars and historians look carefully at the manuscript during this time. They made suggestions and corrections that have been incorporated. The text itself has been edited in an attempt to retain the style of Oliver's writing but at the same time make it more palatable to modern readers. Some family history was removed to make the story of wider interest. His transliteration system has been used throughout to allow the reader to more easily pronounce native place names and personal names.

Almost four decades have passed since Dad's words were penned to paper. It was Oliver's pleasure to write down these memories of our valley's past and the farm's history, which needed to be told. It has been our pleasure to humbly complete his task.

Marie Weeden
January 12, 2003

CHAPTER 1

Adventure Calls

Awild new land it was, the young colony of British Columbia in the mid-nineteenth century, known only to the natives and to fur traders until the discovery of gold precipitated an influx of miners into this land of raging rivers, towering mountains and lowland meadows. Word spread quickly. Thousands of men who dreamt of easy wealth joined in the rush for gold in the Cariboo region. They made their way upriver during the four years after news of the discovery of gold on the sandbars of the Fraser River reached the outside world in 1858. From the gold-fields of California and Oregon many pushed north on foot through the Washington territory, where their inroads into the country were partially responsible for the Indian wars then taking place. Many miners came by ship from San Francisco and Victoria.

Scores of them drowned in the impetuous Fraser, when floating debris and snags rammed their boats or capsized their canoes caught in the grip of treacherous undercurrents. Their passing went unnoticed, but news of the wealth of the country reached and stimulated the interest of established families of Canada West and Canada East living along the St. Lawrence River.

In the spring of 1862, my grandfather Allen Wells, a young man from one such family, sat quietly as a passenger in a native river canoe. He had embarked from the settlement of New Westminster en route to the goldfields of the Cariboo. The canoe made steady progress against the strong current of the Fraser, paddled by a native guide who deftly stroked his paddle.

The young Allen Wells in Napanee before he headed west via the Panama to the new Colony of British Columbia at the age of twenty-five. COURTESY OF CHILLIWACK ARCHIVES

It silently skimmed over the quiet yet rippling surface of the river. Before them a broad expanse of water disappeared from view, obscured by the morning mist. The river seemed a sleeping giant. It was in full freshet, but with the tide moving upstream, the river's current had lost some of its power. Only the soft roll of the undercurrents, their eddies occasionally coming to the surface, tested the strength of the paddler.

For centuries the native paddler's forebears had used the Fraser's great waterway as their main source of food and for travel. One hundred miles upstream at "the falls," where the town of Yale was to rise, was a great salmon fishery. Native people of every village set their course towards Yale during the summer months. Each fishing season more than two thousand canoes breasted this strong current to carry the *STAW-loh* (Stó:lō)[1] or river natives to their summer camps in the canyon of the Fraser, where they caught and dried salmon for their winter supply of food.

In fall and winter months the river was also used by war parties of Coastal tribes who raided the *STAW-loh.* Because of the gold rush, the river was dotted with canoes as it had been of old but now the strong, measured strokes of the native paddlers transported miners with their supplies. Excitement was in the air. The gold rush to the Cariboo was on! Although steamships and paddle wheelers had been plying the river as far as Fort Langley for some time, never had there been the demand for transportation service that there was now. Every native was taking advantage of earning money.

Coastal tribes used the Fraser River as a means to raid Stó:lō villages. PAINTING BY PAUL KANE, 1846. COURTESY OF STARK MUSEUM OF ART

Allen Wells was one like thousands of others who started west to the goldfields from Upper Canada. Armed with a strong spirit of adventure, he wished to try his luck gold mining and eventually carve out a place of his own in this unknown yet promising land. The surrounding foothills, with their unbroken stands of giant evergreen trees, seemed to express the magnitude of this unknown country, and to him its unlimited possibilities. He came from Napanee, where a generation earlier, timber had meant success and prosperity.

Here, within his gaze, he saw an abundance of timber on hills towering above the obviously fertile soil that lay just above the flood tide on which their frail craft travelled. Who was this lone traveller? Not a seasoned

As Allen journeyed east from New Westminster he hired a native canoe guide to take him as far as the Harrison River.

miner, nor a migrant. Allen had come from a family of United Empire Loyalists, men and women whose sense of patriotism to the British Empire had brought them north from New York and other eastern states into Upper Canada during the Revolutionary War. Earlier many of the Loyalists, who were Puritans, had fled to the New World for religious freedom.

Allen had been born in 1837. His father, also named Allen Wells, was a farmer of Napanee. His mother was Martha Casey. Her grandfather William Casey, a Loyalist, had come north to Canada with a brother in 1780. Young Allen, christened Allen Casey, had married Sarah Hodge of Denmark, New York, in May 1856 and for three years they had made their home at Newburgh, Canada West, where he was engaged in the harness trade with his brother John. Napanee and Newburgh were centres of culture where schools had been established under the guidance of the Wesleyan Methodist Church. Temperance, a factor in the founding of Newburgh, was supported by the formation of societies such as the Society of Total Abstinence and the Newburgh Sons of Temperance. The lessons of dignity and sobriety were so deeply ingrained in Allen's mind that they were later to prove him worthy of the tribute paid to him by the Reverend Edward White, "He is incorruptible and will always remain so."

Also deeply ingrained in Allen's nature was a desire to strike out on his own. With enthusiasm he responded to the popular call "Go west, young man, go west!" At twenty-five years of age, he left his new

The first town of Barkerville as it looked to Allen when he arrived from his trek of three hundred miles north hoping to find gold. Established in 1862 and soon B.C.'s largest community, it was largely destroyed by fire in 1868 but subsequently rebuilt. COURTESY OF B.C. ARCHIVES, A-00355

bride behind and ventured forth into the great unknown. He travelled via New York, through the Isthmus of Panama, then overland to San Francisco, by ship to Victoria and on to New Westminster via steamer. That journey in 1862 would have been a long and difficult task.[2]

From New Westminster he struck out alone with his native guide up the Fraser River intent on reaching the goldfields of the Cariboo. Fort Langley, outpost of the Hudson's Bay Company's fur trade empire, eventually came into view. The guns of the fort had been used twenty-four years earlier to disperse raiders from the Coastal tribes. The fort protected local natives and made the river a safe place for trading in furs. Farmlands and livestock were visible in close proximity to the fort.[3] As their canoe passed beyond the fort, the river again became a giant force cradled in a wide valley between the mountains of the Coastal range.

Big Jim, Allen's guide, deftly swung the canoe, as occasion demanded, to take advantage of quieter waters. As the Coast Mountains confined the river, the current stiffened and the ominous roar of the Fraser River in freshet must have brought a feeling of awe-

some wonder to the lone traveller. He must have marvelled at the skill with which his pilot pitted his strength against the river's current.

Occasionally Big Jim edged the craft into the perimeter of a giant whirlpool, which hurled them upstream in a great sweep. Gradually the river's current grew even stronger. Big Jim, whose tribal name was *shee-AHT-luhk*, swung his canoe into the deep water close to the rocky bluffs of Sumas Mountain, where they found the current to be slower. Soon the main current had to be breasted again as he set a course to cross the river's main channel. This strenuous and dangerous feat brought the reward of an easy passage up the quiet waterway of Nicomen Slough, where the Fraser flowed during periods of high water.

Opposite the mouth of the Chilliwack (*ch.ihl-KWAY-uhk*) River, Big Jim crossed the main channel again, then, allowing for drift, entered the mouth of the Chilliwack. Along these banks his tribe had lived for many years. Here, at his home village of *skwiy-HAH-lah* (Squiala), the native showed his passenger his sleeping quarters, shared a meal with him and indicated they would leave at sun-up.

That night, surprisingly to him, Allen heard the

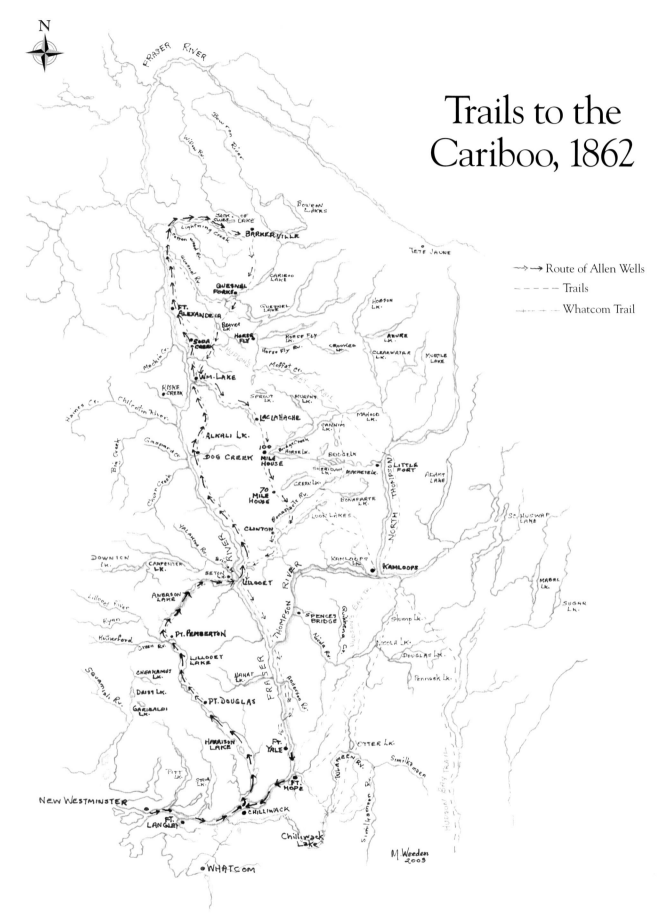

Trails to the Cariboo, 1862

➝ ➝	Route of Allen Wells
– – –	Trails
–·–·–	Whatcom Trail

sounds of cattle and learned that settlers had already taken up land here on the Chilliwack prairie. In the morning they were off again. *Shee-AHT-luhk* exerted his powerful frame to send the craft across the mighty Fraser in order that he might deliver Allen to the Scowlitz tribe, whose great river canoes would transport him up Harrison River and Harrison Lake to Port Douglas. Thus Allen pressed on towards the goldfields, but as he left the banks of the Chilliwack, an image of rich level farmland, already growing tremendous crops of wild hay, was indelibly fixed in his mind.

Shee-AHT-luhk paddled the canoe up the Harrison River to the village of Scowlitz (*SKAW-lihts*). Here, several long cedar-plank native houses had been converted into welcome stopping places for canoe travellers. Men were leaving the houses and assembling their supplies on the riverbank, preparing to load big canoes for the trip to Port Douglas. These canoes would carry ten men and half a ton of freight. Six paddlers took their places as each canoe entered the slow-flowing water. Their even strokes, spaced by the rhythm of their

> **A. C. WELLS,**
> **Saddler and Harness Maker,**
> **YALE, B. C.,**
> HAS CONSTANTLY ON HAND A FULL ASSORTMENT OF
> **Saddles, Harness, Whips, Collars, Fittings, Leather, &c.,**
> which he will sell at the Lowest Possible Prices for
> **C A S H.**
> MAKING and MENDING done with promptness and efficiency.
> ORDERS from all parts of British Columbia solicited.
> Yale, B. C., March 27, 1865.　　　　ap1tc

Allen sold his claim, "Wake-up-Jake," for a grubstake and returned from Barkerville on foot. In 1864 he opened a harness shop in Yale (advertisement above).

canoe song, drove the heavy craft steadily up the short river into Harrison Lake. A challenging paddle up the lake followed and as night fell, the song of the paddlers could be heard at the head of the lake, where Allen found himself in a boom town, Port Douglas.

The Royal Engineers had laid out the townsite and built a church, St. Mark's. Allen likely looked up the parson rather than the bartender, for next morning his travelling companion was an Anglican minister. They had much in common: no money to pay packers, a vocabulary void of blasphemy, a determination to press on up the trail, and a shared respect for the Sabbath, the day on which they rested.

The trail to Barkerville, close to five hundred miles, began here for Allen at Port Douglas. It had been built in 1858 by five hundred miners brought from Victoria on the Hudson's Bay Company's steamer, the *Otter*. Each man had pledged a bond of five pounds for the privilege of working on the trail. They were supplied with meals only and had to promise to stay with the job until the trail was completed to Lillooet.[4] There they would receive a grubstake to go on to the

The fledgling town of Yale in 1858 at the time of the influx of thousands of gold-seekers. COURTESY OF B.C. ARCHIVES, A-03579

Sarah Manetta Hodge, wife of A.C. Wells, was born in New York State. She met Allen and his brother John at a boarding house in eastern Canada where she and her sister were living. Allen was fond of telling how he and his brother, at the request of the landlady, went to assist two young ladies in the same boarding house to lay down a carpet in their room, which resulted in two weddings – of the two brothers, Allen and John, to the two sisters, Sarah and Catherine. Photo taken ca. 1859. COURTESY OF CHILLIWACK ARCHIVES

Cariboo. Mules had been brought to assist them in the heavier work, but mostly they used pick and shovel. Thirty-three bridges were built over the seventy miles of trail. At Seton Portage, the men built a wooden railway so mules could pull cars full of freight from one lake steamer on to the next. These steamers had been built on-site at three lakes. They were the *Melanie* on Lillooet Lake, the *Lady of the Lake* on Anderson and the *Champion* on Seton Lake.[5] These boats saved men like Allen from having to hire a canoe as they followed the trail. There were twenty work crews, each one under the command of a captain of the Royal Engineers.

A stagecoach with a four-horse team on the Cariboo Trail. The BX stage raced along the rocky route from Yale to the northern goldfields, stopping every thirteen miles for a change of team. Allen Wells made the harness used for the first team. COURTESY OF VANCOUVER CITY ARCHIVES

Allen walked most of the entire five hundred miles of that rough trail to Barkerville carrying his heavy supplies on his back. Arriving at Barkerville, he staked and worked his own claim, but failed to strike it rich.[6] He turned to construction work to maintain himself but eventually, tired of that life, he traded his claim to two Americans for a grubstake which he expected would take him back to civilization again. In 1863, he returned via the tortuous Fraser Canyon route to Yale. The trail was difficult, the weather turned foul, and Allen, accompanied by Mr. John Forsyth, who was previously a neighbour of Allen's in Newburgh, Ontario, made very slow progress.[7] Food ran out altogether while three days' travel still lay ahead. Fortunately, one of the party shot a bear and its hind shank was the men's daily menu for three rugged days of travel along the narrow canyon trail.

At Yale, Allen discovered there was a demand for a skilled harness maker and he lost no time in getting started in his old trade. Settling in Yale, he sent for his wife, Sarah, to join him when he had a home ready. The American Civil War was being bitterly contested when Sarah, accompanied by Allen's sister, Jane, along with Susan Forsyth (John's wife) and her sister, left their Ontario homes to go west. On a similar route to that taken by Allen, they travelled by way of New York and Panama, crossing the isthmus on a narrow-gauge railway (built in 1855), then by ship to San Francisco and finally on to Victoria. There, Allen met Sarah and brought her to their new home in Yale. Jane Wells also settled in Yale with her brother Allen and Sarah. It was 1864.[8]

While residing in Yale, Jane fell in love with and married Charles Evans, local magistrate and the bookkeeper for the Barnard Express Company. This company had been preparing for the opening of the Cariboo Road, and its horses and stagecoaches were ready to go into service.

J.W. Winson walked the old Cariboo road from Yale in 1926 and took an excellent series of photos. This one shows the sturdy rock work done by the Royal Engineers. Note the well-worn footpath. The Alexandria Bridge was being rebuilt at the time. COURTESY OF NEIL SMITH

In his small harness shop, Allen must have taken pleasure in working again with heavy leathers creating harness, bridles, lines and strong tugs for these handsome new stages. People described them as the autocrats of the road.[9] Allen was asked to make the harness for the team that pulled the first four-horse coach over the Cariboo Road in 1863. The route started in Yale, then passed along the edge of the Fraser Canyon to Spences Bridge, Clinton and on to Soda Creek. Robert Stevenson, partner of "Cariboo" Cameron and later to become a neighbour of Allen, was a passenger in that first stagecoach. He watched Allen make the final adjustments to the harness for the driver, Charles Major, whose capable hands were to handle the lines that would control this first team to speed a stagecoach over the new road. With the opening of the road in 1863, Yale was fast becoming a centre of trade. Located as it was at the head of navigation, it was now the gateway to the Interior. ᘛ

CHAPTER 2

A Lovely Valley

J K. Lord, naturalist to the Boundary Survey Commission of 1858–60, first described the beauty of the Chilliwack Valley. His description is given here.

These large grassy openings, or prairies, are situated near the Fraser River, on the Western side of the Cascade Mountains. Small streams wind and twist through these prairies like huge water snakes, winding out here and there into large glassy pools.

The scenery is romantic and beautiful beyond description. Towering up into the very clouds as a background, are the mighty belts of the Cascade Range, their misty summits capped with perpetual snow, their craggy sides rent into chasms and ravines, whose depths and solitudes no man's foot has ever trodden; and clad up to the very snow-line with pine and cedar trees. The Chilukweyuk River washes one side of the prairie.[10]

View from the foothills overlooking the Chilliwack Valley.

In his next chapter, Lord depicts in vivid terms the enchantment of this wild new land in late summer.

My canvas house is pitched in a snug spot, overshadowed by a clump of cottonwood trees growing close to a stream, that like a liquid crystal ripples past in countless channels, finds its way between massive boulders of trap and green-stone, rounded and polished until they look like giant marbles.

Towering up behind me are the Cascade Mountains. Before me, stretching away for about three miles is an open grassy prairie, one side of which is bounded by the Chilukweyuk River, the other by the Fraser. At the junction of the two streams, at an angle of the prairie, stands a Native village, the rude plank sheds and rush lodges; the white smoke, curling gracefully up through the still atmosphere, from many lodge fires; dusky forms of the savages as they loll and stroll in the fitful night, give life and character to a scene indescribably lovely.

The "Indian" summer is drawing to a close; the maple, the cottonwood and the hawthorn, fringing the winding waterways, like silver cords, intersecting the prairies, assumed their autumn tints; and clad in browns and yellows, stand out in brilliant contrast to the green of the forest. The prairie looks bright and lovely, the grass, as yet untouched by the frost's fairy fingers, waves lazily; wild flowers of varied tints peep out from their hiding places, enjoying to the last the lingering summer.

Two years after Lord pitched his tent, Allen had stayed overnight at *skwiy-HAH-lah,* the village mentioned by Lord. There, he had seen cattle grazing on land cleared by Jonathan Reece and Isaac Kipp, men whom he later met at Yale. By 1865, the road to the Cariboo was well used and thousands of people were

The paddle steamer Onward *taking on freight at Emory Bar, near Yale, B.C., ca. 1870.* COURTESTY OF B.C. ARCHIVES, A-00102

flocking into the interior of the country. An unprece-dented demand arose for food supplies and for freight teams. Reece and Kipp along with others had already purchased land and began raising cattle, realizing that the true wealth of the country was in the gold of the earth – the products of the soil.[11]

Charles Evans, Allen's brother-in-law, also realized what an asset farmland might be in supplying require-ments for a stagecoach business. He successfully pur-chased a previously pre-empted large tract of land about 1865 that lay between two tributaries of the lower Chilliwack River. This area had been originally pre-empted by John Corry in 1863 and David Seaton in 1864. Both Charles and Allen were frequent trav-

ellers back and forth between Yale and the valley by paddle wheeler. Working together they began to estab-lish the Evans farm.

On a ridge at the Evans place stood a little log cabin, built earlier by Royal Engineers doing a boundary sur-vey in 1858–59. Assisted by Allen, Isaac Kipp and John Forsyth, Charles started to build barns on his property and then a more adequate home. The small engineers' cabin, which remains a designated historic building restored by the Evans family in 1952, was used by Allen Wells when he was managing the Evans farm for his sister and brother-in-law.[12] Past this cabin moved the cattle drives of Reece and Kipp as they came north off the Whatcom Trail. Miners from the

U.S.A., en route to Yale, passed this way. Surveyors, telegraph trail workers, natives and missionaries – all moved along the trail that ran near the little cabin on the ridge.

These narrow, difficult valley trails passed through heavy timber over rough hillsides and through precarious wetland tracts. Some of the nearby land was inhabited by the Chilliwack natives, who earlier in the century had been living in the more mountainous regions of the southeastern Fraser Valley. These hills had provided a haven from marauding Cowichans and Coastal tribes. The Chilliwacks eventually moved to the flat land and on occasion received armed protection from Fort Langley. As every pioneer would testify, the success of their own endeavours often depended upon the help and co-operation of their native neighbours. They were loyal friends and excellent craftsmen.

Allen must have been happy at last to be on the land. Before the end of the year 1866, he was raising cattle for Charles and sending horses from the farm to the Barnard Express Company at Yale.[13] The land was rich in nutrients and ready for the plough, but being so near the Fraser was unfortunately subject to regular flooding. Eventually Sarah and their daughter Lillie, who had been born

Charles Evans, who met and married Allen's sister Jane in Yale.
COURTESTY OF CHILLIWACK ARCHIVES

in Yale in March 1865, joined Allen at the Evans farm. High water came in spring of 1865 and much of the lower land of the Evans farm was flooded. Buildings thereafter were constructed on higher land, above the average high-water level.

During his time at the Evans farm, Allen was making plans and took first steps towards establishing a farm of his own in this fertile valley. As usual the river waters rose very high again in the freshets of the spring of 1866, and Allen became more resolved to have land of his own well above the high-water line.

One fine spring morning, the little log cabin at the Evans farm was astir with excitement. "Big Jim will be here with a canoe after breakfast," Allen told Sarah. "Today, I am going upstream to find land, and we will build a home where high water will never reach us." Big Jim arrived in a twenty-foot shovel-nosed canoe, ready for the upstream trip in search of land. They drifted down the Atchelitz, into the Chilliwack and for a time were on deep water. Soon they reached the mouth of the *kehts-ih-SLIY-ee* (Kateseslie), a tributary Big Jim said would quickly take them to higher land. Their direction was southeast as they paddled up a winding stream. Where their course turned south would one day

This ticket was issued for Allen and his horse to embark on the steamer Onward *in 1870.*

Sarah Wells came from Ontario to join her husband in the West ca. 1864. COURTESY OF CHILLIWACK ARCHIVES

become the centre of the Chilliwack/Sardis clover-leaf interchange on Highway 1. There was a large open tract of land at this site, already staked by Matthew Sweetman. Half a mile farther upstream, the water-course became a spring water creek and the prairie land gave way to brush and timber.

At a spot near the junction of present-day Knight and Vedder Roads in Sardis, Big Jim gave up the paddle in favour of a pole and indicated that shallow water meant land above the high-water line. Leaving the canoe on the bank of the stream (where Vedder Road now intersects with Gaetz Avenue in Sardis), Allen and Big Jim began walking. Allen knew that the land on which they now stood had been staked by Sergeant McColl, a surveyor for the Royal Engineers. McColl died soon afterwards, and subsequently his widow had offered to sell the land to Allen. After careful inspection, Allen decided that this land looked promising to him, and so, undoubtedly with some excitement, he resolved to purchase it.

Big Jim and Allen continued on foot to the west and finally turned south, soon coming to another spring-fed stream – the *kwa-kwa-LEET-sah* (Co-qualeetza), as Big Jim called it.[14] Travelling farther south on a well-used native trail, they came to clear spring water rushing over gravel. The trail crossed over this shallow stream, and Big Jim told Allen that they

This cabin, the oldest non-native building in the valley, was constructed by the Royal Engineers in 1858 during the international border survey. It was located on the property eventually owned by Jane Evans, the sister of Allen Wells. Allen stayed here while managing the Evans farm for Jane.

J.K. Lord described the Chilliwack Valley in 1858. This scene depicts the Cascades, looking eastward towards Cheam peak. PHOTO BY CASEY WELLS

now stood on land several feet above high flood water. Although this land required some drainage, Allen knew for certain that he wanted this to be his home.

A mile or so to the east, beyond high timber growing beside the banks of the *ch.ihl-KWAY-uhk* River, stretched open prairie land. On either side farther east the Cascade Mountains rose majestically to wall in the valley. To the south, on higher ground, forests obscured the mountains. And in the west, patches of open prairie were flanked by heavy brush. Alder and maple trees were found in the open, and on the ridges were giant firs that rose to heights of three hundred feet. Tall spruce and cedar trees grew in profusion on the marshland.

More alder and maple, bordering patches of prairie, were evident to the north. Cottonwoods lined the banks of numerous sloughs. Through this wilderness area, Big Jim guided his companion along trails familiar to him, trails that traversed the higher land alongside the watercourses.

Continuing on about a mile to the northwest, they came upon two small streams draining a large beaver meadow. These streams descended over low falls into the *koh-KWAH-puhl* (Co-coep-ul), merging to become a single large stream with high banks. Lying across the stream was a huge but slippery cottonwood log – a natural bridge on the trail. Walking across this log required great skill and dexterity, as if one were walking a greased pole. Allen never did decide whether *luhk-ah-kuhk* (Luckakuck), meaning "to straddle" in Halkomelem, referred to the log straddling the stream or to an unfortunate traveller straddling the slippery log! The two men managed this crossing and continued downstream. Soon Allen recognized that the open prairie land lying ahead was within a mile of the Evans farm.

While Big Jim retraced his steps, taking the canoe back downstream, Allen headed across the prairie to scout out and mark a trail back to the Evans place. He was to travel over that trail almost daily during the coming year. Arriving back at the Evans farm that night, elated but very weary, he told Sarah that at last he thought he had found a place where they could build their own home. He felt his days of searching to find a special place in the West were over. Every thought and effort he would now direct towards establishing a home in this challenging wilderness – on land beyond the boundaries of established white settlement. ❧

Lillie Jane Wells was born in 1865 in Yale, where Allen and Sarah lived for three years. After moving to the Chilliwack Valley as a youngster, she was sent to school in Victoria. Family legend has it that she was the one who named her parents' farm "Edenbank." COURTESY OF CHILLIWACK ARCHIVES

CHAPTER 3

A Home in the Wilderness

To the pioneer, "staking the land" consisted of squaring a cut-off tree stump and recording on it a description of the land claimed. On August 23, 1867, Allen submitted his Crown grant application. It read: "I desire to pre-empt 320 acres of land situated on the Luckakuck River, which may be shown on the above sketch."[15]

Having staked this land, Allen set to work late in 1866 to build his first home. As yet, there was no road of any kind in the settlement. Lumber for building was rafted across the Fraser from Harrison Mills using native canoes in the same manner that

The little Atchelitz church was the first church in the valley and was built by donation of money and labour on land given by the Evans family in 1869. According to the Chilliwack Progress, *the first monetary donation was from Chief Atchelalah.*

natives moved their own possessions from place to place. Planks were first laid across two large canoes – each capable of carrying two tons of cargo – and lumber was piled on the crosswise planks. It was rough lumber that made its way up the Chilliwack after a crossing of the Fraser. Part of the shipment was taken up the Atchelitz for use at the Evans home and part was taken up the Luckakuck as far as possible and piled on the stream bank. From there, Allen hauled his lumber to the building site on a stoneboat. The pioneer's usual means of conveyance in those days was to spike planks made from long poles across two skids or runners, similar to sleigh runners. This vehicle was pulled short distances by horse or oxen.

Allen and Sarah began to build their home on the site of the present Edenbank house. The walls were made of one-by-twelve-inch rough lumber standing vertically. These boards were later covered with cheesecloth and papered on the inside. Outside cracks between boards were covered with wooden strips. The nearby spring water stream provided sparkling clear,

cold water. A wood-burning stove provided heat, and a privy was located at the edge of the forest.

Some of the stock that Allen purchased first for his operation and also for the Evans farm had been driven north from Bellingham via the Whatcom Trail. The cattle arrived in Bellingham by ship and were unloaded individually with slings and then had to swim ashore. Isaac Kipp with his cousin James would drive the cattle to the Chilliwack area using dogs to help herd them. At this time both Isaac and his cousin Jonathan Reece had farms where the present city of Chilliwack is located. Their homes were near the mouth of the Chilliwack River on a high bank of a slough known to the natives as *wuh-THAY-ee* (Water Lily Slough), adjacent to the Yale trail.

On his new land Allen soon erected a small barn to provide for the cattle and fenced an open meadow. By the spring of 1867, he was ready to move his family and accumulated possessions from the Evans farm to the new home. This move was recorded in later years by his son Edwin, who wrote, "In 1867, my father and mother, with my sister, Lillie, then only two years old, came up a trail following the bank of the Kate-sesliyee."

The diary of Reverend Edward White, pioneer Wesleyan Methodist missionary, who then lived in New Westminster, provides the first glimpse of life at the Wells family home. Dated April 28, 1867, is recorded the following: "Preached at Brother Wells at 8 P.M. Eleven whites and seven natives. Went home with Mr. and Mrs. Kipp – stopped all night. This is a promising settlement." A subsequent entry dated June 19 and 20, 1867, throws additional light on the pioneer Allen

The pioneer A.C. Wells and his wife Sarah and daughter Lillie in the front garden of their first home at Edenbank, on the bank of the Luckakuck.

Wells and the task to which he had set himself.

> June 19, showery, started this A.M. at seven o'clock; left on steamer "Onward" to go to the Chilliwack settlement. We arrived at Brother Wells at 2:30 P.M. and spent the afternoon and evening agreeably. The farm and stock have greatly improved since I was there a month ago. There is prospect for a good settlement, but years will pass before it gets school, church, etc.
>
> June 20, we started in company with Wells at 3:00 P.M. to Kipp's in a canoe. In the evening, Brothers Wells and Forsyth came over and a few others came in, to whom I preached from Galatians 6:14.

Of Allen and Sarah, Reverend White wrote, "They are the salt of the earth."

A smallpox epidemic ran rampant among the natives in the Fraser River valley during 1867. Reverend Thomas Crosby, another Wesleyan Methodist minister, was supplied with vaccine by the government to help stem the spread of the disease. During his visit to the valley that year, the reverend came to the Wells home one day greatly disturbed and asked Allen to come with him to Squiala. Together they were taken by Big Jim downriver to the native village. As they approached, the sound of drums reached their ears. The chanting of the medicine men and the wailing of the lamenting mothers could be heard long before they rounded the bend in the river. As the plank houses of the village came into sight, they were horrified to see the natives throwing their children into the cold river waters.

To the natives, the fever in the children was the result of evil spirits having entered their bodies. They were desperately trying to drive them out by casting the children into the river. Previously in Nanaimo, Crosby had had numerous experiences that had tested his courage, fearlessness and good judgement and had been able to win the natives' respect. Because of Crosby's persuasive manner, reason again prevailed that day. Subsequent vaccination of the native children later proved to be one of the avenues through which many natives accepted the Christian religion.

Reverend Thomas Crosby was later sent by the Wesleyan Methodist Church to be a resident missionary among the natives of the Chilliwack Valley. Allen had been influential in Crosby's appointment and the minister journeyed to the Wells home when he left Nanaimo for the valley. Alone, with his luggage in a native canoe, Crosby crossed the Strait of Georgia, ascended the Fraser River, the Chilliwack and the Luckakuck, finally arriving at his destination in a drenching rainstorm, one long week after leaving Nanaimo.

Crosby's ability to stir the minds and souls of his parishioners with his preaching of the gospel was so great that the settlers became eager for easier communication between those who lived in the Sumas area and those who lived along the Chilliwack River. With this in mind, a road "bee" was organized in 1868 to clear a road and build bridges to connect the two settlements. This was the first road to be built in the valley.

Allen and his neighbours along the Luckakuck and Kateseslie streams cleared an additional road from their own newly established homes to join this first road. These ultimately provided wagon road connections to the Fraser River at Sumas Landing and also a connection to what was to become known as Chilliwack Landing or "The Landing," near the mouth of the Chilliwack River.

The rich loam at Allen's new farm produced excellent potatoes, beans and carrots. Tall hollyhocks and climbing roses stood against the new house. A picket fence enclosed the yard. At night, a coal oil lamp burned in the window so that Allen might more clearly see his way up from the barn when chores were finished for the day.

Work began at daybreak. Allen toiled alone, with keen axe and strong right arm. Brush was slowly

Cattle and oxen were much in demand in the bustling settlement of Barkerville during the gold-rush years. COURTESY OF B.C. ARCHIVES, A-03787

cleared from the meadowlands, where pasture, although marshy, was sufficient for the cattle. Tough vine maple was used to build fences and enclose newly cleared fields. The fences were strong and lasting when well constructed. Each branch was set firmly in the ground, one on top of the other, patterned much like feathers in a quill. Thus the lighter clearing was accomplished, and fenced-in cattle were much more easily found than those that roamed at will.

The cattle were a heavy breed, mostly of Durham (Shorthorn) blood, originating from the Hudson's Bay Company's farm at Fort Vancouver on the Columbia River. The females were used for milk production while the males became oxen. Allen raised and trained them as teams to drag heavy stumps into burning piles. Some supplied meat for the beef-hungry miners in the goldfields. A well-broken team of oxen, three or four years old, would sell for $300 to $400 for use on freighting wagons or logging teams. This was the first major source of cash income for Allen and Sarah.

When the cows calved and there was milk in larger quantity available, great skimming pans were set in a cool and shady spot, allowing cream to rise to the surface. Sarah would skim it off and churn it into butter, which was kept icy cold in the creek. The skimmed milk went back to the calves, or to pigs penned behind the barn. At night the hogs were enclosed within a sty to protect them from bears and wolves lurking in the surrounding woods.

The Collins Overland Telegraph Company had been busy since 1864 with the construction of a telegraph line from New Westminster to Alaska. When the line came through the valley in 1865, it followed Atchelitz Creek, crossing the Evans property on its way to the Chilliwack River, which it crossed near its mouth. The line then passed along the banks of Water Lily Slough. By 1869, when Crosby became seriously ill with a fever after enduring a week's canoe trip in stormy weather, it was possible to wire to Yale to ask a doctor's advice regarding his illness. For six weeks the beloved reverend was confined to his bed in the Wells home and for seven or eight days was not

A painting done by E. Tate (Mrs. Charles Tate) of the first Wells home, dated 1887.

One use for well-broken teams of oxen was to pull timber out of the woods. A trained team three or four years old could be sold for $300 to $400. COURTESY OF B.C. ARCHIVES, C-00570

expected to live. Finally he showed signs of improvement. Much credit for his recovery was due to Sarah's good nursing care.

Day after day Allen laboured to carve out their home site. Gradually he could see positive results. Any money coming in from the sale of oxen was used to purchase necessary equipment and livestock. Since the fields were not yet drained and the roads and trails boggy, he used teams of oxen rather than horses. Their cloven hooves could be extracted from deep mud, which would have mired a horse quickly.

The natives accepted Reverend Crosby's religion and were the first to offer contributions of labour to build a little church.[16] This building was completed in 1869 on the banks of the *A'tsel-ihts* (Atchelitz). The trail to the little church from the Wells farm became very well worn, leading through timber to a stream, where Allen kept a canoe cached. On the way to church he would paddle, while Sarah held a line to their horse swim-

ming behind. Reaching dry ground, Allen would drag the canoe, tied by a rope to the horn of his saddle, to the next stream. Natives and whites gathered at the little church each Sunday to sing and worship together and establish lasting friendships. Allen was treasurer of this, the first community endeavour.

The year 1870 was a special year for the young Wells couple, for that year many more of their own cattle were purchased in Oregon and Allen had the task of driving them from Whatcom County to his farm. The original landing warrant, which recorded the duty paid on these cattle, is still on file. Under the colonial seal it reads:

> Landing Warrant. Permission is hereby
> given to A. Wells to land the following
> packages of merchandise in British
> Columbia by Road (trail) from Whatcom;
> 16 cows, value $500, duty $32; 3 steers,

value $100, duty $9. Total value $600, duty $41.

Signed by A. Grier – for the collector of Customs, Chilliwack.

Dated Jan. 15, 1870.

En route to the Wells farm, the cattle crossed the Sumas grasslands, which provided natural rough grazing even during winter months.[17] Skirting Vedder Mountain by using the trails opened by the Cariboo cattle drives, they arrived at their new home in the barn on the banks of the little *kwa-kwa-LEET-sah* (Coqualeetza).

The cattle didn't hold the spotlight for long at their little home in the clearing. In July, Sarah bundled up her little Lillie, summoned Big Jim to take her out to the Landing and boarded the steamer to go down the Fraser to New Westminster to await the birth of her second child. In August she returned home with their new son, Edwin. Now Allen worked with even greater zeal, for a son and heir had been born.

A larger herd of cattle was Allen's goal – a symbol of accomplishment and of greater things to come. He planned for the erection of a large barn. Eventually it was to be known as the straw barn, but its original plans called for a centre structure of two large haymows with a driveway in between. On three sides, surrounding this centre portion, were lean-to shed/barns, which would house cattle and horses in individual stalls. There was a four-foot passageway in front of and behind the stalls. Window spacing pro-

vided light by day and the pioneer lanterns, hung on a high peg, lit the dark winter mornings and evenings. By lamplight that winter, Allen laid out his plans for this barn and estimated the requirements in timber and boards.

Axemen would be needed to fall and square the timbers and to cut the rafters. David Bicknell, a new neighbour, had established himself on higher land to the south. He was willing to haul in the timbers with oxen, after they had been squared ready for use. Allen had observed the careful work of the natives, who were expert axemen. He now went to them for help. Among the great axemen of that day was Thompson Uslick. Arrangements were made for Allen to pay him with bags of flour. The two became good friends. His son, Harry Uslick, also became a fast friend of Allen and later of Allen's son, Edwin.

Big Jim also came to help with the barn construction, as well as Billy Sepass, Long Charlie and Short Charlie, Captain John, George Cooper and David Commodore, all friends of Allen and converts of the Reverend Thomas Crosby. These men squared the timbers, mortised the beams and made ready the tenons and pegs. Eventually the big day came and a barn raising in the old Upper Canada style was called. Next, cattle stalls were built and soon fitted with wooden stanchions to hold cows during the winter months. Halters were made for the horses, utilizing rawhide and lace leather. These halters were strong enough to secure an unbroken colt, as Allen's son and grandsons discovered over the years. ༄

Chapter 4

Battling High Water

Tragedy struck in 1871 when Charles Evans met an untimely death in Yale. The exact circumstance of his death is not known but he did die from a gunshot wound. He was responsible for handling much of the gold that was being transported by stagecoach through Yale. Being suddenly widowed, his wife, Jane, was anxious to move her young family out of this frontier town. Allen offered to accompany his sister to the new home which was already built by 1867 on the Evans property and to assist her in getting re-established. A large river canoe, crewed by six natives, was arranged for transport. And so, early in 1871, Jane Evans with her family of three small children and a native nursemaid, accompanied by her brother Allen, left Fort Yale for the trip down the treacherous Fraser River to the Chilliwack. Jane brought many of her household possessions with her. Experienced rivermen as the native paddlers were, it was nevertheless a perilous journey for a young family setting out to establish a new home.

Ten hours later, their canoe swept around a giant whirlpool at the mouth of the Chilliwack River and entered the clear water of a mountain stream. At *SKWIY-ee* (Skway), on the north bank of the river, natives could be seen making canoes. For generations they had carried on this trade and were very skilful and accomplished. Many natives in the big village of *koh-KWAH-puhl* (Kwow-kwaw-a-pilt), by a nearby slough, were busy working on construction of a house of worship. It was to be the first Roman Catholic church of the white man's God to be erected in their midst. Under the direction of the Catholic priests, these builders of plank houses proved to be superior workmen. Their own great ceremonial hall and numerous large plank houses were located along the banks of a broad, deep channel, where the waters of the Fraser flowed in periods of flood and high water.

Next their canoe passed *skwiy-HAH-lah* (Squiala),

to which a few years earlier Allen had accompanied the missionary Thomas Crosby in answer to an urgent call for help. Soon the family group was passing another native village, *A'tsel-ihts* (Atchelitz), where the natives had a huge dance hall erected. This structure remained for years as the last example of a building constructed with native lumber. The great canoe then entered the tributary of the Chilliwack River that gave this little village its name. Just beyond the village was the future home of this pioneer family of Jane Evans, her sons Allen and Charles and daughter Nellie. Here too, Allen Wells earlier had made his home for two years, between 1865 and 1867. In this land, so beautifully described by J.K. Lord, the Evans family would eventually hold twelve hundred acres between the Atchelitz and the Luckakuck, both tributaries of the Chilliwack River.

In the early 1870s, the fields of the Wells farm were finally cleared and drained. The big beaver dam at the northwest end of the farm was opened and a large marsh quickly drained. The native people were on hand to take the beaver for their skins. Grain fields were sown to oats, and soon flocks of Canada geese were winging in on their migration and feasting on this new delicacy. Timothy, alsike and red clover were grown for hay. The virgin land was so fertile that heavy grain stalks would rarely stand erect as they ripened. Oat fields often yielded one hundred bushels and hay four tons to the acre. What a contrast to the shallow Northern Shield soil Allen remembered from Napanee. New roads built in the settlement all led to the Landing, for most produce could find a market if it reached the riverboats on the Fraser.

For a few years grain was threshed on the barn floor or in the yard by using horses circling a post four abreast. They trampled the grain from the hand-tied bundles, previously cut with a cradle. This grain was worth an amazing $100 a ton, a fine reward for the long, tedious hours of hand labour. At first hay was cut with the scythe, hand raked with homemade wooden rakes, then put up in large coils or cocks in the field and allowed to cure before stacking. The natives quickly learned the white man's ways and were glad to work for wages. Young Billy Sepass grew adept at swinging a scythe or cradle. The old Irishman James McConnell would walk eight miles to and from the farm to swing a scythe or cradle all day till darkness came.

With prosperity came pleasures too. In August 1871 the neighbours made their way towards the falls of the Luckakuck.[18] It was a special occasion, the first picnic to be held by the pioneers. They came however they could to the Wells farm, or more correctly to the clearing in the woods near the falls. All were dressed in their Sunday best for the event. The Millers and Chadseys arrived from Sumas, carefully and comfortably transported by wagon. The Evanses and Forsyths came by canoe, as did the Sickers and the Bicknells. Tablecloths were spread on the grass and great quantities of delicious home cooking were laid out. The picnic was a wonderful success and would become an annual event. Each year afterwards, when the hay was safely gathered or stacked, everyone would assemble for this big social event – the haymakers' picnic.

Meanwhile Allen's farm was developing rapidly. Timber was cut, land cleared and split-rail cedar fences built to replace the ones of vine maple. The big "straw barn" had been built a hundred yards from the river, at the edge of a boggy area. Behind this, the hogs were busily helping to clear land by rooting out skunk cabbages. If these animals wandered too far into the woods, they were occasionally caught by bears, and they frequently returned suffering from a loss of neck flesh and blood, with possibly a shoulder bone exposed.

Allen would apply a dose of coal oil to the wound to kill the swarming maggots and initiate rapid healing. A high split-cedar fence was built around the farm's chicken house in an attempt to keep out wild animals, hawks or sometimes a great horned owl whose hooting was often heard in the quiet of the night.

Molly was the first saddle horse on the farm. Her name was remembered almost with reverence. Although she was Sarah's horse, she was used by everyone for any emergency. At first the only bridge across the Coqualeetza in front of the house was the large trunk of a cedar tree that had been felled over the stream and stretched from high bank to high bank. Flattened on the top for walking, it measured fifty feet long. If Sarah wished to visit a neighbour when the river was too deep to be forded, she and Molly had to use this log bridge. They would cross individually and wait for each other. Their destination over lonely trails might be the Evans farm, three miles away. If the water was not too high, Sarah on occasion would ride five miles downstream to visit Susan Forsyth.[19]

One day in September 1871, a "bee" was called at the place where the Chilliwack River joined the Fraser. Allen and his neighbour John Sicker took their axes and paddled down to what was to become the Methodist campground. There Reverend Crosby had pre-empted land at a site where the old Hudson's Bay Company fishery had once stood. Among the neighbours who that day lifted up their axes on the thick trees were David Miller, Jonathan Reece, Isaac Kipp, James Kipp, Donald McGillivray, Chester Chadsey, James Chadsey and Volkert Vedder.

In 1870, at age 18, Horatio Webb had arrived in the valley. His background was English and he had worked for a time in New York. He proved to be a most thoughtful and helpful neighbour. His capable hands assisted with the construction of both the house and barn at Allen and Sarah's farm. On October 15, 1875, Horatio married Lucinda (Lucy) Ada Hopkins of New York and brought his bride to the valley. Three days after they arrived, the fall rains began in earnest. Day after day heavy cold rains blew in on storms from the Pacific Ocean, just sixty miles to the west. Dark moisture-laden clouds hung over the Cascade Mountains and continuously dropped snow at higher elevations. Each time the timber-clad mountains came into view, they were blanketed with even deeper snow.

Sarah crossing the log bridge over the stream with her horse, Molly. Pat Erickson's sketch has captured the careful steps of Molly over the narrow log bridge. Note the sidesaddle and the stump Sarah would need for remounting.

By the end of November, snow lay twelve to fifteen feet deep in the upper valleys. It was the heaviest snowfall the pioneers had seen. When Allen came in to breakfast on the morning of November 25, it was snowing heavily in the valley. Snow continued to fall throughout the day and into the night, until it reached a depth of thirty inches.

For two days Allen worked steadily to make his stock comfortable in their barns and shelters in preparation for the winter's cold. On the night of November 27, on leaving the barn he stopped to listen. He felt a sense of foreboding. Nothing moved, yet there seemed to be an ominous feeling in the air. Soon, coming from the south, he felt a surge of warm air and the trees surrounding the clearing stirred. Then he heard the wind. He waited and listened. The wind velocity increased and became a strong chinook; it was blowing strongly from the direction of Cultus Lake and from southwest over Sumas Lake. He had not long to wait before the heavy snow started tumbling from the trees. The wind whined through the tall firs. The temperature suddenly rose. Before long everything was dripping wet.

Allen started towards the house, where Sarah joined him at the door. Together they listened to the frightening noise of the wind. They had a certain feeling that there would be too much water in the Coqualeetza by morning. The bridge Allen had recently built over the stream was a substantial one, with three logs as stringers stretching from bank to bank. Onto this he had spiked the best of split-cedar planking. When daylight came, he rose quickly and went outdoors. He noticed the river running high, but the rain had stopped. The south wind was still warm, and half of the heavy snow had disappeared. During the day he tended stock and dug ditches to keep runoff water moving away from the buildings.

That evening the Webbs came over for a visit. When they left at midnight to walk home, Allen and Sarah took up lanterns and went with them down to the bridge. The water was very high and running close under the stringers. The two couples stood on the bridge for a time and watched the swollen stream. It had risen only a little since the rain had stopped. The chinook, however, was still blowing, and as they listened to the wind in the trees, they realized there was another heavier sound. It seemed to gather volume and filled the air with a fearful roar. They knew it was the Chilliwack River they heard – some two and one-half miles to the south and sixty feet above the valley floor, tumbling wildly from the Cascade Mountain ranges.

Since Allen had settled on his farm by the Coqualeetza, there had been several occasions during

Lillie Jane Wells was educated in Victoria and later married William Townsley in England, where they remained and raised their three children.

the winter months when the Chilliwack River had risen high enough to send some freshet water down the Coqualeetza past the front of the farm. The usual source of the Coqualeetza was spring water arising one or two miles to the south. The upper reaches of the Chilliwack River drained an extensive eastern watershed about thirty miles deep into the Cascade Mountains, stretching to a width of about fifteen miles.

That night as Allen and Horatio watched the swollen Coqualeetza, they discussed the likely possibility of the Chilliwack River again breaking through in their direction with even greater force. The two men decided to take the split-cedar decking off the bridge. Even if the river took out the timber supports, they would have at least saved the planking. Working in the dark with only the light from lanterns held by the women, they removed the planking and carried it to high ground many yards from the stream, safe from being carried away.

Later, heading home, the Webbs managed to cross the river by walking the timbers to reach their own side of the constantly rising water. The weather remained warm all that night. During darkness the roar of the river penetrated even into the cabin as Allen and Sarah, probably sleepless and frightened, listened and waited, wondering what morning light would reveal.

After the death of her husband Charles, Jane Evans moved from Yale to the Chilliwack Valley to live on a farm not too far from her brother's.
COURTESY OF CHILLIWACK ARCHIVES

The Evans barn pictured in October 1987. Up in the peak is the date of its construction, 1888. COURTESY OF NEIL SMITH

At daybreak, the two neighbours met again at the river, which was now a thundering, raging torrent between them. The channel had widened to one hundred yards, and with the rushing waters, logs and whole trees were careening down from land upstream. In the night, a great log-jam had formed at the "crossing" (Vedder), blocking the old channel and forcing the river to find a new channel north, which it cut with amazing rapidity as it rushed down an incline, falling more than sixty feet in two and a half miles.

Allen shouted across the river to Horatio, who finally understood that he wished him to go to the native village at Skowkale and get help. Horatio returned by midday with two natives, Sepass and Uslick with their canoe. In places, the stream, now a wide river, was running ten feet deep, undercutting the bank and taking out many yards of good land. Allen was anxious to save five acres of newly established orchard land that was also threatened.

For days they worked, attempting to shore up the banks – men and teams against a relentless torrent, often labouring in the cold water. The excitement and strenuous work somewhat offset the bitter cold of the water, which was running thick with mud. David Bicknell, the neighbour whose property was upstream, joined in their efforts to keep the river running a straight course. To do so they had to remove the huge uprooted trees that were continually being carried down by the freshet and lodging on gravel bars. If allowed to remain, these trees quickly formed the base of a log-jam, turning the river towards the opposite bank and creating more havoc.

The natives, who were daring but experienced rivermen, pitted their skill and strength against the river as they ventured out again and again into the rushing current to fix a line to a large tree or log. The rope was attached to a cable that was then pulled to the tree and secured. This enabled teams to drag the tree across the current to a section of the bank needing protection. The tree would be anchored with its roots upstream. Allen and David

Frederick W. Lee painted the Luckakuck, Vedder Road and the Edenbank bridge in 1907 – a quiet, pastoral scene. But the stream could grow to a raging torrent in times of high water, as when a chinook melted a heavy snowfall late in 1875.

Bicknell were frequently in the river up to their waists. On one occasion, Bicknell's powerful grip on the cable was all that saved him as he was swept out of sight in the murky waters. When Christmas Day came, the men were still busy in the river.

Christmas celebrations were a very important time to the pioneer families and were not to be ignored. Thus the women and children started off to have the midday Christmas dinner at the Forsyths' under the care of Reverend C. M. Tate, who was driving Mr. Webb's team and wagon. Crossing a slough, the team became mired down and considerable time was lost getting them out of the mud. All bridges were out, so they proceeded on foot. At the Luckakuck, Matthew Sweetman took them across the river in his little canoe. Sarah and her son Eddie, then five years old, were taken by canoe to the Forsyths'. Mrs. Webb and Lillie Wells walked with Reverend Tate. They had had so many difficulties on the way that it was well after Christmas dinnertime when they arrived. At the farm, meanwhile, Allen and the other men never left the river.

After the flooding subsided, the deep channel through which the Luckakuck now flowed provided excellent drainage for the front of the farm. Allen asked the natives to trap more beaver, which were causing additional flooding of his land to the west. He then removed all the beaver dams and the whole farm felt the benefit of natural drainage into the Luckakuck.

In 1873, the Township of Chilliwhack had been incorporated as a municipality. It derived its name from the native word *ch.ihl-KWAY-uhk*, used to refer to the Chilliwack River, its valley and its native residents. The native name, which had been in use during the fur trade period of 1827–57, was soon changed to Chilukweyuk, then to Chilliwhack, and finally to Chilliwack. An official municipal assessment notice of 1876 regarding the farm reads as follows:

Owner, Allen C. Wells, Free-hold. Age 38. P. No. 675, Group 2. Lot 38. Number of Acres 310. No. of acres cleared 100. Value of Real Property $3,000. Value of Personal Property $1,000. Total taxes due $12. Number of resident persons 8. Religion, Christian. Number of Cattle 30; Number of hogs 15; number of horses 5. Dated Oct. 2/76 District of New Westminster.

Prior to 1874, when the New Westminster to Yale Wagon Road was established through the valley, mail and news of the outside world came to the settlers only once or twice a month. Old *Sah-MAHT*, a Sumas native, came with the mailbag from Miller's Landing on the Fraser River. When the water was high he came by canoe, and at other times he travelled on foot over the trails. Allen would select his mail from the bag and old *Sah-MAHT* would then continue on his

The Agassiz-Rosedale ferry stranded in ice on the Fraser ca. 1929. During the nineteenth century, the river regularly froze over.

rounds to other settlers' homes. After the road was completed from New Westminster to Yale, Bill Bristol carried mail for Barnard Express, which held the contract from New Westminster to Barkerville. Once, back in 1862, the Fraser River had frozen over, a phenomenon that reportedly lasted for five months. Mail was then easily taken over the ice by either wagon team or sleigh.[20]

One day in 1869, Sarah received a letter from Ellen Robson, who had become her good friend while they both lived in Yale. It read in part:

> You don't know how pleased I was to receive your good long letter and how often I read it over... for we often think about you and wonder how you are getting along. How I would like to see you and have a good long talk. How much we would both have to tell... Oh how I should like to see your little Lilla, is she the only Lilla still?... You don't know how often I think of all my British Columbia friends and wonder if I shall ever meet any of them again in this world. Give my love

to Mr. Wells and a kiss to little one...
Your affectionate friend, Ellen M. Robson

Ellen's letter accompanied a letter from her husband, Reverend Ebenezer Robson, to Allen. Reverend Robson's first charge in the Methodist Church had been to establish a mission in Yale.[21] In later years he was happy to be able to attend Sarah and Allen's fiftieth-anniversary celebration, as at the time he was posted to the West Coast.

In the summer months, gardening at the pioneer home was a special joy to Sarah. As their house and farm grew in stature, so her flower garden bloomed in greater profusion. She and Lillie enjoyed working together in their cozy home, creating exquisite Battenburg lace and linens and spending time in the garden. As yet there wasn't a senior school in the valley, so Lillie spent her high school years with family friends in Victoria. Lillie passionately missed the farm and its lovely setting. Each time she came home for holidays, the homesite looked more beautiful to her. One day she said to her mother, "This must be like the Garden of Eden, on the bank of a stream. Let's call it Edenbank!" And so they did.

Sowing the Seeds for Success

The "home in the wilderness" gradually became a farm home in a pioneer settlement. As new roads and markets became established, Allen's farm rapidly developed. He embarked on his projects with great initiative and ambition.

Although Allen had not had formal schooling beyond elementary grades, he recognized the value of education. The pioneer's reference journals to which Allen subscribed early on were *The Family Herald*, founded in 1869; *The Farmers' Advocate*, founded in 1886; and *Hoard's Dairyman*. When the day's work was done, Allen would make himself comfortable in his chair by the stove, turn up the lamp and pick up his reading of the latest advances in farming methods.

An early issue of *The Farmers' Advocate and Home Magazine* lists subjects that represented the thought given to agricultural advancement prior to 1900. Notices of livestock meetings included those submitted by breeders of Shropshire and Cotswold sheep, Shorthorn and Aberdeen Angus beef, and Clydesdale horses.

A selection of A.C.'s books including his well-worn copy of Feeding Animals. *For fifty years he consulted his books by lamplight, always eager for new agricultural knowledge.*

As he read by the light of his fireside lamp, it is safe to say that little if anything of importance escaped Allen's eye or failed to register in his mind as he studied and planned for the future. He made much practical use of his magazines and reference books, evidenced by the fact that his farming enterprise went ahead successfully.

Among the most useful books in his library was *Feeding Animals*, by Elliott W. Stewart, published in 1883. In this volume of more than 500 pages, the most modern knowledge on such diverse subjects as the composition of animal bodies and the digestion and composition of feeds was supplemented by information about livestock housing, soil management, and the feeding of dairy cattle, horses, sheep and swine.

The books *Horse Doctor* and *Cattle Doctor*, by George Armitage, were other books Allen consulted frequently as he accumulated more livestock on the farm. The success or failure of his livestock operation depended upon his ability to diagnose a sickness in his animals and to administer suitable treatment and

When Allen read about the usefulness of silage on a progressive farm, he located plans described in eastern farm papers and built the first upright silo in the valley. He designed a horse-powered leather conveyer belt to be used with a treadmill to get the silage up into the building. At the time of this photo by Ron Gray, the Fraser Valley College had chosen the farm as its Chilliwack site and requested that Ron photograph the farm and buildings in detail.

medication. Later he was able to teach both his son and his grandsons much about veterinary medicine.

Another very useful volume, which he won at the 1881 Chilliwack Exhibition, was the illustrated *Stock Doctor and Livestock Encyclopaedia*. Its pages soon became well worn with use.

In the early development of farm herds, two of the most destructive diseases were bovine tuberculosis and contagious abortion. As late as 1894, family scrapbook clippings on the subjects indicated that there was little knowledge of how to control these diseases. Contagious abortion spread like an uncontrolled plague among dairy herds. Some farmers noticed that cattle living in open sheds, where there was an abundance of fresh air and sunshine, suffered less from diseases than those housed in a warm humid environment. Many diseased herds were slaughtered before it was also discovered that an immunity resulted in those animals that recovered and were retained in the herd. In herds where diseased animals were slaughtered and replaced, many of the new animals in turn would quickly become infected. This was a double tragedy to struggling young farmers.

The construction of the Canadian Pacific Railway through the Fraser Valley took place in the mid-1880s and stimulated a market for dairy farm products. Allen recognized that the production and sale of butter and cheese, which allowed for better retention of soil fertility, was a more desirable mode of farming than his previous dependence on hay production, which lessened soil fertility.

Before 1886, with no rail connection to eastern Canada, as Ontario was then called, B.C. farmers had to concentrate on products that could be marketed locally. After the railroad was finally built across the country, Isaac Kipp shipped apples, cherries and plums from his orchards as far as Nova Scotia. At Edenbank the dairy herd was producing more milk during the summer months than could be handled by skimming in the old manner. But, as the local farmers discovered, there was no market for milk. Butter was eventually shipped by riverboat to New Westminster and also to Victoria in great firkins.

After his battle with the river in front of his farm was over, Allen set about planning the establishment of a larger farm with suitable buildings to allow for livestock expansion. During the winter of 1884–85, he wrote down his future plans.

In Ontario, Joseph Yuill had written to *The Family Herald* concerning the requirements of winter dairying. On reading this article Allen visualized the fulfilment of a plan that had been formulating in his

The horse barn, ca. 1970. The turn-of-the-century buggy, similar to ones used by the Wells family, was purchased by the Weedens and driven many times to Buggy Club breakfasts at the Royal Hotel in Chilliwack. Also visible is the mower used at Edenbank (far left) and the workbench where saws were sharpened and tools repaired (right). Not seen to the left are the original stalls for the Clydesdales.

mind for months. The recommendations, given here in part, were to be closely followed at Edenbank:

> It is a great mistake to milk the Beefing breeds. Have your cows calve in October and November and stable them; have warm, dry, well-ventilated comfortable buildings. Keep the cows clean and give them a good bed; milk punctually to the minute, and do the same in feeding.
>
> Let the same hands milk the same cows in the same order. Try to make your cow as comfortable as possible while you are milking and if she kicks over the pail, do not take the milking-stool and beat her. You will never cure a kicking cow in that way. If you want to get the most out of your cow, be gentle with her.
>
> If you have a cheese factory within reach, get your cheesemaker to fix up his factory with the proper appliances to make butter in winter and cheese in summer.

Yuill also recommended the feeding of silage to the herd to reduce the cost of winter dairying. Using prices of the day, with wild hay at $5 per ton and silage at $1.50 per ton, he estimated the cost of producing one pound of butter at 8.3 cents when using hay as roughage, and 5 cents when using silage. Butter at the time had a retail price of 25 cents a pound.

After reading Yuill's recommendations on winter dairying, Allen made up his mind to build a creamery. He decided, as suggested, to produce butter during the winter months and cheese during the summer, using the river for cooling and a windmill pump for the water supply.

Allen and Sarah discussed more plans for the farm. They decided on a horse barn just northwest of the house, with a stone walk to approach it, and a wagon shed south of the house with room for two farm wagons plus a dump cart, a democrat and a buggy.

The farm lane running east to west, which became a beautiful wagon road later, had not been established at that time. There was only a wagon road along the bank of the river, serving the newly cleared fields at the front of the farm, both to the north and south of the buildings.

The young orchard, which had escaped the river freshet of 1875, was now bearing fruit, much to everyone's satisfaction. It now covered ten acres, upstream from the farm home. There were several long rows of apple trees. Northern Spy and Kings were the favourite apples for fall and winter use. The harvest apples, Yellow Transparents and Gravensteins, were enjoyed during the late summer and harvest season. Russets, after being covered with straw, were carefully "pitted" in the ground for winter use. They maintained a crisp freshness for eating in hand and for using in a favourite dish, baked apples. Winesaps were for late winter use in the root cellar. Then there were Bartlett and Seckel pears, Italian prunes, German plums, and Bing and Royal Anne cherries kept in storage.

Downstream, along the riverbank, the wagon road passed by the half-acre garden plot. Still surrounded by stumps, but well fenced and tilled, it produced quantities of vegetables and small fruits. In the fall, a stoneboat would be used to transport produce to the root cellar.

The root cellar was built behind the house for fruit and vegetable storage. Its walls were of mortar and stone, some eighteen inches thick, resisting the winter cold and summer heat. It was above ground, but well insulated and ventilated, and measured twelve by twenty feet.

Allen must have had a feeling of well-being when he walked into the root cellar in the late fall. Before him he would see great bins of apples stretching back from the centre aisle and large trays, each holding a separate variety of fruit. Underneath the fruit, just above the cool earth, were trays of pumpkins and squash and more bins with potatoes. Overhead hung huge cabbages, head down. Their garden companions, Brussels sprouts, were still growing in the garden. They would be harvested during the winter months, after a touch of frost. Carrots and beets were placed snug underground in a pit beside the Russet apples, for they too needed cool, damp earth to keep them crisp. The family's winter supply of fresh fruit and vegetables was thus safely put away.

Beyond the vegetable garden to the north, the wagon road wound along the edge of a large meadow. Farther on, downstream, it led to one of the hay barns erected to shelter hay off the land first cleared but which now housed young cattle during the winter. At this old barn a river steamer later would tie up to put off cattle to safety during the great Fraser River flood of 1894. Nearby Allen would build his retirement home at the turn of the twentieth century.

Allen's grandsons often heard and remembered the story of how one hot July day in the late 1880s, Allen rode Molly down to the hay field beyond the old barn. As he was riding along to see how the haying crew was progressing, he noticed dark clouds gathering in the west.

The hay in the field had been gathered into large stooks, or coils, each of which contained about five

The farm lane, cleared in the late 1880s, cut a straight path to the rear property line almost a mile long, opening up all the land for production.

hundred pounds of well-cured feed. That day, the crew was "stacking." As he drew near, a scene of great activity met his eyes, for "Old David," the native in charge of the young riders, had also noticed the summer storm blowing in and had shouted, in the Chinook jargon, "*Mika-hiy-yahk-klah-tah-wa-snass chchlo,*" meaning "Hurry! It is going to rain."

It was a huge field, in the centre of which a large rectangular stack had already been built up to a height of ten feet. On the stack stood David. A few years before, Allen had given him this simple biblical name. In Allen's mind the name David symbolized strength, for had not David met and defeated Goliath? David's true name was *sel-AHK-ee-ah-tihl.* With him in the crew was Sam, a Chinese of strength and character, who had already proven his worth working for Mr. Dunville. He was therefore known as Sam Dunville. There were many Chinese in the valley then, who had worked on the recently completed Canadian Pacific Railway right-of-way. Many of these men had turned to agriculture, and Sam's long stay at Edenbank was to be three score years.[22]

Allen rode up to the stack to pass the men a cold drink. A half-pail of cold spring water was always refreshing and nourishing. Often two handfuls of rolled oats were added and mixed in during the ride from the spring.

Clarence Midgley was working on the stack when Allen arrived. A pony pulling a coil of hay on a "bucking pole" came in on the run. Clarence slung the hay quickly up on the stack and set the sling ready for the next rider to drop another load. To speed up their work, the crew had divided into two competing teams, natives and whites, so a race was on!

Allen's son, Edwin, had Jack Stevenson and young Charlie Evans on his team, three boys who had been raised on horses. Their endurance and horsemanship were being severely tested. The friendly rivals were Jack and Harry Uslick, sons of Thompson Uslick. Their teammate was the native Dan Milo. The Uslick boys' name had changed little from their father's name of *way-OO-sehl-uhk* (Uslick).[23] Dan Milo's father, *sloh-kwih-LAH-loh,* who frequently worked for Allen, originally had a name that seemed very difficult to

The first creamery on the farm (left) was built on the Luckakuck. Butter was produced during the winter months, cheese during the summer. One can see the tracks where the teams and wagons crossed the creek and, in the background, the big barn constructed in 1894. This photo dates from ca. 1910. COURTESY OF ARCHIE W.S. KENNEDY

pronounce. As he was frequently in their home, Sarah asked for permission to call him Milo.

Allen had a soft spot in his heart for Dan. When Dan rode in with his load, Allen noticed that his horse was just a colt, possibly only a two-year-old. The colt was obviously exhausted by the furious pace and by the heat of the day. While Dan was getting a drink, Allen slipped the harness and saddle off the colt and onto his own horse, Molly. Dan was soon quickly away with the strong and seasoned mare without having lost his place in the race. In the field, being quickly stripped of its coils, two men, Commodore and Billy Sepass, were kept busy setting the bucking poles under the coils. William McGillivray, for whom he had worked, had given Commodore his name but his native name was *seh-EE-eh-KWEHL*. He was descended from *eh-KWIV-ehl,* a war chief of the *STAW-loh* tribes. Commodore married the daughter of a chief of the *ch.ihl-KWAY-uhk* tribe and according to tribal custom had come to live with her tribe. The Sepass family migrated into the Fraser Valley about 1848. The Sepass family name, *see-PAH.S,* was recorded by Paul Kane, at Kettle Falls on the Columbia River, as Chief-of-the-waters.

As the riders returned to the field for more coils, their empty poles dangled behind the galloping ponies. The poles were picked up by others who slid them under another coil. Quickly an attached rope was circled around the coil and attached to a ring on the end of the pole. Again, pony and rider took off on the run for the stack. After watching a few minutes, Allen left the field, not too concerned about the outcome of the race, for he had done what he could to balance the odds in favour of the native riders.

Before the imminent rains struck, the hay was all stacked and secure from damage. The friendly bantering among the young riders passed almost unnoticed by the older men as they made their weary way back along the dirt road to the farm home and supper.

As the haying season came to a close, Allen spent a day blazing a straight line west along the centre of his property for three-quarters of a mile to the back line. During the coming winter he would keep several men employed clearing this path. He wanted it a width of thirty feet in preparation for the establishment of a farm lane. Little did he realize that as the century went by, the trees he planted along the lane would grow to great heights and become magnificent specimens that would give much pleasure to others. When work began on the lane, the first major problem was the crossing of a large swampy area. It was almost a bottomless marsh. Here oxen were used, as horses were unable to work in the mire. Slabs of rough cedar were dragged to the site to build a base for a corduroy road. Brush was then laid down and straw piled deeply on top to support the oxen while they worked. The wooden slabs were then set in place, and a thick gravel layer poured over them to provide a solid roadbed. Work progressed onto higher ground farther west. There, timber had to be felled and stumps removed. After this was done with the help of strong teams of oxen, there were huge piles of brush, limbs and tree trunks, all of which had to be destroyed by burning.

Midway to the back of the farm, two watercourses crossed the property from south to north. One of these was on higher ground, where for a time the freshet waters of the Chilliwack River had cut a deep channel. Near the east bank of the deep channel, on the high ground, a group of young trees formed a grove of alder, birch and maple, through which the farm lane had been cut. These trees were spared the bite of the axe and were left to grow by the sides of the lane. In later years, during the summer heat, man and beast would often take time to "rest a spell" in the shade that the trees completely spread over the lane. They were tall, slim trees, with clear, smooth bark and limbs that of necessity had grown skyward as they reached and fought for the forest light.

A low, broad watercourse had at one time led into beaver ponds in the north part of the farm. Here again another roadbed was laid on corduroy slabs. Farther along, the land was higher and fresh springs of water could be channelled off to become a perpetual asset to the farm. At last the lane was cleared and the farm took on a new perspective. With completion of this major project, the entire farm was now accessible. Prairie patches became pastures and the heavy timber promised new areas for cultivation. Allen's plans for a greatly expanded dairy operation now had a firm foundation in available pasture. With determination and tenacity he faced the tremendous tasks of clearing, draining and fencing all the farm. His son Edwin long remembered the cherished dream his father kept before him and his comment, "Edwin, once we get the farm cleared, drained and fenced, we will then be in a position to make some money!"

The Lee brothers had come out from Ontario and were now busily engaged as contractors in the valley. Allen asked them to call and together, in pursuit of Allen's new goal, they planned the construction of a creamery. He and Sarah discussed the plans enthusiastically. The creamery would be twenty-four feet by forty feet and would be insulated. Its walls were to be filled with sawdust for insulation against both heat and cold. There would be two floor levels above a mortar-and-stone-walled basement. The structure would be built into the high riverbank, allowing wagons to unload their heavy cans of milk just above ground level. The wagons would then be driven around to the back of the creamery to receive an allotment of skim milk or whey. There was to be equipment for making cheese as well as butter.

Allen was to purchase and deliver all the necessary material and provide skilled labour. Will Newby, a former CPR construction man, had recently married a daughter of Allen and Sarah's neighbour David Bicknell. Will and his bride had moved to a homestead, and he was eager to earn cash for carpentry work. Another neighbour, Jim Bellamy, also did some of the carpentry. Clarence Midgley and Joe Teskey, men

land. As charcoal was the only saleable product of the entire operation, the huge log piles were covered with soil before being set on fire. Gradually the fires turned the logs into charcoal. Fire was also used to clear land of brush, and, if carefully managed, a fire was the pioneer's helper.

With prospects for better returns from butter-making, Allen turned his attention to improving the butter-producing quality of the milk from his herd. At that time, the Jersey cow was the most popular dairy breed in eastern America. Herd production was measured in pounds of butter per week. Mary Anne, of St. Lambert, Quebec, was the outstanding Jersey cow of the day, and her production was recorded as

Two farmhands joke as they stook oats to allow the crop to dry. (Note the "floating" hat.) During threshing, the oat seeds were separated, pouring steadily into sacks, and the straw from stems and leaves was blown up into the barn through a long tube. Gordon is driving the binder in the background; Tom Bowers is on the right.

familiar with the river, were sent to haul large boulders from the "crossing" at the Chilliwack River.

Lumber had to be hauled by wagon over a rough road from Popkum, where Will Knight operated a lumber mill. This was a twenty-mile round trip on roads at times almost impassable. Horatio Webb undertook to haul the lumber. Occasionally he had to camp out overnight on his return journey.

While construction of the creamery went ahead, Allen drew up plans for a hog barn with a capacity for thirty fattening hogs to be fed skim milk and whey from the creamery operation.

During the winter months, land clearing kept the men busy. Fires were a common sight by night and day, as great piles of logs were burned to clear the

36 pounds 12½ ounces of butter in one week. A beautifully proportioned cow, her picture appeared in one of the contemporary farm publications. Seeing this article encouraged Allen to bring pure-bred Jersey cattle into his herd to increase butter production.

The 1886 completion of the Canadian Pacific Railway also provided direct contact with livestock breeders of Ontario. Allen lost no time in making a trip east to secure improved stock. Among the first cattle he brought west were three Durham bulls. This was a general-purpose breed, later known as "milking Shorthorns." One of these bulls was purchased by Chester Chadsey of Sumas and Allen retained one. In 1955, J.W. Hall recorded some of his impressions of the early cattle at Edenbank.

The last remaining team of Edenbank Clydesdales enjoying a well-earned rest ca. 1950 under the shade of trees planted by Allen more than sixty years before. Edwin purchased two Clydesdale mares from a shipment imported from Scotland and gained much pleasure from the breeding of their progeny.

From these bulls of Mr. Chadsey and Mr. A.C. Wells, particularly the Wells' place, was raised one of the finest herds of dual-purpose cows I have ever heard of. They were all large animals, all heavy milkers, and all quiet dispositions. I know this as I milked twelve of them morning and night for three years. There were sixty cows in the herd then.

These Durham cattle established Allen's herd as the major dairy herd for which he had been striving. Further improvement to the herd took place with the purchase of a Holstein bull by the name of Zad. This was a three-year-old bull George Chadsey bought in Washington State. Unfortunately, the coming of Zad led to a tragedy at Edenbank. The bull was being housed in a large box stall in the horse barn. When noon hour came, the man who usually watered the bull was late in returning from a field at the back of the farm. A Chinese hand, by the name of Foo, decided to let the bull out for a drink at the water trough. When he went into the pen to drive him out, Zad charged him. The bull carried Foo between his horns and crashed him against a beam that crossed the back wall of the stall. John Coatham was unhitching a team nearby at the time. He grabbed a heavy neck yoke, which he had just dropped, and rushed to help Foo, whose loud scream for help came from the barn.

John was a large and powerful man and meeting a bull's charge did not daunt him. After pinning Foo against the wall, the bull is said to have backed up to lunge again. Foo made a leap for the door, but collapsed just before he reached it. John struck the bull's head as he charged and actually felled Zad with the force of his blow. Although he had not been gored, Foo was so badly crushed that he died almost instantly.

Foo was given a Chinese funeral by his fellow countrymen. As the funeral procession moved slowly to the graveyard, they left a trail of pieces of white paper behind to prevent evil spirits from following the deceased.[24] Afterwards, Zad became an evil spirit in the minds of the Chinese all over the valley and he had to be guarded day and night to prevent his being poisoned or killed. The Chinese believed that unless the animal was destroyed, his spirit would enter Foo in the next world. Eventually Zad was sold, without having left any good influence on the stock at the farm.

Soon after this, Allen decided again to try to improve the butter-producing quality of the milk from his herd by the purchase of several Jersey cows from C.L. Street. Mr. Street had settled on the Sumas-Chilliwack road and had started a herd of pure-bred Jerseys. About this time, Allen went east again to purchase more livestock and brought back six bred heifers and an Ayrshire bull. The Ayrshire breed had been strongly recommended by Joseph Yuill. In order to finance the purchase of pure-bred cattle, Allen held

A.C. Wells, "the father of dairying in B.C.," had a herd of sixty dairy cattle by the mid-1880s. His progressive methods included the building of a creamery and an upright silo, the first in the valley.

a sale of stock that year which netted him $3,000. These particular Ayrshires proved to be a poor investment, for their yield of milk was only about one-half that obtained from the Durham cows.[25]

Deciding that all his herd needed testing for bovine tuberculosis, Allen found that his young herd of Ayrshires all reacted and had to be destroyed. Unfortunately, at the time there was no government compensation for animals killed for this reason.

In the spring of 1892, Charles Reid seeded a newly cleared thirty acres at the back of the farm by hand. He would walk over the fields, swinging his arm in wide arcs, allowing oat seed to escape over an extended forefinger. With each alternate step he would reach for more seed into an open bag hanging from his neck. Using his skill and the momentum of his swinging hand, he spread grain evenly over the soil. The field was harrowed afterwards to cover the oat seeds.

After this, Reid repeated his measured walk, back and forth over the field, this time scattering grass seed over all the newly harrowed land. Some of this seed would yield plants that would remain untouched by the plough for seventy-five years. In years to follow, this thirty-acre pasture was known as "the Big Meadow," a pasture some of which has yet to see the plough [1967]. When seeding was completed and after the harrowing, the fields were rolled to firm down the seedbed. Allen made a log roller for the purpose from one of the big Douglas firs cut during land clearing. All this hard work seemed worthwhile when fall brought a record yield of grain.

Harvest time brought the familiar sound of Fred Collinson's heavy steam-powered threshing machine, lumbering up the driveway. During the warm fall evenings, preparations were always made for the busy day ahead. A team of horses pulled with every muscle to get the water wagon up the steep grade of the bank after being filled in the stream. Wood had to be hauled and stacked where the old steam machine would sit during the following day's threshing, separating oats and blowing straw into the big straw barn. In the farm kitchen, Sarah and Mrs. Tyson prepared great quantities of food to feed the hungry men. At five o'clock in the morning, Collinson threw in the wood and fired up the steam engine. By the time breakfast was over, "steam was up" and work began. The threshing crew began work on loads of sheaves already on the wagons and by the time the dew was off the stooks, neighbours were arriving with teams and pitchforks ready to help. Several teams and wagons came from close neighbours the Higginsons, Stevensons, Knights and Evanses and from the Coqualeetza farm. These, together with three other farm teams, provided a total of six teams hauling sheaves from the field and another one hauling grain away.

It took many men to thresh in those days. In addition to the seven teamsters, nine more men were required. Three "pitchers" loaded the wagons in the field. A "band-cutter" cut the strings on the sheaves as they entered the machine. A "spike-pitcher" assisted the teamsters to unload, and one man tended the grain at the sacks while three men "mowed" away the straw. Allen kept himself free for any possible emergency. On occasion he would go into the mow with Molly when the quantity of straw was so great that it had to be trampled down by a horse. By nightfall, Molly would be on top of twenty feet of straw in the mow. With encouragement she would take a long slide down the straw chute to a great pile of straw below and a soft landing.

About threshing days, J. W. Hall wrote:

One episode on the Wells farm remains quite vivid in my memory. One fall, they were threshing and must get through that day as the machine was promised for the next day. This same machine kept breaking down and delaying the threshing all day long, and when it came milking time, Mr. A.C. Wells came to another boy, William Latta, and myself and told us to go in and start milking the sixty cows, and that the other milkers would come in as soon as they finished the threshing.

The machine delayed them so much that they did not get done threshing until midnight and the other milkers by that time were too tired to start milking. Consequently, Latta and myself just managed to get through those sixty cows in the morning in time to start again at number one!

For several years, Allen had been experimenting with silage production. Clover and grass silage were made simply by cutting in the month of June and stacking it green. Over the stack, soil was spread to a depth of two feet, to stimulate a curing process. Allen was delighted to find that the cows relished the silage and milked well while feeding on it. He therefore made a pit silo by digging into the old riverbank. This gave him a twelve-foot-deep pit on the one side and a four-foot

Allen introduced the first cream separator in the area, called a De Laval. It stimulated wide interest, and other farmers came to see it in operation. Ray Wells remembered that the parts were taken to the house and washed by the women in an old hotel sink in the kitchen. The skim milk was fed to the pigs and calves.

wall of soil on the lower side, from which he could feed during the winter months. He constructed great V-shaped racks that he set up on posts on the gravel bars of the old riverbed to feed the dairy herd during the day.

Corn was being raised in the United States as fodder in 1891. Such varieties as Northwest Dent were being recommended as sufficiently early maturing to ripen in Canada. After obtaining information about an upright silo built in eastern Canada, Allen constructed, that year, the first such building to be made in the West. The silo was sixteen feet square and was set on a mortar-and-stone foundation. It still remains secure on this foundation today [1967]. The shiplap wallboards were laid on upright two-inch-by-twelve-inch planks. Two thicknesses of shiplap, with tarpaper between, made the inside walls airtight. There were false corners inside, rounded to prevent loss by spoilage. The outside covering was of standard siding of the day. Doors on the south side at four-foot intervals to a height of twenty-five feet provided openings through which fodder was carried into the silo. Before storing, it was put through a cutting box driven by tread power from a team of horses or a bull. The team walked over treads of oak planking, which rotated under their feet. The fodder was then finally conveyed to the silo on a carrier ingeniously constructed by Allen using leather belting, onto which he had riveted crosspieces to carry the fodder up an inclined trough.

By this time, Coqualeetza Indian Residential School had been built by the Methodist Church on land Allen had sold to Horatio Webb in 1878. The Methodist churchmen wished to

The posts for this lengthy cedar-slab fence along the Luckakuck were driven in with a horse-powered piledriver. It was built to protect the farm's vegetable garden and orchard from extreme water after heavy winter rains. The mile-long fence guarded the riverbank from further erosion. Vedder Road is on the left.

purchase an additional fifty acres of the north end of Allen's farm, and he agreed. A substantial part of the food supplies required by the school was purchased from Edenbank. Because of this extra capital and available market, Allen was able to go ahead with his plans for a new barn for his dairy herd.

The freshet waters of the Chilliwack River still frequently did great damage when they flowed into the Luckakuck during periods of heavy winter rains. In the fall of 1887, another heavy freshet almost took the lives of Horatio Webb, his wife and their son as they were crossing the Luckakuck. They had been visiting Allen and Sarah. Again, the river had come rushing down in a tremendous freshet and all bridges had been swept away. Two natives in a stout canoe, Sepass and Milo, had taken the family across the fast-flowing river to visit Edenbank. When they left for home, Sarah and Allen accompanied them to the river and watched from the bank as they settled into the canoe.

The natives paddled out into the swift current and were soon caught by it. However, they managed to set a steady course across, aiming to put ashore in a backwater several hundred yards downstream. While still in heavy current, the canoe struck a submerged object, splitting the bow. Water rushed in. Sepass, who was in the bow acting as pilot, dropped his paddle and threw himself face down into the bow of the canoe, encircling it tightly with his arms. He was able to hold the canoe together until Milo could beach

the craft safely. Horatio shouted back across the river to Allen and Sarah, "Indian Billy says, 'Mrs. Webb *yahka skookum tumtum*,'" meaning "She has a strong heart." The Webbs were safe thanks to the quick thought and action of their native friends.

Before attempting to build any more structures on the farm, Allen decided he must establish some permanent safeguard against the river. After consultation with William Hall and other retired members of the Royal Engineers, he resolved to build a cedar-slab fence six feet high that would confine the main current during freshets. Allen hired natives to split cedar logs. They would haul logs to the bank and sharpen them into large posts, twelve inches in diameter and twelve feet long. Some of the cedar logs were also split into slabs three inches thick and twelve feet long, varying in width from six inches to sometimes two feet.

These twelve-foot-long slabs were to be spiked onto the posts, which had been pile-driven into the sand and gravel of the river bottom. William Hall directed the construction and operation of a piledriver. After each tripping of the driver, a team of horses would relift the heavy weight using a block and cable. By moving the piledriver forward on heavy skids, a line of posts was driven along the edge of the wide riverbed for a distance of approximately one mile. The cedar-slab wall formed a smooth solid barrier against the river current, protecting the riverbank from further erosion. ✍

CHAPTER 6

Father and Son Work Together

As Edwin entered his late teens, he became in every way an accomplished assistant to his father. He loved working with horses. He enjoyed especially the excitement and satisfaction of breaking in a colt, whether to saddle or to harness. Most of the earlier light horses were known as cayuses, descendants of horses brought in for use in Hudson's Bay Company pack trains, for boundary line survey work and during gold-rush days. They were tough and hardy for riding or driving. Horses of heavier weight and a better class of driving horses were brought west from Ontario via the CPR.

"Eddie," as his father affectionately called him, was trained to ride English style, sitting upright in the saddle and "posting." He loved riding or driving a good horse with plenty of spirit. In the fall of 1884, it was his pleasure to enjoy the rugged life of a livestock exhibitor. At exhibition, he competed with, and had opportunity to see, the finest livestock of the day and the best agricultural produce, for Chilliwack, New Westminster and Victoria quickly were becoming the focus of major agricultural exhibitions. Eddie was sent to New Westminster to high school to continue his education. A bit homesick, he missed not only his home life, but also the friendship of a special girl, Gertie, Isaac Kipp's daughter. Correspondence brought the two to the realization that they meant much to one another.

Following graduation from high school in New Westminster, Edwin took a diploma course at the Ontario Agricultural College in Guelph and one term of a business course at MacDonald College in Quebec. He returned to Edenbank well equipped to carry on the advancement of the farm.

Meanwhile, the romance between Edwin and Gertie Kipp continued and flourished. In the spring of 1893, an announcement carried news of special interest to two pioneer families: "Mr. and Mrs. Isaac Kipp request your presence at the marriage of their daughter, Gertrude, to E.A. Wells. Wednesday evening, March 8th, 1893, at 7 o'clock."

The following year, 1894, was a year to be remembered at Edenbank. Two events were of particular importance. Firstly the planning and construction of a truly huge barn and secondly, in July, the birth of Gertrude's first child. Ray was the first of their family of all boys, which finally numbered seven. He was a challenge at times to both his father and grandfather, as he had his own very strong views about life. Always "a character," he was able to spin a good yarn, especially about horses, which he too loved.

Gertrude (Kipp) Wells and Edwin after their marriage in 1893.

This scene depicts the unloading of cattle from a riverboat that tied up behind Coqualeetza school during the 1894 flood. Neighbours who were flooded out kept their cattle for some time at Edenbank.

With great anticipation, plans for the big barn were drawn up and approved. The Lee brothers held the contract and were to supervise the barn's construction. The creamery and other farm buildings had already been completed. Provincial records indicate that A.C. Wells & Son at their Edenbank creamery produced over 16,000 pounds of cheese and 3,000 pounds of butter. This, it might well be said, was accomplished in spite of "hell and high water," for in that year the Fraser River rose to record levels. At the Mission City gauge, the river rose to 25 feet 2 inches in the spring, a level that has never [in 1967] been repeated.

Fortunately, Edenbank was well above the high-water line. The Fraser rose higher and higher until the waters of Sumas Lake stretched unbroken for miles, joining waters at the far eastern end of the valley. Flood waters skirted the northern end of the farm, which was twelve feet lower than the rest. A great many adjacent farms were flooded out. Cattle from both the Evans and the Kipp farms were brought to Edenbank by sternwheeler. The boats were able to steam right up the Luckakuck to discharge their cargo at the old hay barn at the lower end of the farm. Afterwards, two other herds sought refuge at the farm for the duration of the flood. These extra herds were there until well into the summer of 1894.

Letters written after the '94 flood by Allan Brooks, who later became a famous bird illustrator, give some idea of the devastating effect that the flood had on valley farmers. In a letter of 1896 Brooks wrote:

> I, Kipp and Evans have had to borrow money from the natives for the last two years to pay their hired help. Wells built a splendid barn last summer. He still had more hay than he had room for. He now cannot sell his hay for even $5 a ton – and I hear he's going behind. Ashwell and Henderson are ageing very fast as they have so much money out on property that would not realise the mortgage if sold, owing to drop in prices of land.[26]

The newly erected cattle barn, ca. 1895. Constructed at a cost of just over $3,700, it could hold 100 cattle, including 75 milking cows, and 500 tons of loose hay in its lofts. James Bellamy is holding the team. A.C. Wells is dressed in black, young Ray Wells is wearing a bonnet, and Edwin Wells is on the right holding a bull. Photo by Mr. Booen, a commercial photographer.

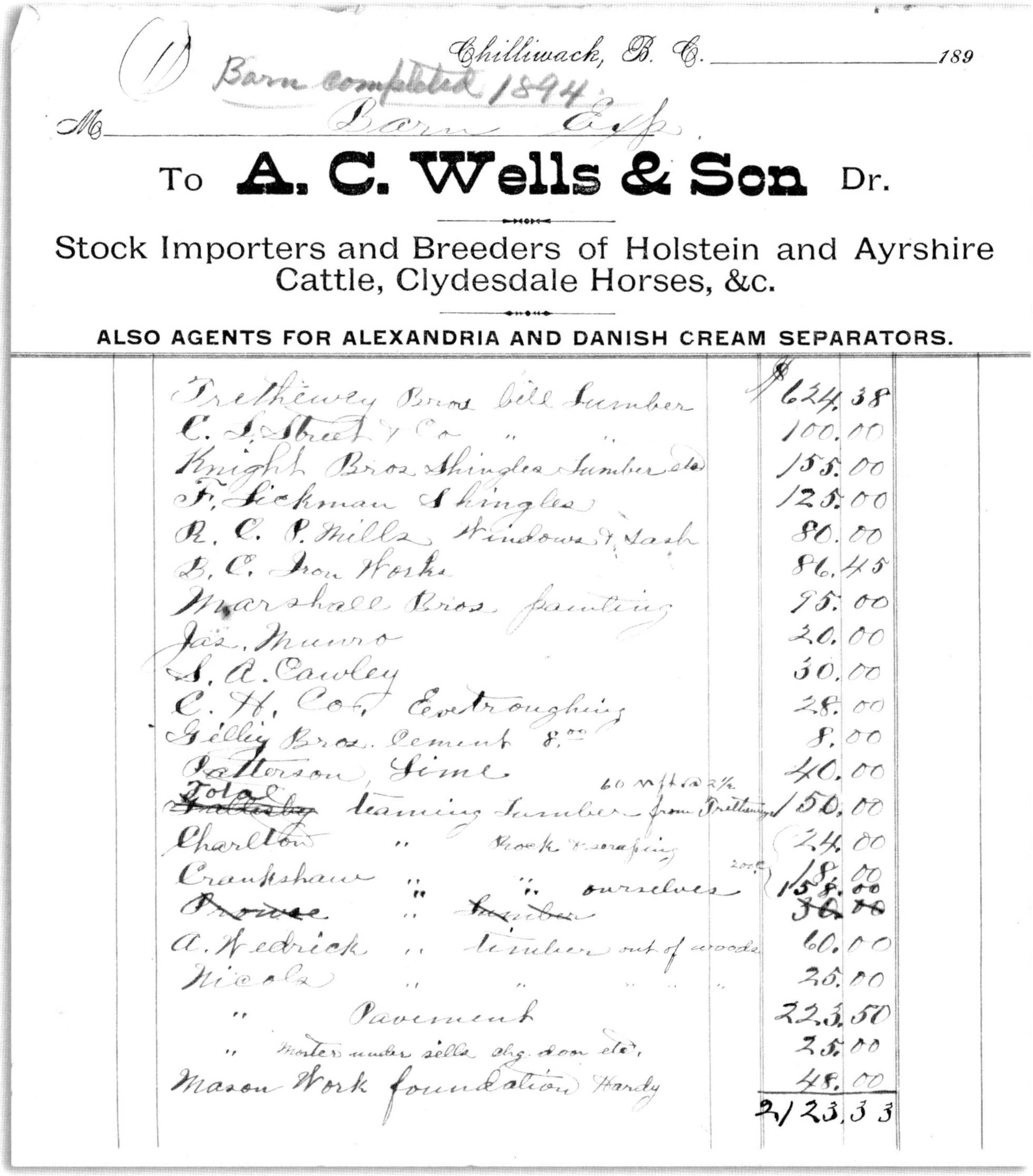

(1) Barn completed 1894

Chilliwack, B. C. _____ 189_

M_ _____ Barn Exp.

To **A. C. Wells & Son** Dr.

Stock Importers and Breeders of Holstein and Ayrshire Cattle, Clydesdale Horses, &c.

ALSO AGENTS FOR ALEXANDRIA AND DANISH CREAM SEPARATORS.

		$	
Trethewey Bros bill Lumber		624	38
C. I. Street & Co " "		100	00
Knight Bros Shingles Lumber etc		155	00
F. Lickman Shingles		125	00
B. C. P. Mills Windows & Sash		80	00
B. C. Iron Works		86	45
Marshall Bros painting		95	00
Jas. Munro		20	00
L. A. Cawley		50	00
C. H. Co. Eavetroughing		28	00
Gilley Bros. Cement 8.00		8	00
Patterson, Lime	60 m ft @ 2½	40	00
Total teaming Lumber from Trethewey		150	00
Charlton " Rock & scraping		24	00
Crankshaw " " ourselves	200	158	00
Prouse " lumber		36	00
A. Hedrick " timber out of woods		60	00
Nicola " " " "		25	00
" Pavement		22	50
" Mortar under sills chg. door etc.		25	00
Mason Work foundation) Hardy		48	00
		2123	33

Partial construction costs of the large cattle barn at Edenbank erected in 1894, noted in farm records.

While other valley farmers, because of the '94 flood, were enduring the greatest agricultural setback they had known and many were bankrupt, Allen held firm to the course he had set for himself. He believed that his own fortune as a farmer would change for the better by careful decisions. His eventual successes would later gain for him the title "the father of dairying in B.C."

Plans for his "Big Barn" contained several innovations in dairy barn construction that as yet were not common, even in established dairying districts in eastern Canada. His barn was to be 125 feet long, 72 feet in width and 60 feet high, with a hip roof. The stable would hold 100 cattle, 75 of which would be milking cows. Overhead, the lofts would hold 500 tons of loose hay. It was to be a bank barn, built into the sloping riverbank. This would facilitate the construction of driveways up into the loft area on one side.

The foundation on which the walls would stand was of mortar and stone. On this foundation, a base

An after-haying picnic celebration was held each year at Cultus Lake. This photo, taken in 1902, includes young people from the area. Mildred Wells and Ernest Farrow were courting at the time and here Mildred (seated second from the right) is holding Ernest's hat. He is sitting hatless in the middle.

beam fourteen inches square was laid the length of the barn. The walls were insulated with sawdust ten inches thick to a height of the twelve-foot stable ceiling. The haymow floor was a double layer of one-by-ten-inch boards resting on heavy hewn timbers. The floor of the barn was composed of cedar blocks. These blocks were set together like cobblestones on top of a sand and gravel base. Over all this, sand would be worked into the cracks together with hot tar. The cedar blocks were twelve inches long.

Construction started in 1894, when J.W. Hall set to work to haul sand and foundation gravel to the chosen site, next to the first barn Allen had built. With an old horse named Scamp, Mr. Hall transported hundreds of cubic yards of gravel and sand from the nearby riverbed, using a dump cart which held 1¼ cubic yards in each load.

One hundred cubic yards of rock and stone for the wall foundation were hauled 2½ miles from the Chilliwack River. This hauling was done by such distant neighbours as Peter Crankshaw and Mr. Charlton. Timber, from which the hewn beams were cut with a broad axe, was hauled from the foothills, where trees

Young Ernest Farrow (right) came from England directly to work at Edenbank. Here he and his good friend Andrew Atcheson have had a professional photographer take their photo with the Fraser River for a backdrop.

growing in dense forests gave the logs a uniform thickness. A. Weadrick, a pioneer of Promontory, and Nicol of the Vedder River area hauled out the timber to be used for the heavy posts and beams. Jack Stevenson and others cut cedar blocks that had been hauled to the construction area by J.W. Hall. Again, old Scamp pulled the dump cart.

When the logs arrived at the building site they were squared with broad axes in the capable hands of Billy Sepass, Dan Milo, Commodore and Uslick. Harry Kah-Piht and August Sam had a busy job splitting the cedar to make the blocks.

The framework of the barn construction was held together by mortise and tenon joints secured by wooden pins. Bracing struts were set into place as the framework was assembled and ready for erection. The braces were not held in place by any pin or spike, but depended entirely on the mortise and tenon joints for support. This special craft work was done by Arthur Pearson, James Bellamy, Clarence Midgley and William Hall.

Week after week, the materials were assembled in preparation for actual construction. Lumber and shingles were hauled from the Tretheway Mill in East Chilliwack, the Knight Mill in Popkum, the C.L. Street Mill and Lickman's at Atchelitz. Glazed tile came from the B.C. Pottery, and cement and lime from Gilley's & Patterson's in New Westminster. At last the day came when construction really commenced. The Lee brothers proved themselves as master builders.

Lying assembled on the ground was a whole post and beam unit. Lifted by cable and pulley, it was swung into an erect position to form a frame for the end of the barn. When this had been secured, another unit was swung up approximately twenty feet from it. Connecting beams were raised and set in place and braces fitted into position. Again, more units were raised up and the combined units were held more firmly by the main sills and purlins under the hip of the roof. These were long beams, specially hewn for their position, extending half the length of the barn in an unbroken straight line. Finally, seven units of the frame had been swung up, aligned and pinned in place.

Now the full magnitude of the barn could be appreciated. From ground level to the sills at the base of the roof measured 30 feet. The barn's peak rose to a dizzying height of 60 feet. The finest of fir lumber in boards 20 feet long soon covered the walls, and two-by-six-inch rafters rose by the dozens to carry the roof, so that, when completed, it was strong enough to carry snowdrifts six feet deep. One hundred squares of the best cedar shingles completed the roof and remained in service for seventy-two years.

The hip roof "Big Barn," rising to a height of sixty feet, incorporated an indoor silo and a modern ventilation system. It was constructed with the assistance of Native axemen and carpenters. This sketch by Oliver Wells shows the fork lift used to fill the mow.

A modern ventilation system was installed, which provided a continuous supply of fresh air. The air came in through eighteen-inch passages formed of glazed tiles, then through smaller lines up under each manger. The warm and foul air of the stable was drawn off through wall vents, carrying it up through the overhead mows, to be released above the roof.

"Bidwell" stalls were installed for the cattle. They provided an adjustable manger for each cow, as she stood, untied, in a wooden stall, a chain behind her. When she was ready to be released, a door swung open at the side of the stall, allowing her to turn and walk out. Even the feeding of the calves was made easier, by having them enter individual stalls when it was feed time. A gate was then swung down behind them and their buckets were placed in front in a frame, which prevented upsets. For the convenience of feeding, a silo was built indoors, beside the feed room at the north end of the barn. The granary, which held 30 tons, was situated above, with a chute to send the grain down easily. The silo, 18 feet in diameter and 30 feet tall, held 150 tons of silage. It was built of special lumber ordered from Ontario, as silo lumber

Hay was cut in early days by scythe and cradle to form swaths. It was then expertly coiled in the field by hand to finish drying. In the late 1890s, three to six teams of workhorses hauled wagons that each carried 1½ tons. "Pitchers" forked the hay onto the hayrack-equipped wagons, still the case during the 1940s (above).

tongue and grooved was not yet available in the West.

Early in 1895, a grand opening was held to celebrate the completion of the barn. Brass bands played and neighbours and friends came from far and near to enjoy the fun. That summer yielded a record crop of hay, as if nature itself was celebrating and set on filling up that barn. Two crews of men were kept busy all season and one thousand tons of hay were harvested.

One crew was kept busy cutting and making hay in the fields. As soon as good weather came in July, both A.C. (Allen) and Edwin, now a man of twenty-five, set quickly to work mowing the first big field. This crop was mostly timothy and alsike. A good general rule for reaping hay of good quality was to start cutting when the joints in the stems of the timothy were firm yet would still part when pulled.

After one full day's mowing, the two had cut sixteen acres. While the dew was still on the hay early the next morning, a first round was started with horse and "tedder," kicking up the hay to lie loosely for quicker drying. If the weather held, the tedding would be finished and Edwin would have that field raked into windrows before the dew fell the second night. On the third morning, Allen liked to have his crew start coiling before he joined Edwin mowing in the next field. It was in the coil that hay was cured, or

allowed to sweat for about three days before it was ready to haul. Then the great mows in the big barn could be filled.

There were many men at Edenbank who became well known for their ability to coil hay. It was a very important part of the harvesting. A well-coiled haycock could repel rain and prevent crop loss from a rainstorm. The men worked in separate rows as they moved forward down the field, doing six or eight rows at a time, crossing the windrows as they progressed. The Chinese farmhand Sam Dunville was the expert and teacher. If a greenhorn came to help with the haymaking, he was sent along to work with Sam until he had learned to do the job well and keep up with the rest of the crew.

A second crew started when hauling commenced. Three teams of heavy workhorses were harnessed up to wagons and hay was hauled to the nearest barns. When a field was farther away, six teams were needed to keep the field and barn crews busy. What a sight it was, under the long rays of an afternoon sun, to look down the long farm lane and see row after row of haycocks, and watch the wagons coming and going in steady procession.

Besides the teamsters, the hauling crew had two "pitchers" to fork the hay up into the wagon. Each wagon, with its hayrack in place, would carry about

1½ tons into the barn. The teamsters built the load so that the hay could be lifted by cable in huge fork-fuls, swung high above the mow along tracks fastened to the roof beams, then dropped. A teamster would stand on his load, carefully adjusting and fitting the hay fork each time. When the hay had been hauled upward and somebody yelled "Trip!" he would jerk a rope and down would go the hay. As the hay dropped it would be "mowed" away by one or two more men. Usually, Sam liked to have this job, as it was he who later would be moving the hay out to a baler operating below.

As each wagon was emptied it was carefully backed off the ramp. This could be a thrilling experience to watch – horses backing against the hames leathers, drivers shouting "Back" or "Easy," taking care not to edge over the ramp's twenty-foot drop-off. The team would then be driven back down to the field, where a crew of pitchers would be ready to load another wagon.

Thus the work went on as the generally hot weather continued. Load after load was pitched, driven up into the huge new barn, unloaded and stowed away. Day after day, new fields were mowed, tedded, raked and cocked. At last, at the summer's end, 250 acres had been cut, and 1,000 tons of good hay safely put away.

Allen had planned to sell 750 tons of this hay for a profit, but because of the serious setbacks experienced by farmers due to the '94 flood, no one was in a position to buy. The hay was worth just $5 a ton. The eventual price they were able to sell the huge crop for is not recorded. Nevertheless, when haying was finished, the event was celebrated enthusiastically,

as it had been for years, with the fun of the annual haymakers' picnic.

It was a great day to look forward to. There would be a huge feast at the lakeshore of Cultus, and after-wards games and races for everyone. All the children would dash towards the water for their swim and after-wards watch excitedly as the men matched their strength and talents in a tug-of-war or a game of horse-shoes. The trip along the six miles of wagon road was a treat in itself. The ladies were dressed in their best-starched dresses, the children shouting with excite-ment, and even the horses were specially groomed and decorated with big red poppies and ribbons in their bridles. The trail wound along the Chilliwack River, crossed it, then passed over another bridge at the Vedder. It went through Soowahlie Indian Reserve, and through heavily timbered mountainside. The road was so narrow that if another wagon was met, one had to be unhitched and lifted into the brush to allow the other to pass.

Farther on they would ford Sweltzer Creek and again drive through heavy timber beside the creek to the lake. Their destination was the deep lake tucked in behind the foothills, fresh and cool on a hot summer day. Those at the picnic in '95 might have been those who had also sat at the huge table at Edenbank dur-ing haying season.[27]

After a day filled with fun and fellowship, the women would prepare a hot cup of tea and prepara-tions would be made for the long, rough ride home and of course the waiting chores. Natives who helped with the haying seldom joined the picnic, however,

The new Eden Bank Creamery Company building was located at the present intersection of Spruce Drive and Vedder Road in Sardis, on the northwest corner. Note the milk firkins sitting on the deck. Later this building became James Chambers's store, the Edenbank Trading Company, and now it is owned by Bill Towler, who keeps it in excellent condition. A.C. Wells is standing left centre of picture.
COURTESY OF CHILLIWACK ARCHIVES

The interior of the Edenbank creamery after 1910, when power came to Sardis via the B.C. Electric Railway. Before electricity became available, the butter churn was run by steam separator. Note the pulleys and belt, the wooden butter boxes, and the two butter moulds lying on the desk.

many of them joined in the camp meetings between seedtime and harvest.[28]

With many new farms developing, and with increased production in many herds, a need for a community-owned creamery became so acute that in 1896, some of the neighbours joined with the Wells family in setting up a co-operative company. It was named the Eden Bank Creamery Company Ltd. Joining the endeavour with Allen Wells were Mrs. Jane Evans, Shelton Knight, William Blanchflower and C.T. Higginson. Thus was formed the first farmers' co-operative in western Canada. Jack Stuart became the first secretary, and many years of prosperity followed for the company.

Mrs. Pashley had been the first butter and cheese maker to manage the creamery Allen had built on the farm in 1885. When the new co-operative took over operation and management, Ted Smith became the butter maker. Ted had received his training at the Dairy School of the Agricultural College in Guelph, Ontario. The creamery was equipped with a No. 1 separator with a capacity of 300 gallons per hour and a churn with a capacity of 400 pounds of butter.

On August 12, 1897, Allen wrote to William Townsley, his son-in-law living in England, "The Kootenay mines have improved our prospects very much. We hope to sell (them) our hay for $10 a ton, f.o.b. here."

By the fall of that year, Edenbank Farm had acquired a Canada-wide reputation. The editor of *The Farmer's Advocate* visited B.C. on a national tour and one of his farm visits was to Edenbank. In the November 20, 1897, issue of this magazine he described Edenbank and Allen's achievement.

> The Edenbank farm and setting are excelled by few in the Dominion in culture and appointments. Mr. A.C. Wells is an enterprising and influential man in the community, being Reeve of the Municipality, taking a leading part in many public enterprises for the public good, widely read, and up to date in methods of farming.

It had been just thirty years previous to the editor's visit that young Allen Wells had walked with his family up a small trail to the little house he had built in the clearing, in a wilderness of timber and swamp. ❧

CHAPTER 7

Family and Community Life

The pioneer farmers of Chilliwack were among the first to recognize the desirability of establishing an agricultural exhibition in order to display their livestock and produce. Jonathan Reece offered his barns for exhibition use. In 1873, A.C. Wells became one of the directors of the newly formed Chilliwack Agricultural Association. The prime object of the association was to encourage the development of improved livestock and field produce. Allen too became an enthusiastic exhibitor. Livestock and farm produce soon travelled from Chilliwack to New Westminster by boat, then on to Victoria to compete with the best livestock of the province.

The church camp meetings, held between seedtime and harvest, were an annual event in the lives of the pioneer families. Allen, like others, had a small building on the grounds where the camp meetings were held under the direction of Reverends Crosby and Tate, the Wesleyan missionaries. These men were successful in the conversion of many natives to Christianity. Crosby was a kindly but domineering figure

This sampler was made in 1813 by Martha Casey, Allen's mother, at age ten years. In 1904, Allen sent it to England to his granddaughter May with a letter telling her about his mother and the hard time experienced by the Loyalists. COURTESY OF SARAH REAY

who held full-scale revival meetings. His powerful voice, in all sincerity, would boom out, "Praise the Lord, Hallalooooooyah" whenever a worshipper felt a need to acknowledge his sins and ask forgiveness.

Young and old looked forward to these gatherings. Natives and whites came by riverboat and canoe from points as distant as Nanaimo and Yale. One camp was established in 1870, near the junction of the Chilliwack River and the Fraser. Another was established in 1882 approximately three miles up the Chilliwack River. These meetings continued until 1910 and for the children, it seemed like a big picnic where they met and made many new friends.

Weekly prayer meetings were also part of regular family life on the farm. Allen remained a faithful church attender, and Lillie and Eddie would often attend with their parents. The church and their faith were a constant focus in their lives.

When the town of Chilliwack became the established centre of the valley communities, Allen assisted with the building and support of a new Methodist church there.[29] For a time, he acted as choir leader since he was a lover of the "grand old hymns." He also

Cattle being taken to exhibition. With a bull tethered to the back of the wagon, the cows were willing to follow behind.

Isaac and Mary Ann Kipp, ca. 1885, are seated on the porch of their home on what was later Hodgins Avenue in Chilliwack. Their son Will, nearby with the crutches, was badly injured while rafting in the flood of 1884. The rest of the group are relatives and friends. This house, built ca. 1880, was the Kipps' second home. Their first, made of logs, was the first pioneer home built in Chilliwack. Modified slightly over the years, this house now operates as a bed and breakfast.

led classes in the new Wesleyan Methodist church and was a staunch supporter of its principles.

When he became magistrate in 1884, he was respected by all, admired for his stand on moral issues by many and feared also by a few. He was a powerfully built man and as magistrate walked unafraid down the streets of Chilliwack. In those rugged days, knuckle-dusters were worn by those who still clung to the old frontier idea of "might is right." On one occasion his life was actually threatened, and for a time he drove into town via Main Street rather than Yale Road, where he knew he might be shot easily from ambush. When accosted on the board sidewalks in town by a ruffian who threatened to "smash" him, his quiet but firm answer was, "Go ahead; it won't change the law."

The reader will recall that Gertie Kipp married Edwin Wells and her father was Isaac Kipp. Isaac and his wife, Mary Ann, whose maiden surname was Nelmes, had a family of ten children. The Kipp house (still standing today on Wellington Avenue in Chilliwack) was of sufficient size to accommodate this large family.[30] The house had eight bedrooms, a large dining room, a parlour, kitchen and dairy room. The latter had room for necessary farm equipment such as skimming pans, churn, dairy utensils and pails. Cleanliness and sunlight were relied upon to produce the finest quality of butter. A successful farmer himself, every week Isaac shipped 100 pounds of butter along with thirty dozen eggs downriver by boat to New Westminster. Twice yearly, Isaac would go for supplies and come back laden with everything needed for the family for the next six months. In the fall, a steer would be killed along with six pigs, and the meat would be cured for winter use. As a family member, Gertie would have been very involved with household and farm chores from an early age.

Besides a strength of character and a thoughtful nature, Gertie, as Edwin's new bride, brought an immense beauty and charm to Edenbank. In the years to come, her pioneer upbringing on the Kipp farm and the fact she had been raised in a large family would be of great value when it was necessary for her to take an active role in farm management.

As for family members, hired help had to be provided with comfortable sleeping quarters in the pioneer home. Beds, like most furniture, originally were made out of available material. Rough lumber, carefully smoothed down, or split cedar was favoured for bedsteads. Woven wire was used for bedsprings, and mattresses were filled with clean straw from the barn or "pugh-lah," the down gathered from the bulrushes in marshes.

Even before the turn of the century, sheep supplied wool for the pioneer home. This represented real luxury. Gertie replaced the "pugh-lah" in the mattresses with soft wool and made a woollen quilt for every bed. Within a few years, she had made no less than twelve quilts. She took pleasure in making the guest room especially attractive and comfortable, as many a visitor proclaimed.

Because four extra dairy herds arrived at Edenbank for safety during the '94 flood, these herds together with the Edenbank herd greatly increased the output of the creamery at Edenbank. The area and surrounding farms entered into a period of comparative prosperity and the farmers' co-operative begun in 1896 was successful.

Allen was recognized as a community leader and in 1897 was elected Reeve of the municipality as well as its magistrate. Edwin by then was quickly assuming a major role in the farm management. This led to a partnership between father and son. Edwin's sister, Lillie, had taken a trip to England a few years previously, and there she had met, fallen in love with and married William Townsley, the son of a landed gentleman.[31] Lillie remained in England for some time and had three children, May, William Allen and Edward Ernest Townsley.

Farm stationery first appeared in 1894. While primarily for farm use, it was no doubt of particular interest to Lillie when her husband received a personal letter from her father. The letterhead featured a picture of an Ayrshire cow and had special typesetting for many of the words. Chilliwack, B.C., was noted as the postal address. The letterhead read:

> Eden Bank Farm
> A.C. Wells & Son Proprietors
> Stock Berkshire Pigs
> Importers & Breeders of Ayrshire Cattle
> also Agents for Alexandria Cream
>   Separators

In the letter to William Townsley, Allen referred to knowledge of agents from B.C. in England to promote sales of B.C. mining stocks. He warned his son-in-law

A wonderful group photo of the Kipp family. Back row left to right: Allan, Frank, Gertrude (Kipp) Wells and Arthur Kipp. Middle row: Jenny (the first white child born east of New Westminster), Mr. Isaac Kipp, Mrs. Isaac Kipp, Will and Fred Kipp. Seated: Alma (Kipp) Chadsey and Nellie Kipp. Isaac was heard to say that his house was often full of music, with the piano playing in one room and an organ in another.

that he himself would not buy these stocks. He referred to the very small proportion of successful claims being established by thousands of Klondike gold-seekers. He inquired whether William ever thought of coming to B.C. to live and spoke enthusiastically of opportunities in business, particularly the salmon-canning business. Regarding an abundance of salmon he wrote, "This year, the salmon were so plentiful that the nets were out only a short time in the day, and then the salmon accumulated so much that large scow loads were taken to the salt water, spoiled. They are sure of the finest fish known: the average price paid for them by the Cannery was 5 cents each."

His letter closed with a personal note, characteristic of a deeply felt yet rarely disclosed love of family. "Tell Lillie I will write her soon. Kiss the children for me. Please remember me kindly to your father and mother." Signed, "A.C. Wells."

Land clearing was still a major undertaking on local farms to bring more acreage into production. Following the completion of the CPR, many Chinese workers took up residence in the valley. A Chinatown sprang up beside the old Westminster/Yale Road, between Chilliwack and Edenbank farm.[32] Industrious Chinese labourers walked daily to work in the surrounding countryside. They carried their necessary requirements for the day in their accustomed fashion, dangling at either end of a pole balanced over their shoulders.[33] One behind the other, maybe half a dozen or more Chinese would be seen walking in single file to work, chatting animatedly in their native language. They came to Edenbank, to assist other Chinese who

Edwin Wells and his sister, Lillie, when he visited her in England in 1902. He was delighted by his carriage rides around the nearby estates. His letters home were full of enthusiasm and love for his family. Sadly, when he returned to Toronto, he received word that two of his small boys had died of diphtheria.

had taken a land-clearing contract with A.C. or Edwin. One such contract has been preserved. It reads:

This indenture made this 6th day of Dec. 1900 between A.C. Wells & Son of Chilliwack B.C. on the first part and Kwong (Chinaman) of Chilliwack B.C. on the second part:

Witnesseth that the said A.C. Wells & Son for and in consideration of the covenant hereinafter mentioned and reserved on the part of the said Kwong all that parcel of land being part of Lot – 8 acres more or less, said land being the uncleared portion of the S.W. Corner of the said lot – to have and to hold for the space of 4 years from the date of this indenture upon the following conditions, to wit

The said Kwong agrees to clear the said land of all brush and timber and the said lot shall be free of all roots, sticks etc. at the end of the term –

It is also agreed that the said A.C. Wells & Son provide for the hauling of the said produce from the said lot to the present Chilliwack Landing at the rate of $1.00 per ton (providing two tons can be hauled at a load), and also for the ploughing, harrowing etc. @ $4.00 per day (8 hrs. in a day). In witness thereof we set our hands and seal.

Signed & delivered in the presence of Liester Frost
A.C. Wells and Son

By the spring of '98, many changes had taken place at Edenbank. During the previous year, Allen had had carpenters busy again in construction of a retirement home. It was north of the original farmhouse on a bank overlooking the Luckakuck. An attractive two-storey home was built on a mortar and stone foundation, eighteen inches thick, enclosing a basement. Central heating, an added luxury, came from a wood and coal furnace, a major advancement for the time. Allen built himself a modern chicken house, incorporating into the construction some features

Allen Victor Wells, 1896–1902.

Carmen Willard Wells, 1898–1902.

that would be adopted into common use only seventy years later. He also had built a horse barn and buggy shed, for his "driver," a beautiful mare. For years he drove over to the old farm almost daily to keep an eye on progress. He kept twenty ewes in a specially constructed sheep barn at the retirement home. When asked what he enjoyed as a hobby, he modestly said, "My enjoyment has always been in the satisfaction of seeing things accomplished." His grandsons were always fascinated by an automatic gate he designed and installed at the entrance to his driveway.

At Edenbank, Edwin, although still relying on his father's good advice, was now managing an extensive farm operation. He developed into a natural and enthusiastic exhibitor, making every effort to show fine livestock and farm produce. The Chilliwack Agricultural Association prize list of 1900 showed active support by A.C. Wells & Son in a full-page Edenbank Farm advertisement. It referred to the pure-bred Jersey cows, Ayrshire cattle, Berkshire pigs, White Plymouth Rock fowls, White Peking ducks and White Embden geese of Edenbank. The association solicited correspondence from readers and advertised the Eden Bank Creamery, operated by the farm. A.C. contributed a special $10 prize for the best display of farm produce at that exhibition.

In 1901, A.C. Wells & Son purchased six pure-bred Ayrshire cows in Ontario. These cows became the foundation of the famous herd later developed.

New Westminster became the leading and most important centre for agricultural exhibits and displays and the gathering place for leaders in agriculture. Here Allen traded a ram lamb for the biggest show pumpkin, grown by Mr. Kelleher of Matsqui. While at the Chilliwack Exhibition, he helped host Premier Richard McBride as well as Mr. Ladner, for whom Ladner district was named, and other pioneer farmers.

Many notable agriculturists and breeders were Allen's early competitors, among them Herbert Page, noted breeder of Holstein cattle and Percheron horses; Mr. Shannon of Cloverdale; Joshua Wells of Wells Landing (later to be known as Hatzic); and Mr. H. Vassey of Nicomen Island. Exhibition times were important occasions to allow the farmers to

The Wellses were particular about their hired help, preferring "a respectable, gentlemanly, clean lot of men." Standing left to right, 1899: Gertrude, Edwin, young Ray, Harry Weeds, C.L. Reid, Frank Blackstock, Archie Atkinson, A.C. Wells. Seated left to right: Young Allen, Ernest Farrow, Mr. Clark, Foo, Frank Twigg, Fred Hussey. It was Foo who was fatally injured at the farm in an attack by the bull Zad.

show their best livestock and produce. They seemed to be times of never-ending effort day and night and rarely were there enough daylight hours to train animals to lead or to groom them before they left for competition.

In a typical trip to the Chilliwack Exhibition, a wagonload of hay would be followed by a wagonload of hogs and sheep. The bull was usually tied to the tailgate of the wagon and acted as a lead animal to the twelve or fifteen cows, heifers and calves, which were driven in a herd along the road. Sometimes the animals following the wagon would give trouble to the rider on horseback who was trying to herd them along. In this fashion they travelled to the fairgrounds or to the Landing, where they might encounter difficulty loading the animals onto the riverboat if their destination was New Westminster. Such difficulties might be intensified by darkness. When the cattle came off the boat at New

Allen's retirement home and a stopoff in his buggy for his horse to have a drink.

Westminster, there was another drive to be made, this time up through the city streets to Queen's Park.

About this time an influx of settlers made it opportune for A.C. Wells & Son to sell ninety acres of land at the upper or south end of the farm along Steven-son Road. The price paid of $100 an acre was a record for the time.

In 1902 Edwin enjoyed a visit with his sister, Lillie, at the Townsley estate in Yorkshire, England. The village of Fogathorpe was within the estate boundary. Old country customs, titles and class distinction were a bit unfamiliar to the young farmer from the West. During his visit he noticed that the Irish did indeed love potatoes, as he had always heard. They seemed to be the staple diet of Irish labourers working in the harvest fields. He also noted that his sister Lillie served tea to the workers in the fields, rather than bringing them their customary draught. He thought his father would surely approve! Edwin said her buttered scones and winning personality were an added treat that the workers appreciated so much that they didn't mind missing their usual draught.

The pastoral landscape of the English estate left a lasting influence on Edwin. In the years that followed he tried in part to duplicate what he had seen. He also learned one very worthwhile basic rule of haymaking in rainy weather: if the weather is wet, keep turning your hay to keep it fresh and free from mildew. He often said he was sure that in England, in a wet year, when the men were turning the hay with only a pitchfork to help them, "They could have moved it to the barn if they had turned it in the same direction each time!"

A terrible tragedy occurred at home while he was overseas. His two young sons, Carmen and Allen, ages four and six, were stricken with diphtheria. They died within a day or two of becoming ill. This was a terrible blow to all the family, and a deep sorrow lingered. In spite of this the daily chores at the farm had to continue.

In 1903, A.C. Wells accepted the presidency of the B.C. Dairymen's Association and became even more involved in community affairs. He took time, however, to write a letter to his granddaughter, May, Lillie's daughter in England, then age twelve, in which he enclosed the gift of a sampler his mother had stitched when she was ten years old.

Edwin, meanwhile, was busy planning for increased production and sale of pure-bred livestock. He aimed at developing the herd into a supply centre to which breeders, wishing for foundation animals, would come for good, reliable breeding stock. The Edenbank creamery by then was producing 118,000 pounds

William and Lillie Townsley, ca. 1910.

or more of butter annually, and the trademark "Edenbank" was becoming known in various parts of the developing province of British Columbia.

A sense of being transported in time to the past is conveyed from reading Edwin and Gertrude's daybook for the first few months of 1903. It tells who does the chores, cleans out the barn (by forkfuls) and feeds and milks the cattle, and it records how much hay the men are busy baling and stowing in the mows of the barns. Notes are made each time someone takes a team and a load of baled hay to the steamer landing. (The hay used at the farm for their own animals was loose hay, and the baled hay gave them a source of income during the winter.)

They were wintering more than 220 animals, fattening pigs and making arrangements to sell and buy stock. When Allen returns after attending a Farmers' Insurance meeting in New Westminster on January 27, 1903, Edwin meets him with the horse and cutter as there had been a snowstorm (a chilly ride, no doubt under the cover of a buffalo robe).

There are several Chinese men working at jobs such as fencing and clearing and helping with chores in the barn. At one point Edwin goes to the blacksmith

The retirement home of A.C. Wells showing the unique Manlove gate. The sign to the left of the gate said, "This gate for buggies only." For years the family heard stories of this marvellous gate, which opened automatically as one wheel passed over the trip. This house has been maintained and is located on Spruce Drive in Sardis, B.C.

A.C. Wells and grandson Ray at a 1907 exhibition in New Westminster with a champion cow, Dentonias Arpeggis.

to have clogs put on a team, so he can help Kwong plow his leased acreage. Gertrude tells about young Ray and also the blond and bright baby Clarence. As the days go by you learn he can stand alone and finally walk around the room. What a joy he must have been to Gertrude and Edwin, for it was less than a year since their two youngsters, Carmen and Allen, had died of diphtheria.

One of the farm geese is killed and Gertie cleans it. She then describes the roast dinner she prepares for twenty good friends, having the day previously baked mince and lemon pies and chocolate cake. She tells of the pleasure of that evening. Often she writes of the community's losses and how she and Edwin visit friends by buggy or cutter. Edwin describes his daily schedule and what the men's jobs are for the day of the week. As spring approaches they tell of how many rows of tomatoes, corn and vegetables such as mangels and sugar beets are planted and when they butcher different meat for the table.

One evening Edwin goes to hear a debate at the Epworth League by Mrs. Street and Mr. Hasham, "Resolved that farmers' wives have a harder life than farmers." Results are in favour of farmers' wives.

Wagonloads of barley are taken to Kipp's mill to be ground for the hog feed. They also boil up as much as a ton of potatoes at a time for the hogs.

Sundays the family always enjoys going to church. One morning, Gertrude writes, Ray and baby Clarence both go to sleep. After church that day she and Edwin have a quiet walk in the garden.

During the week of January 15 the men are working on Allen Wells's driveway up to his new home. They install the special Manlove gate that always fascinated the boys. As Allen approached this gate and ran his buggy wheel over a metal lever, the gate automatically opened.

The diary entries by both Edwin and Gertie give a glimpse into the intimate lives of a young and busy farm family one hundred years ago. ௸

CHAPTER 8

Edwin, Gertrude and Their Growing Boys

When Ray was around age ten or twelve, a devastating event took place in the Edenbank swine herd. There were three hundred hogs at Edenbank and they were an important part of the farm economy. Allen was disturbed one day when he noticed that several of the pure-bred Berkshire hogs were very sick. He got down the old *Stock Doctor* book and learned to his amazement their symptoms were undoubtedly those of hog cholera, a dread disease then known to be infecting valley herds. Government regulations required that all hogs on an infected property be destroyed.

Ray Wells remembered the event clearly years later and described it in graphic detail.

A large pit was dug near the old hay barn, at some distance from the hog barn. The pit was 8 feet deep, 20 feet long and 10 feet wide. A fence was erected around it, sufficiently strong to corral the pigs either into the pit or close to it. The bottom of the pit was covered with lime. The hogs were then driven into the enclosure: old sows with litters of young; feeder pigs and fat hogs ready for market; pure-bred boars and young Berkshire sows. In all, 300 head were driven into the corral encircling the pit. There they were shot, one at a time. If they were not already in the pit when shot, they were thrown in afterwards. The carcasses were covered with a deep layer of lime and then buried under several feet of soil. Fortunately the disease was eradicated. All hog barns and pens were thoroughly cleaned and disinfected before it was possible to have hogs at Edenbank again.

Another major change in life at Edenbank occurred in 1904 when the old Edenbank farm creamery (built in 1885) could no longer handle milk from the greatly increased number of member shippers. A new creamery was built adjacent to the farm.[34] This allowed the retail shipping business to Vancouver to be maintained and for a time the creamery flourished. In 1912, it paid 55 cents per pound of butterfat.

The old creamery building on the farm was converted into a boarding house for farm workers. A couple was employed to operate the house, and the farm paid them their cost of board and lodging.

A boarding house statement is reproduced here, dated August 18, 1908.

Gertrude Wells with baby Oliver, born in 1907, the sixth of seven sons. Her pioneer upbringing gave her the skills to manage a busy household.

An early barnyard scene at Edenbank. In the background, left to right: windmill, butter and cheese factory, residence, horse barn, straw barn, large cow barn (built in 1894). Between the barn and the cedar-slab fence is the dairy herd. In the foreground are gravel bars left by the Chilliwack River after floods in 1887 and 1894. This photo is another by Mr. Booen.

A.C. Wells & Son
July a/c
Board 6 men 15.00 . . . . $90.00
Mr. Barter 4 meals @ 16 cents 65
Mr. David 4 meals @ 16 cents 65
Mr. Thornton 2 dinners @ 25 cents .50
Borrowed by Mr. Wells 50

$92.30

Less Milk 3 qt. for 31 days 5.58
Fruit picked 40 lbs. 40

Pd. by Cheque Aug. 18/08 *Total $86.32*

A letter written and circulated by A.C. Wells & Son is indicative of Allen's careful selection of the type of individual he wanted to work at Edenbank. This letter was written on the farm's letterhead, which now advertised "Edenbank Farm. A.C. Wells & Son Proprietors. Stock Importers and Breeders of Ayrshire Cattle, Berkshire Hogs, Lincoln Sheep." It read, in part:

We would like to engage some competent person, a married woman without children preferred, to run our farm boarding house. We usually have from six to eight men by the month all the year round, and at times a few more. We have always paid $15.00 a month for each man, and 20 cents a meal for single meals. We furnish free boarding house and have a very suitable, roomy building for the purpose; also supply free city water, bedsteads, spring mattresses, wool mattresses, also feather pillows for the men. We also let the free use of a small garden plot for growing vegetables. We always try to keep a respectable, gentlemanly, clean lot of men and have made it a rule, for years, to keep only men who did not make a practise of using liquor, bad language or tobacco. Would be pleased to receive your reply and references.

(Signed) A.C. Wells & Son

In response to the letter, Mrs. Wilbourn with her two sons Ernie and Frank, who were old enough to work on the farm, and her two daughters, Jessie and Nellie, arrived at Edenbank. Mrs. Wilbourn operated the boarding house for several years. The two girls did not long go unnoticed by the up-and-coming young farmers Fred Hubbard and Clarence Newby, who sported the best in covered-buggy comfort for long evening drives with the girls. Soon weddings were announced.

During the early part of the twentieth century, there were few dedicated livestock breeders in either Canada or the United States.[35] Edwin, like his father before him, was an enthusiastic breeder and always strove to improve his already well-chosen stock. He always recognized and appreciated the efforts of others who were leaders in the field of stock breeding and innovators in crop management. He himself introduced new crops, and these varieties were soon able to compete and be tested against the old. Among the field crops, grains were given many trials. Corn, a new crop in Canada, was experimented with yearly. In 1907, Edwin planted five varieties of corn to assess for yield and early maturity: Long-fellow, Canada Yellow, Northern Pacific, Mammoth Cuban and Stowells Evergreen. Bonner oats were received in small four-pound bags from the Dominion Experimental Farm, Ottawa, to be tried and propagated. Root crops were important to the dairy cattle, and several varieties of mangels, carrots and turnips were planted each year, until the most desirable were selected.

The orchard was now producing a major crop. Small fruits were grown, and experiments were undertaken with raspberry, blackberry and currant bushes. Edwin and Gertrude developed a wildflower bed beneath an oak tree to the south of their home. From the surrounding woods and trails they collected Oregon grape, Solomon's seal and ferns. In 1906, twelve rose bushes, purchased in Victoria, were planted in big circular beds, together with four varieties of red and white tulips.

The children were encouraged to take an interest in livestock breeding. Ray became the registered owner of Elmwood River, a Yorkshire boar, bought from the Kelly Brothers in Ontario. By 1908, he sent a Berkshire sow to Dawson along with a number of dairy cows to supply milk for this boom town of the Yukon. Frank Twigg went on the boat with these cattle from the farm.

Edwin was always ready to buy a good horse and loved to hitch up and break a young colt. The ones he selected were mostly of medium weight, often with a

The young Wells boys – Oliver, Gordon, Casey and Ray – with their favourite pony.

Edenbank cows were shipped by boat in 1908 to Dawson City, Yukon. Frank Twigg accompanied this shipment to Elliott Dairy. Later Frank took over the management of the farm for Edwin while the new home was under construction.

quiet nature, although sometimes they proved to be a fair challenge before they were "broke." Bands of horses were always being herded through the valley, often coming from the Interior over the Hope-Princeton Trail. In 1906, all of the young men on the farm rode out to see a band that was spending the night in the open fields just to the east of Edenbank. In the morning, these horses were driven onto a riverboat at the Chilliwack Landing to be taken to New Westminster.

Another son, Casey, born in January 1902, was the blue-eyed baby of the family until Gordon, his brother, was born in January 1905. With big brown eyes, curly hair and a happy disposition, Gordon became the favourite of Jock Stronach, a husky Scot who had come to work at Edenbank. Jock's jovial presence was welcomed in the home, and he soon became a most capable herdsman for the farm.

During the spring of 1907, a telephone line was built into the Chilliwack Valley. By the assistance of that medium, Oliver, the new baby boy born to Gertie Wells on May 21, was able to cry loudly enough in New Westminster to be heard sixty miles away by his father in Chilliwack. Being another boy (number six by then), I often wondered about my welcome, but I was lovingly accepted and because of this was years later able to set my hand to the task of writing the story of Edenbank.

The year 1907 brought a first major win for my father, Edwin, at a provincial exhibition. The Ayrshire herd of A.C. Wells & Son showed at the New

Westminster Exhibition and won recognition as the best dairy herd of any breed. This was a major accomplishment and the first of many laurels for the herd under Edwin's guiding hand.

The 1909 World's Fair was held at Seattle, Washington. Edwin attended to have a chance to see all the herds of international importance. There, from the herd of Barclay Farms of Pennsylvania, he purchased Lessnessock King of Beauty, a mature Ayrshire bull who had been undefeated in major show rings of America. This bull was imported from Scotland. The breeder was J.W. Montgomery of Lessnessock, who for many years would be a leading livestock breeder.

The following show year at New Westminster, prizes for senior and junior herds were again won by A.C. Wells & Son, with A.H. Menzies & Sons of Pender Island receiving second place. In the long-wool breeds of sheep, Edenbank took first and second place. The farm continued to prosper and the land to bring forth great rewards.

John Coatham had for some years been developing a fruit farm on Promontory Heights, about two miles south of Edenbank. His flock of sheep industriously cleared the rough stump pastures of brush there. John also carefully tended the orchard at Edenbank on a share basis. He was a leading orchardist and for a time, his fruit entries from the Chilliwack Valley and foothills presented stiff competition in the district exhibits at New Westminster. Jim Bellamy and Andrew Atcheson were other long-time Edenbank employees who acquired land and established their own dairy farms.

At noon one fine day in 1910 as the family sat down to have dinner, they heard the piercing wail of a steam whistle, a strange new sound near to their farm. They instantly knew its source. For weeks, workers had been laying a rail line diagonally northeast across the farm as construction of the B.C. Electric Railway neared completion. Crews of Chinese working with wheelbarrows and shovels had built the railway bed. Large wooden culverts drained low places, and the line was raised in some places to an even grade five feet above average ground level. All the rails had finally been laid and now the first train was coming through the

sought-after benefit. Sardis residents had sponsored a financial drive, raising $1,200 to help bring the line through their area. Edenbank had contributed a land gift of six acres. When my future wife, Sara, first travelled to Sardis on the B.C. Electric train in 1922, she was told to watch for a large sign on a big barn, "Edenbank Farm."

Many more changes continued to take place at Edenbank. Edwin's adopted sister, Mildred Wells (a relative taken in by the family in the late 1880s due to misfortune in her own), had grown to womanhood, and her hand was won by Ernest Farrow, who had come from England to work at Edenbank. By the time the B.C. Electric had crossed the property, Ernest was

Mr. E.J. Trapp of New Westminster on horseback judging the first prize Edenbank herd at New Westminster, B.C., in 1907.

farm. Everyone dashed down the farm lane to watch the train pass for the first time.

The steam engine blew lustily as it neared the present-day Spruce Drive, north of the farm. Only three years of age, I can remember being hoisted onto my father's shoulders for the rush to the lane gate to watch the big train come in and can still feel that excitement and thrill. For everyone who had laboured for years without the benefit and convenience of electric power, this represented a dream come true. The rail line was finally through, and although steam was powering this first train, high-voltage power lines along the track would soon provide another energy source.

Edenbank was literally hungry for power. The big barn was already wired for electric lights and had a 10-horsepower electric motor waiting for current, to saw wood, cut up mangels and turnips, grind grain, fill the silo and bale loose hay. With the coming of electricity, Gertrude and her family could set aside the old coal oil lamps in use in the house and barns.[36]

The coming of the B.C. Electric had been a much-

busy clearing forty acres of land southwest of Edenbank, adjoining the Charles Evans place beside the B.C. Electric right-of-way (land now owned [in 1967] by John Urquhart). He wished to establish a road, to cross the wet lowland and allow access to other roads. With the coming of the railway, he had only to flag down a train and step on. According to Ernest Farrow's written memories of the valley, previously only the river steamers the *Beaver* and the *Ramona* provided regular transportation in the valley.

Unfortunately, the railway set up unfavourable repercussions affecting the Edenbank creamery. The rail line provided a new shipping outlet for fresh milk from farmers in the Chilliwack Valley. A milk train became a special feature of an express service, and each morning, within a period of a few hours, milk from Chilliwack could be delivered into Vancouver. Shippers were drawn away from the old dairy to retail outlets in Vancouver. The boom in Vancouver lessened in 1912, then went into a slump. These facts, combined with some difficulties in its retail general

Allen and Edwin Wells were among very few dedicated livestock breeders in North America early in the twentieth century, and they were both enthusiastic exhibitors. Edwin here shows Whiterose of Springbrook at New Westminster Provincial Fair, 1912. She was reserve grand champion of all breeds and the champion of Ayrshires.

store, led to the breakup of the Edenbank creamery co-operative. The co-operative founders all suffered financially, and for some members a permanent with-drawal from farmer-owned co-operatives resulted.

Ronald, the last of Gertrude and Edwin's sons and another fair-haired boy, was born at Edenbank in 1911. With five living sons, it seemed to Edwin and Gertie the time had come to build a new and larger home, and long-dreamed-of plans were formulated as they sat around the kitchen table.

They decided, while construction of the new home was taking place, to move temporarily to a cottage in the orchard. Here the Bryant family had lived for sev-eral years after arriving from England. George Bryant, the oldest boy, had become a member of the Eden-bank extended family. He later moved with his mother to take up farming on his own in the Rosedale area.

When George was working at Edenbank, the Ayr-shire show herd had been given added prestige by the purchase of Rose, a grand champion cow. Later [in 1989], Fred Bryant, George's son, an active commu-nity member and agriculturist, recalled his father's memories of days spent at Edenbank.[37]

The land was graced with teams and scrapers to form the spacious lawns and building site for the new home. Father

mentioned that the first Mrs. Edwin Wells [Gertrude], a very gracious and dignified lady with a strong and determined spirit, was the driving force in the preparation and planning for their large new home. While it was before my father's time, I heard of the battles, almost with blows but certainly with force, to divert and control the Chilliwack River, which would have had a bearing on the volume and flow of the Luckakuck River in front of Edenbank.

Recalling other stories by his father, Fred referred to the fact that getting to the Chilliwack fair was a major task.

The animals were herded or led along Vedder Road to the fairgrounds. A team and wagon travelled along as well, perhaps carrying young calves but for sure carrying grain and loose hay, likely straw for bedding, along with milk pails and other equipment. As well, one year, likely 1911 or 1912, my father was given the task of walking home the old bull (herd sire, to be more correct), who likely weighed 1,600 pounds. I do not think that he was part of the main herd

Ray with four-horse team and Fresno scraper landscaping the front slope of the Edenbank homesite towards Luckakuck Creek, ca. 1914.

procession. Dad told it as if he was alone with simply a rope halter on the bull and a wooden staff attached to the ring in the animal's nose. Apparently all went well until they got about halfway home. At the Cottonwood area [now the Highway 1 interchange to Chilliwack/Sardis], the bull became frightened and for a few minutes Dad had all he could handle. He finally succeeded in snubbing the bull, probably to one of those cottonwood trees. And there they remained until the other farm workers finally came to his rescue, bringing a riding horse or two and a lariat.

Both Jock Stronach [Fred Bryant's father-in-law] and Father were young boys who came directly from Britain to work at Edenbank. George travelled across Canada by CPR in 1908 or '09, got off the train at Harrison Mills and crossed to Minto Landing in an Indian dugout canoe. After the long journey he had all of 50 cents in his pocket! By the time these men graduated or completed their years, Jock Stronach was foreman of the fields of Edenbank, with eight men as teamsters and labourers. My father, George, was the barn foreman, with a complement of twelve milkers.

Since 1906, records of production testing was used Canada-wide for pure-bred cattle. Edwin entered cows on test and obtained official records in reports of 1907. Mention is made here of the names of his Ayrshire cows of quality breeding. He purchased these in eastern Canada, and their progeny added greatly to herd improvement. Their interesting names were Nellie Bairns 2nd of Burnside, Bonalee, Evergreen Maid, Coronation and Springhill White Beauty. These cows provided increased financial security and helped Edwin pay a mortgage on the farm and their new family home.

To make sure that the progeny were always equal to or superior to their dams, Edwin was forever searching Ayrshire literature for herd sires with greater potential in conformation and pedigree. Willowmoor Robinhood 18F was purchased from Willowmoor Farms, a world-renowned establishment in Washington State. Edenbank Peter Pan, a specially named son of Beuchan Peter Pan, famous sire of Scottish breeding, also came from that farm.

My own first memories of activity on the farm are vivid. As a boy of six years, I used to climb onto the truck wagon or dray, whose front wheels could be turned completely under the wagon for convenience in city dray work. I remember this wagon, parked under the shed at the end of the big barn during winter months. There, the milk from the dairy was poured from buckets into ten-gallon cans and strained through clean cheesecloth. I remember seeing this rich milk being poured, the warmth of the dairy barn and the contented, well-tended cattle in their stalls. I also have special memories of the many horses at Edenbank raised and used over the years.

One of my happiest memories, along with my brothers, was the arrival of three pure-bred hackney ponies, purchased in New Westminster. They were a tandem trio of high-steppers and beauties all. Johnny Bang was the two-year-old stallion of the trio and was the top horse to we boys' way of thinking for the next seventeen years. The trio had been imported from Scotland, along with a number of pure-bred Clydesdale draft horses. Johnny Bang was bred at Harvieston, Dollar, in Scotland. Mr. Kerr, who managed that famous Scottish livestock breeding establishment, remembered Johnny Bang even forty years after he had shipped the pony from Scotland to Rogers, a New Westminster importer. Johnny was of a fiery disposition. As a stallion he was almost unmanageable even by experienced horsemen. He was soon gelded and in due time became our quiet family horse. He taught us boys just as much as we were able to teach him. Our escapades with Johnny Bang could fill a book, much like stories of "old Molly," who was a favourite and a legend to all. Ray rode to school in Chilliwack each day on Molly. No horse could have been more dependable, nor was her spirit lacking when Ray would race her against the Evans boys.

In 1912, on his decision to fully retire from the farm operation, Allen signed an agreement with Edwin providing him full ownership. By this agreement, A.C. retained a portion of Lot 38 in his own name in order that he might subdivide it during his retirement years. It became known as the Wells subdivision. The approximately two hundred acres remaining were assigned to Edwin. An appraiser was hired to establish the value of farm livestock and equipment. It was agreed that A.C. Wells would receive half of the established value in cash. To facilitate the undertaking, a sale of stock took place which included 11 horses, 35 cattle, 42 sheep and 13 pigs. This sale realized more than 50 percent of the money required for settlement, and Edwin paid the balance by cheque. With this agreement, Edwin became the sole owner of Edenbank and continued the farm and family tradition.

The energy with which Edwin undertook to meet financial commitments and advance his plans proved to be a considerable strain, and he decided to hire a manager temporarily until his health improved. Subsequently, he arranged to rent the farm as a going concern to Frank Twigg, who had worked for some years on the farm and in whom Edwin had every confidence. On September 12, 1912, Edwin made a lease agreement with Frank Twigg to take over management of

Oliver at the head of Johnny Bang with Ronnie on board. Ronnie would ride the pony from the house to Vedder Road to pick up mail from the box.

The Edenbank farm home was designed by renowned Vancouver architect Thomas Hooper. Young Casey took this photo of his three younger brothers just after the house was built. He was fascinated with any aspect of science, including photography, and even took pictures from the top of the house and from the highest trees. Later he developed stereoscopic photography for aerial views of the forested slopes.

Edenbank and one hundred head of livestock.

With his son Ray as companion, Edwin then went to California for a holiday, free from the stress of farm management. On his return and with renewed vigour, he devoted much of his energy to the construction of a new house. Plans were completed according to well-thought-out ideas of both Gertie and Edwin. A Vancouver architect, Thomas Hooper, was asked to prepare sketches for the residence, which he did at a fee of $100. Edwin acted as contractor and made financial arrangements for every phase of the construction.

The house was to be approximately forty by forty feet, standing two storeys high on a basement ten feet deep. A cement-block foundation wall would extend four feet above ground. The first floor would have ten-foot ceilings, the second just eight. Above the attic, the roof would rise to a central deck on top, measuring six feet square. For a number of years, the opening cover or trapdoor from this high outside roof

deck into the attic below proved a very practical place of entrance for Santa Claus with his jingling brass bells at Christmastime.

With the completion of the house, Edwin launched enthusiastically into landscaping. A gardener, Mr. Sherlaw, assisted with laying down of lawns and sidewalks. Edwin and Gertie planned the overall landscape. Edwin supervised contouring of a slope down to the river in front. Ray was the worker who drove a team pulling a slip scraper for many days to slope the bank gently and gracefully down to the Luckakuck stream.

Edwin planted dozens of trees in his "park," which encompassed ten acres around the new home. Beech, willow, silver birch, decorative evergreens and shrubs were set out to form a manicured setting. The final appearance of the homesite when landscaping was complete reminded Edwin of some of the fine English country estates he had visited some years before. ♞

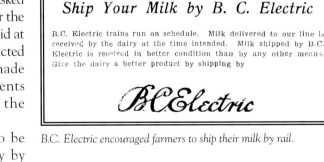

B.C. Electric encouraged farmers to ship their milk by rail.

CHAPTER 9

A Time of Worry

The completion of the new home in 1914 preceded a period of national insecurity. The First World War had begun, and there was nothing to stimulate the Canadian economy. Working classes were still unorganized. In the United States, labour began revolting against poor working conditions and low wages. In industry, tension was rising, and there was open revolt in the agricultural community. Harvest crews in the grain-growing areas of the West were literally "throwing a monkey-wrench" into the threshing machines. Crews staged sit-down strikes and the battle cry of labour was "IWW – I Won't Work."

At Edenbank there was also a rumble of discontent. The Wells family was again managing the farm. Ray, aged twenty-one, was a strong and burly youth in charge of horses

Ayrshire bulls Robinhood and Peter Pan do battle for supremacy of the herd.

and could do any man's job in the field. Gertie and Ray were assisting as farm managers, and Edwin was involved with house building. Haying season was in full swing when suddenly, everything came to a halt. Teams stopped hauling and were tied up. Men left the haymow. Those pitching hay in the field waited and waited, but no empty wagon came back. It was the first and only strike Edenbank ever knew. It occurred possibly because Allen's stern personality and Edwin's influence were not present, or because there was an agitator in the crew. In any case, the men rebelled and suddenly the situation was out of control.

The strike held up the haying for the day. Grandfather came out of retirement to get the work under way again. The agitator, who slept in the bunkhouse with regular hands, continued to make

The ice storm in the winter of 1917–18 caused great devastation in the valley. The new electric power was lost and the trees badly damaged.

trouble. Ray finally could take it no longer and faced him in the bunkhouse to "set things straight." Fists flew that day and the outcome was that Ray's mature adversary decided to seek employment elsewhere.

All his life, Gordon had a love of the land and especially of horses. He was in his early teens during the years of the First World War and was needed to help on the farm, so he decided to withdraw from school. Later, he did take further schooling. His love for all animals influenced his permanent choice of a country life. He had an uncanny sixth sense with horses and happily spent much time working with them from his early youth into his adult life.[38]

Archie Edmondson, a strong young man in his early twenties, was employed at Edenbank for a period during the war years. Farm help was then scarce, so Edwin applied for Archie to be exempt from military service. In those days, when cows were milked by hand, there were few men who could milk ten cows in one hour. Many thought they could, but good milkers would average only seven or eight cows per hour. Archie could milk ten cows an hour

This sign hung above the old root house door. Later the root house was turned into a garage for the first automobile purchased for the farm, but the sign remained for decades.

regularly each hour and often twenty cows in two. He was a favourite hand around the farm and the boys loved his good humour. Archie later drove as a teamster for the Fraser Valley Milk Producers' Association.

By 1918, when the Allies were still hard-pressed, every able-bodied man on two good feet was enlisted. At Edenbank, the farm crew was reduced to a small number. They were Moses Grapit, a seventy-year-old Texan; Wing, of Chinese descent; and Gordon, a boy of fourteen. Gordon fed and cared for twenty-two horses, fed cattle and helped with the milking. Moses cleaned out the barns, and he and Wing hauled roots and pulped them for feed. They pitched out the silage, hay and straw required for each day's feeding during winter. They had to regularly drive to a large pit in a field to load turnips and mangels. One hundred tons were sometimes kept in one long covered pit. Protected by straw and eighteen inches of soil, the mangels would be fresh and crisp. Often, with a cold northeast wind howling and the snow drifting, collecting them became a terrible task. We boys vividly recalled those trips.

The first motor transportation for hauling milk in 1925 was operated by Archie Edmondson, one of the best hands at the farm and fondly regarded by the family. He could consistently milk ten cows an hour. COURTESY OF FRASER VALLEY MILK PRODUCERS' ASSOCIATION

The family at Stanley Park after visiting their very ill mother in hospital in New Westminster. The boys didn't know how sick Gertrude really was.

Many in the family didn't realize that Gertie was becoming ill. Although she still assisted in farm management, she was especially exhausted. That particular winter of 1917–18, cold weather and icy blasts blew in from the east. It was all everyone could do to prevent stock as well as family from freezing.

A silver thaw, a rare phenomenon caused by unusual weather conditions, twice wrought havoc and destruction at Edenbank. In January 1918, rain had fallen in the valley for days and the previously frozen ground had absorbed but little of it. Ditches were filled, and water lay everywhere. A gentle breeze blew from the southwest. For a time it finally stopped, then the clouds lifted and moved inland up the valley. Soon the breeze returned, but this time it came from the northeast, with cold air from the Interior coming down the Fraser Canyon. The temperature dropped to below freezing. Ice began to form, and soon the surface ice was joined by a deeper frost, which falling rain could no longer penetrate. High overhead, more clouds arrived from the southwest and as they rose dropped their moisture into the cold, freezing atmosphere of the valley below. The temperature fell to 28 degrees Fahrenheit and stayed there as the cold northeast wind held steady.

Ice formed on tree limbs, on telephone and power lines, over roads and on the steps of the houses. Soon it was too icy and dangerous to travel anywhere. A person could not stand without exercising great care.

A horse, unless "sharp-shod," could not walk about without slipping dangerously.

In one day, the ice became an inch thick and was still forming. The stock had to be kept in the stables or paddocks. Ashes were spread on the hill down to the road to give temporary relief from slipping. It became evident as darkness closed in the second night without any change in weather conditions that the power might fail at any time. Hand lamps and lanterns were made ready. As morning came, the smaller limbs of trees, covered with thick ice, began to break off. The cold air echoed with the cracking of frozen limbs. A B.C. Electric train crossed the farm the evening of the second day. We boys were able to see the overhead trolley connection spit out a steady stream of flame as short-circuits from the ice became almost constant.

When electric power lines were first brought onto the farm, a 1,200-volt line extended several hundred feet in from the public road, crossing the river to an initial pole, then continued past the boarding house to a second pole. Overhead it connected to a third pole, which stood beside the horse barn. A large transformer was located on that pole.

The weight of the thick ice on the lines finally brought the transformer pole down, along with the "hot" 1,200-volt line. In the paddock, Rose, a 1,600-pound Clydesdale mare, switched her tail against the line. Normally she was very quiet and docile.

Allen and Sarah's retirement home, built in 1897. It featured central heating from a wood and coal furnace, a luxurious advancement for the time.

She received a shock so great that she crossed the paddock in terror and jumped a high board fence without touching it.

One of the power lines over the river broke with the ice. An end of the wire dropped into the stream while the other end lay about twelve feet from the water. Immediately, an arc of light began running over the ice from the end of the live wire to the river, keeping up a continuous flare and lighting up the whole area. Everyone had been warned to stay inside and away from all downed wires. Sadly, word came that Mr. Sayjohn, a neighbour not long arrived from the Prairies who was not accustomed to electricity, had been electrocuted. He died instantly as he picked up two ends of a broken power line, presumably thinking he could join them while wearing leather gloves for protection. Another neighbour almost lost his life by simply getting too close to downed wires.

The third day began in darkness with no power. Every tree was stripped bare of small branches. At Edenbank an enormous limb of a big oak near the house broke off with a loud report and other large limbs followed as oaks, maples, alders and cottonwoods came crashing down in great disarray amidst masses of ice. The ice was now three inches deep on the ground. No one ventured onto the roads or moved about in any way, except to care for themselves and their livestock. Gravel roads, normally rounded a little for drainage, were now like skating rinks. Charles Evans, Jane's son and cousin to Edwin, came around with a sharp-shod team to take milk to the creamery on bobsleighs. He took off his mackinaw coat when he came into the house for lunch and, miraculously, the coat stood by itself – frozen stiff. Almost every telephone and power pole in the valley was down. All the tall ornamental trees in the newly landscaped areas at Edenbank were bent or broken.

Then the temperature rose, and torrents of water came pouring down the mountains into the Chilliwack River. The roar of the river two miles away could be heard from the porch at Edenbank. A call went out for teams and men to help control the flooding. For the next eight hours the river rose a foot each hour. The Teskey farm above the Vedder Bridge lost ten acres of land to the river. Men were stationed on the bridge to keep floating trees from snagging when their big roots were caught. Below the bridge, the dance hall was undermined by the river and finally was carried away. Because of log-jams, the river's flood waters broke through into the old channel leading towards the Luckakuck. People living alongside the stream bed packed their belongings, ready to move if necessary. Fortunately, the river held its main course to the west and Edenbank was spared its ravages. Warm rains continued to melt the ice and the weather moderated. Power and telephone crews laboured for a month before restoring limited power and service to the area.

At about this time, the worldwide Spanish flu epidemic of 1918 was causing immense hardship throughout the nation. In British Columbia there had already been an overwhelming loss of young men due to the war. Now many returning soldiers were becoming ill with the flu and many people died from it. It seemed that with the ravage of flood and ice storm, and now the flu epidemic, this added tragedy was more than most could bear. In Chilliwack, all schools, churches and public gatherings were closed indefinitely. At Coqualeetza school alone there were over one hundred seriously ill flu patients.[39]

At this troubled time Gertrude became very ill, and with apprehension Edwin took her to the hospital in New Westminster. When she said her goodbyes to the family, we boys didn't understand how ill and frail she had become over the previous months. She died a short time afterwards from cancer. This tragic event had a profound effect on the family and naturally created a huge void in the lives of Edwin and his young family of five boys. Gertrude had been a wonderful wife and mother and a carefree, happy and fun-loving person. She had always provided much support to the family and worked diligently to help where possible in all farm activities. She would never be forgotten, and her spirit would live on in the memories of her family and many friends.[40]

Personally, I knew our mother had always provided a special joy to our lives. She added such a happy presence in the home. I can remember how often we gathered around the piano to sing while she played and sang as well. In the ensuing months my father and Wing kept a kind eye on us and soon Mrs. Bradshaw came to help manage the household. We then started again to have a better sense of security.

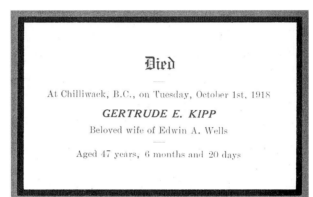

Died

At Chilliwack, B.C., on Tuesday, October 1st, 1918.

GERTRUDE E. KIPP

Beloved wife of Edwin A. Wells

Aged 47 years, 6 months and 20 days

A memorial card of Gertrude (Kipp) Wells, 1871–1918.

෴

Two years passed and one day in 1920, now a teenager, I was standing alone in the driveway leading up into the big barn. I was casually watching two massive Ayrshire bulls. Robinhood was moving back and forth along a single fence, which was all that prevented him from getting at Peter Pan. They were both full-grown bulls, each weighing close to two thousand pounds. Robinhood must have been resentful of the fact that he, with all his twenty or more grown daughters, should have had this upstart Peter Pan come and presume to be a superior bull to head the herd.

While I watched, Robinhood moved to a gate, well hung on strong hinges, that separated the two paddocks. His big horns were tools of destruction that he could handle with terrible power as well as with delicate precision. He set his horns in the gate and easily lifted it off its hinges. Letting it fall, he slowly walked into Peter Pan's paddock. With neck bowed and head down, he snorted. Peter Pan also carefully lowered his head, pawing the ground in defiance, and held his position, not fifteen yards away. For a few minutes the two beasts pawed and snorted. While slowly backing away from each other they continued to snort, roar and paw the ground in their mutual challenge. When they were about twenty yards apart, they each held their line for a minute and then charged.

Until then, I had been completely fascinated, watching in awe. When the charge came, I knew it was too late to do anything but watch. Heads lowered, the bulls ran at full speed and crashed head to head with a resounding thud. For a second they faltered and then each, as if by mutual consent, backed away. At about fifteen yards they lowered their heads and again charged headlong at one another. They were fighting this time in earnest. In the furious onslaught, each tried to gain the advantage by getting under his opponent. Their only protection against each other was their massive horns, burly necks and tough shoulders. They fought fiercely but quietly, straining continuously to find a weak spot in the other's defence.

For a time, Peter Pan held his own. Then, slowly, he gave ground. He went to his knees in an effort to get under Robinhood to lift him, but he could not. If he turned to try to get away, such a move might be fatal, exposing his belly and flanks to powerful horns. He held on defiantly but finally retreated. Gradually, Robinhood forced the younger bull towards a corner formed by two rail fences. Peter Pan must have realized the danger of being cornered, for he made one more attempt to back up his adversary but again failed. When he tried to break loose and escape, Robinhood caught him broadside with both horns, low down on one side. The force of the blow threw Peter Pan against the fence, breaking three rails. With a final lunge, he escaped with two long, bloody gashes in his hide.

Fortunately the horns of Robinhood had not pierced deeply and Peter Pan survived. He never tested Robinhood again, but it was only half a victory for

The bull Willowmoor Robinhood 18F, shown here dehorned, was a most remarkable contributor to the improvement of the Ayrshire herd.

Robinhood. He had done too much damage with his horns, so after this incident he was put into a dehorning chute and Dad took a fine-tooth butcher saw and cut off the horns. I weighed them afterward and found they were three pounds each. When the tourniquet to control excessive bleeding was removed, Robinhood regained his freedom. He was allowed out into the fields, but thereafter his movements were hampered by a heavy leather halter, which also acted as a partial blindfold.

The daughters of Robinhood were wonderful producers and of good conformation. This bull remained head of the herd for several years, vanquishing Peter Pan in every way. Robinhood's progeny raised the herd to new achievements in the dairy world.

Edwin joined with other farmers in B.C. to form what was known as the B.C. Field Crop Union, a group of men dedicated to improvement of field crops through experimentation. Because Ayrshire cattle were becoming popular, Edwin and other prominent breeders established the Ayrshire Breeders' Association of B.C., whose aim was to promote advancement of the breed. He became the first president.

During the war, conditions had worsened in the dairy industry. Edenbank had been shipping to an independent retail dairy in Vancouver. Edwin knew he was being badly done by at times, and when cans came back from Vancouver unwashed or poorly washed, the shipper sometimes also suffered by a low grade for his milk. At one time, he became so disgusted with dirty cans being returned that he put ashes in them and sent them back to Vancouver with a demand they be washed properly.

During 1917, farmers in the lower Fraser Valley decided to organize a co-operative of milk producers. Although still a young lad at the time, I was taken by my father to an organizational meeting in the old Chambers Hall in Sardis. Edwin joined the co-operative, and in 1917 he became a shipper and shareholder of the Fraser Valley Milk Producers' Association, to which Edenbank milk was shipped for more than forty years. In 1920, Edenbank was the second largest shipper of milk in the area. The Edenbank creamery and cheese factory was taken over by this co-operative in 1919, thus ending the name of Edenbank Creamery. Their products had been on the market since 1885.

With continuing good health, Sarah and Allen Wells celebrated their diamond wedding anniversary in May 1919 with family and many friends. A write-up of the event follows, excerpted in part from the *Chilliwack Progress* of May 20, 1919.

The home of Mr. and Mrs. A.C. Wells, Sardis was the scene of a delightful celebration on Saturday, when the host and hostess gathered around them the members of their family in a happy reunion in honour of their 60th Wedding Anniversary. The rooms were banked with flowers from relatives and friends and the long table from which the wedding banquet was served, bore masses of red roses. At the place of honour, before the bridal couple, was an Indian basket filled with Lilies of the Valley and Wild Solomon Seal, the gift of Mrs. J.A. Evans. Letters and telegrams poured in from the many friends of the family and a large number of well-wishers called during the afternoon and evening.

The same article described A.C. as "always a man of outstanding Christian character, farsighted energy, and undaunted perseverance, foremost in whatever occupation he takes up, and as a neighbour, a reliable guide, counsellor and friend."

Adding to the couple's happiness was the fact that

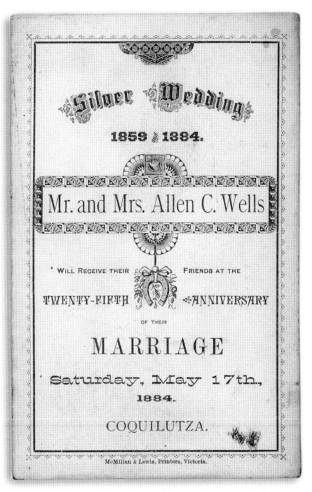

An announcement of the silver wedding anniversary of Allen Casey Wells and his wife Sarah.

A.C. Wells and Sarah at their sixtieth wedding anniversary party in 1919. Sarah recalled on that occasion how, traversing mud and water, it would take most of a day before roads were built to visit her sister-in-law Jane Evans at her farm.

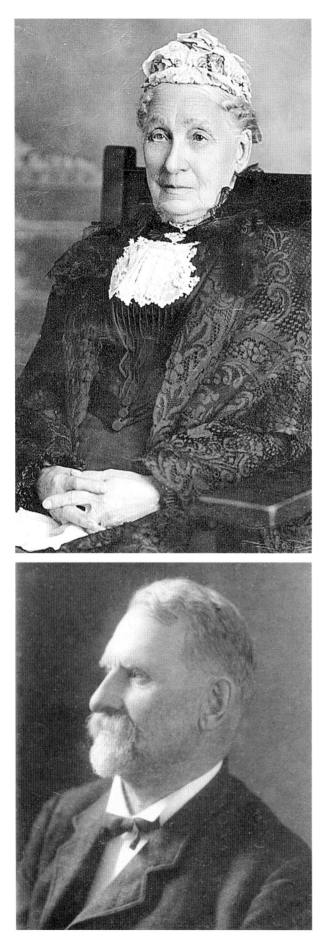

their daughter, Lillie, with her husband and family, were there for the festivities and had decided to make their permanent home in Canada. Lillie, William Townsley and their three children eventually settled in North Vancouver.

Allen's wife, Sarah, died in 1921. She was dearly missed by her husband, family and her many friends. Allen himself was then aged eighty-four.

In the spring of 1922, A.C. invited the B.C. Dairymen's Association to hold their annual convention at his home. Over fifty members were in attendance. It was a great reunion for many of the earliest pioneers in the valley. Two months later the pioneer Allen Casey Wells died peacefully at his home on the farm he had established some fifty-five years earlier, after arriving at the wilderness site in a native canoe. One of the many tributes spoken in the couple's memory was "Their home radiated a simple piety and was the centre of boundless and genial hospitality." ꒰

Top: Sarah Manetta (Hodge) Wells came west on the long journey through the Panama to join her husband in 1864, during the Civil War. Bottom: This formal portrait taken in the last few years of his life shows that A.C. Wells was a man of great vision and determination.

CHAPTER 10

Farm Chores for Teen Boys

argaret Smith stood in the upper window of the newly constructed Coqualeetza Industrial Institute in Sardis and looked out over the scene below her. It was early in 1894, and the waters of the Fraser in flood were high and still rising. She was then teaching at the institute.

Each day was bringing added hardship to the pioneers as flood waters spread out over the whole valley. A great sheet of water could be seen from Coqualeetza, encircling the outskirts of the little village of Sardis. Margaret could see the waters spreading west for ten miles to Sumas Mountain, past the Fraser River to the mountains beyond and, to the east, reflecting the sky and foothills below Mount Cheam.

Much later, in 1920, Margaret recalled these images as she prepared to return to Sardis to marry Edwin Wells and become a mother to five young men. She knew that Gertrude Wells, Edwin's wife and the mother of the five Wells boys, had battled cancer and passed away at any early age in 1918. She understood what a hollow her death had left in the family. Margaret had previously met Edwin while still

Margaret entering notes on the animals' performance. She was very meticulous and kept comprehensive records.

a young woman and teaching at Coqualeetza in the 1890s. For several years afterwards she had been a dedicated missionary teacher for a Chinese mission in Victoria. Now, at age fifty-five and a spinster (and much to the astonishment of her young niece Sarah McKeil, living in Victoria), she had been asked for her hand in marriage and had accepted the proposal of Edwin Wells.

On her return to Sardis, Margaret assumed a new role as Edwin's wife. She adjusted easily to her duties and to the home life at Edenbank and in a short time developed a fond attachment to and love for Edwin's young family. As well, she felt very familiar with the Sardis community and renewed many old friendships.

It was in her nature to have some worthwhile project under way. The Ayrshire herd quickly came under her observation, in regard to cattle lineage and production. On January 1, 1921, Margaret made her first herd book entry. The page was divided into four columns, with the headings (1) Date of Birth; (2) Tag No.; (3) Name; (4) Sold to. She listed the cattle born each year, including their

Farm mares were bred by a "travelling" stallion arriving behind a stud cart.

Stockmen and cattle in the new paddock at Edenbank just north of the horse barn, ca. 1915. Ray Wells, in left background, is riding the horse Dan, which went as a remount (replacement officer's horse) to World War I. George Cook, herdsman, is the one wearing a bowler hat in the centre. Gordon is the young boy in the centre and Oliver is the youngster on the right. A news article of the time pasted into Margaret Wells's scrapbook noted "that even the younger sons still going to public school each accepted his own responsibility and knew the details of his own branch thoroughly. 'They are the greatest asset we have,' said Mr. Wells, 'and we hope soon to change our letterheads to read E.A. Wells and Sons, Edenbank Farm, Sardis' " (Farm and Home, May 12, 1921).

registration numbers, and the names of their sires and dams. This became a regular project. Margaret then turned her attention to the family groups within the herd. These she listed separately, together with their official production records. Herd sires came under close scrutiny, as well as production records of progeny. Edwin appreciated her energy and organizational ability. Their mutual keen interest in his livestock breeding enterprise proved of great benefit for the herd.

Within a year, Margaret had completed an inventory of the entire herd, and within a few years, had undisputed proof of the superiority of the bull Robinhood as the best sire of high-producing daughters. As a result of her analysis, many cows, even show cows, were sold to the butcher if they lacked an ability to produce at least four hundred pounds of butterfat per year. All the farm records came under her close study, and once Margaret was heard to remark with wry humour, "I believe the hogs are keeping the cattle."

The home life at Edenbank gradually returned to normal after Margaret's arrival. Her own home train-

ing had been similar to Edwin's. As well, their church backgrounds had provided similar teaching, so their basic ideals and principles were much the same. Having a stepmother following the loss of our own mother was a stabilizing influence for the family.

Help-wanted notices were often placed in British newspapers by Edenbank and by other local farmers. As a result, Edenbank was fortunate to have many men of British origin on the payroll in the early 1920s who were willing and able workers. Their services were supplemented by the help of the three youngest Wells boys, who were beginning to take on more responsibility on the farm.

Cyril Roberts, who had come from England and was first a herdsman at the University of British Columbia, was engaged at Edenbank as herdsman. Under his guidance, the herd made rapid progress. In keeping with the times, he started milking some of the cows three times a day and soon had Little Queen of Beauty producing seventy-six pounds a day, a record for the time.

Sandy McFarlane, an Irishman, kept the team-

Edwin arranged for a new family portrait of Gordon, Oliver, Edwin, Ronnie and Margaret Wells ca. 1921. By this time Ray had married Alma Campbell and was living on his own.

work in hand, and William Stevenson, a Scot, who was a painter by trade, learned to enjoy driving old Beauty, the imported Clyde mare. In the fall, they would haul tons of mangels and turnips in the dump cart. Casey and William Stevenson got to betting on how long the famous Irish rebel, de Valera, would fast before he died. We boys affectionately knew William Stevenson as McSweeney, or called him Steve. In later years, when he went back to his old trade, he helped to redecorate the old home where he had spent so much time. He would expertly hang long strips of paper across the broad ceilings of the Edenbank house.

Our father began experimenting in the vegetable garden with new varieties of grasses and clovers. Working with Mr. Sutton of the B.C. Field Crop Union and others, he noted that on the old Maritime farms, land was being limed and many rundown pastures rebuilt. He laid out a pasture-management program as a result of his studies. He divided the larger pastures into smaller ones, then began field rotating his grazing animals. This, along with clipping, harrowing and fertilizing, proved of great value in increasing land production.

Feeding the pigs was a daily chore for the boys.

During our early teens, life on the farm for Gordon and me was never dull. On school days, we got up early enough to do farm chores before breakfast. In the spring and fall, Gordon had to "run in" the horses, brush them off and harness up the teams. Afterwards he went to the cow barn to milk his share of the cows. I fed milk to about thirty calves off milk stands in the barn, or fed them a homemade gruel of wheat, flax and "hulless" oats. I would carry two pails to the house containing the meal. Wing, the Chinese cook, then poured boiling water into each pail. I'd stir up the gooey mush and add cold water to make the pails full of a lukewarm nourishing drink for about five calves. Using a Dutch-style shoulder yoke, which had been beautifully fashioned by Chief Billy Sepass, I carried the two heavy buckets back to the barn.[41]

After feeding the calves , I fed great pens of chickens and rabbits. We were in for breakfast by 7:45 A.M., departing for school at 8:20. With schoolbooks and lunches we climbed into the two-wheeled cart, to which Gordon had hitched Johnny Bang. By 8:45, this fleet-footed pony had covered the three miles to Chilliwack. After a quick unhitch and tethering of

the horse we were in school on time, by nine.

When haying season was in full swing, Gordon, myself and Ronald, even at eight years of age, had our own work assigned. Gordon and I would mow and haul in hay with other men and teams. Young Ronnie would go out with the tedder and rake hay to help it dry. When the teams started hauling in, Ronnie would be lifted up on top of Nellie, the "horse fork" animal. He rode back and forth all day, pulling up the hay with a cable hitched to a hay fork. The fork was hitched to solid "breeching" (pronounced britching) that circled around Nellie's hindquarters, held by a draw-ring. At times, on the approach to the barn, Nellie had to pull downhill.

One day, young Ronald had a near-fatal accident. It happened when Nellie had been harnessed for the day's work. Neither Gordon nor Edwin was there to check that the bellyband, holding down the draw-chains, was securely fastened. If a horse is pulling and has its wind cut off by a collar on which the hames are fixed, it invariably continues to pull until it "chokes itself down." This happened that day when a downhill pull lifted the collar. Nellie choked when she was pulling hard. As she went down, the weight of the load on the fork pulled her over backwards. Ronald was caught under the horse, and the two points of the hames pressed deeply into his chest, fortunately not hard enough to cause a puncture. Before night, with his usual smile, he was riding again.

Edwin never burdened us boys with more work than we could manage, but of Gordon and me, it was expected the work would be completed, and done well. The feeding and care of livestock was an ever-challenging education which both of us accepted with keen interest and ready co-operation.

In the practice of medicine and surgery, Edwin had become an experienced hand and did not shield us from veterinary operations. Rather he taught us to meet any necessary emergency such as setting a broken bone, putting a dislocated joint back in place or helping a cow that was having difficulty calving. It was all in a day's work. Once, while quite young, I was asked to hold the "twitch" (a nose hitch for controlling a horse) while Edwin operated to remove a growth from the side of the neck of his much-loved driving mare, Tear-a-Way. She was nicknamed Pet and her fast gait could take Edwin to town in just a few minutes.

Horses supplied all the power for hauling, piledriving, haying and field work for almost ninety years and were not replaced until after the first tractor was purchased in 1950.

Tear-a-Way, Edwin's fast-paced mare, took him to town on many occasions. A horseman would note the growth on her neck, which Edwin himself later removed by surgery. COURTESY OF NEIL SMITH

A four-inch growth had developed on the animal's neck. After carefully examining its nature and the manner in which it had developed, Edwin decided it needed removal. Taking necessary hygienic precautions with carbolic acid or Creolin as disinfectants, he prepared his knife and opened up an incision twelve inches long, extending over and beyond the growth. Lacking chloroform to alleviate pain, a twitch had to be applied to the horse's nose. The device consists of a small loop of cord attached to a wooden handle approximately three feet long. The loop encloses the soft upper lip of the horse and is tightened by rotating the wooden handle. A nose twitch will reflexly quieten a horse's nervous system, and while pain is not entirely relieved, a horse will stand quietly while an operation is performed. I held on tightly to that twitch as I watched my father's skilful surgery.

Pet took her operation standing up. Edwin also worked standing. After making an incision, he bypassed large veins as he went in and around the growth and removed it by carefully severing its attachment. A thorough cleansing followed by carbolic solution, and

nothing remained except to sew up the opening, which he did with a strong needle and linen thread. It was a difficult and bloody operation, but quite successful. After that anything seemed possible to me.

We boys also received lessons in the art of home butchering of hogs, sheep and cattle. Home butchering was usually done in early winter. At first, the killing of a butcher hog was an experience that made us boys shudder, but it was a usual farm practice and gave desired results. A pointed knife, with a strong blade and sharp point, was taken in hand and when the hog stood quietly, the knife was sent deep into the lower throat to cut the jugular veins close to the heart, releasing a heavy flow of blood. The hog was allowed to walk about freely for a few minutes during which time its lifeblood quickly escaped, then the animal dropped lifeless.

A barrel filled with very hot but not boiling water was at hand. Using a mechanical lifting device, a 200-pound hog, freshly killed, was lifted into the barrel and dipped for sufficient time to loosen the hair. The animal was then lifted onto a platform, where it rested while the hair was scraped off, leaving the skin clean and white.

Then on to the actual butchering. A stick called a "gamble," about two feet long, notched at each end, was set into the opening at the hock joint. The carcass could then be lifted and hung from a stout beam on the ceiling. With deft fingers and a sharp butcher knife, Edwin would dress out the hog, removing the offal and retaining the heart and liver for early eating.

For two or three days, the carcass would be hung in a cool area, then carried into the basement of the house. Edwin taught us how to cut up and cure pork. From the sides, bacon sides were trimmed out and smoke-cured. The hams would be pickle-cured before smoking, using brown sugar and saltpetre. The feet were carefully prepared for a special dish as was the head meat, from which headcheese was made in great quantity.

The killing and butchering of lambs was harder on us young boys and for a time we were sent away when a lamb was killed. Eventually we had to learn the method. My father would lay the lamb on its side on a gate, place a knee on its neck to make sure it could not move or get up, then carefully send a sharp-pointed knife deep into the throat, through the jugular veins on both sides, carefully avoiding the windpipe. Even with a clean and correct thrust, it was always a long wait for the lifeblood to flow out and disappear between the gate boards. With life gone, the fresh carcass was placed on its back between two blocks set on the gate for skinning.

Edwin demonstrated how to cut the carcass. A cut was made through the skin, but not into flesh, from knee to brisket, hock to crotch. He sent the knife with ease through the joint at the knee and hock, or "false joint." The belly line was opened skin-deep, end to end. A gamble stick was set in place and the carcass pulled up, using a rope thrown over a high beam. Hanging thus, the skin was quickly pulled and punched off without bruising the meat. The belly line had been opened carefully to let out the offal. Lastly, the liver and heart were saved for the first feast of the newly butchered lamb.

After the carcass cooled, it was carried to the basement, where a heavy table and butcher's block were available for further cutting. Edwin did this with a keen feeling of pride in his work, as he taught us how each fine cut of meat was the result of a careful division of the quarters, loin and sides. Frequently, a veal was killed and dressed in much the same manner as the lamb.

With ten people to feed each day, it was a general custom to butcher a steer or heifer for the family whenever meat supplies were running low. Butchering a larger animal involved lifting a carcass by ropes and pulleys. It was much heavier work throughout. In warm weather, much of the beef would be preserved in salt brine as corned beef. It was a dish that was not appreciated by the young people. My own children were never served corned beef!

The propagation of livestock became common knowledge for farm boys. We not only raised rabbits, but also were responsible for turning the rams out to the ewes each fall. The propagation of hogs was a more complex business. Mature sows were expected to have two litters of young during the year. This entailed taking the weaners from their mothers at six weeks of age in the fall and breeding the sows again for spring farrowing. Before the little ones were weaned, those males that were not to be raised and sold as boars had to be castrated into barrows. There were generally twenty or thirty to be done each spring and fall. Edwin had long experience in this field, and he insisted that each of his sons had to take his turn in learning how to do both pleasant and unpleasant tasks.

After a sow was separated from her young, it was fun to learn how to catch a piglet without making it squeal. When its head was turned away into the corner of a pen, I learned to step forward and quickly catch a piglet by one hind leg. With a quick lift into the air there would not be the slightest squeal. I would then quickly flip it onto its back while at the same time catching it between the feet. In this position, the little one was helpless to do anything except loudly squeal. With the careful hand of a veterinarian and a razor-sharp knife, it took only two minutes before the pig was castrated and again on its feet. The squealing stopped and it was now a barrow.

Old Tornado, the big Yorkshire boar of the farm, had been herd sire in the hog barn for several years. His offspring came twice a year, in litters of twelve or even more. He had so often been master of his pens that he came to feel he should be master of all. His tusks had grown to a length of five inches, protruding

Tear-a-Way, nicknamed Pet, standing proudly with her foal.

out at right angles from his lower jaws. With these weapons, he could tear a hole through almost any fence to get to his sows. Over the years he became extremely vicious and was almost unapproachable, for his tusks could slash the flesh of man or beast.

Men had been known to use bolt cutters to cut the tusks out of old boars. Edwin decided on a simpler way for both himself and Tornado. Placing the boar in a narrow chute, he reached over the side and carefully and quietly set a cold chisel on the protruding tusk. A sharp crack on the chisel with a hammer and one tusk, which was solid ivory, flew off. After a vio-

pounds. He decided to castrate him even though the task looked formidable. Such an animal is a tremendously powerful beast while he has his feet under him, and to get Tornado off his feet and tie them securely together was no easy task. We boys watched the subsequent performance, assisted where possible, and amidst ear-deafening squeals the operation was completed. When Tornado was released, he was completely subdued. He spent the remaining weeks of his life fattening for market.

The development of pure-bred Clydesdale horses at Edenbank was one of Edwin's greatest pleasures. He

The Edenbank Ayrshire herd, shorn of their horns in March 1927, were the second largest pure-bred herd in Canada by 1922. Here they are shown on permanent pasture in 1930.

lent squeal, old Tornado settled down again. It was some time before the chisel could be set again on the other protruding tusk, but eventually, Tornado stood still long enough for another sharp crack and the ivory flew again. I gathered up the sharp tusk points and put them away. Years later, when watch fobs were all the rage, I had gold tips and a fine gold chain attached to one tusk-point to make a unique watch fob much admired by my friends.

Eventually it became necessary to dispose of Tornado. As an old boar he was neither saleable nor could he be given away. Castrated, he would be worth two cents a pound. Edwin estimated he weighed 750

loved a good horse, whether light or heavy. Pure-bred Clydesdales were his pride and joy. His purchase of Beauty and May after their importation from Scotland to New Westminster in 1909 gave him his start. Occasionally, a stallion was kept at the farm, but when we boys were in our teens, a familiar sight, and one which was always heralded with the noisy call of the stallion and the mares, was the approach of a visiting stud.

Tom Devillin, who was later secretary of the Clydesdale Association of Canada, was then "travelling" a beautiful Clyde stallion in the Chilliwack Valley. With a nice driving horse hitched to a two-wheeled cart, Tom went from farm to farm where mares were to be

Edwin's family at A.C.'s retirement home ca. 1930s. Left to right: Oliver, Edwin, Gordon, Margaret, Ron.

bred, leading his beautiful stallion behind him. His calls were weekly, although more often than not the mares said, "Not this week!" When the next spring came, there were generally two or three beautiful new Clydesdale colts on the farm eligible for registration. Because this was no boy's job, the men attended to the necessary arrangements when the teams were in at noon. Out behind the barn, over a stout high gate, the mares were given the choice to say Aye or Nay.

When Saturdays came, all too often there was wood to be cut, straw to be put through the cutting box or calves to be tagged. In the fall, which was also soccer season, mangels had to be hauled in. Every Saturday during the harvesting of the root crop, four loads of mangel tops were hauled out and spread on the pastures for the cows to eat over the weekend. This all had to be done before we boys headed to the sports fields. The family respected the Sabbath, so no work was allowed on Sunday, other than regular morning and evening chores directly concerning livestock.

CHAPTER 11

Horse Tales

In the spring of 1920, a foal was born in the big pasture field of the late former reeve Earl McLeod – a little "dark bay fellow" with darker mane and tail and four black socks. He carried a beautiful head and when his mother, a well-bred black standard-bred mare (a granddaughter of the world-famous Dan Patch), started going places, wee Dan would throw up his head and show a stride that spoke of strength and determination.[42]

For two years Dan ran free without feeling the restraining hand of man. Possibly he often watched the evening shadows creep up the mountains surrounding the valley and wondered what lay beyond those hills. Little did he dream he would walk those ridges and gaze far to the west, seeing out over the Pacific, and north, east and south as far as the eye could see, mountain range after mountain range.

During the same spring of 1920, on the Tzeachten Indian Reserve, about five miles west of the pasture where Dan began life, another foal was trotting along beside his mother. He, too, was a dark bay with darker mane and tail, and his three dark socks had the company of one white one. His mother was a good agricultural mare with a will to work and a desire to protect her own. When she ran in with a bunch of horses the wee colt, Red, trotted contentedly along and would watch his mother lay back her ears and drive the bunch clear of him. For two years Red cavorted about with his mother and learned there wasn't a fence they could not jump if the grass looked greener on the other side.

Dan's two years of freedom came to an abrupt end when he was corralled. He tried to clear the six-foot gate, but just couldn't make it – then Gordon's rope circled his neck and he was snubbed down. A hackamore halter was quickly fashioned on his head, and when the gate swung open Dan left the corral in a break for freedom. His hopes were short-lived. When the rope snapped tight, he found himself snubbed to the horn of a saddle under which was a horse that knew his stuff.

Edwin Wells loved to hunt and ride in the mountains and often went with his native friend, Chief Billy Sepass.

On the two-and-a-half-mile trek to his new home at Edenbank, Dan spent about half the time on his hind legs trying to free himself of the rope. When Gordon finally led him into the corral at home he was heard to remark, "There's a real horse – look at that head – and talk about power and determination – he's got it." With a feeling of pride and satisfaction, he looked forward to the coming days when he would develop this beautiful two-year-old into a perfect saddle horse.

Red's freedom terminated in a very different manner. Running with the band of horses on the native reserve, Red had developed a crafty nature, ever avoiding capture. Seldom was he seen without his ears back driving a bunch ahead of him. However, one day, Bridge Bailey, a respected local horseman and packer, managed to get close enough to Red to throw a rope on him. He was snubbed to the saddlehorn, saddled and bridled. When the rider hit the saddle, Red was given his chance to fight for freedom. Putting up a valiant effort, he nonetheless failed to dislodge his rider. Joining in with a party of riders, Red was finally willing to go with the bunch. That first day he went up over the foothills across the ridge trail, down into

Gordon Wells loved his horses, the rivers and mountains.

Bridge Bailey and Ray Wells(right), both skilled horsemen, shoeing a wild one at the Allison Ranch up the Chilliwack River. Old Ed Allison was a skilled packer and took many trips into the Red Mountain gold mine, as did Bridge Bailey. They guided heavily loaded pack horses over the Chilliwack River on a narrow log bridge.

the Chilliwack River valley and by night had covered about forty miles. He was broken – yes, partly – but Red was tough and he would remember. Another day would come.

Dan's training began in the corral, where he had nothing to think about except his trainer. It was not long before he was halter-broken and had lost all fear of Gordon, his trainer. Then came the "trips." He was led out onto soft ground, one front foot was tied up to a bellyband, then his head was pulled round to the same side, with no one nearer than at the end of a thirty-foot rope.

Dan found he had to submit to the ropes, but not without a determined struggle, which often took him up into the air to come down in many a queer position. He learned he had to go down when the word was given. His lessons were always thorough, but only one at a time, and care was taken to preserve his noble

spirit. Finally, Dan grew quiet enough to lie quite still while he was "gone-over" with ropes, raincoats, tin cans, firecrackers and anything else that might frighten a horse. Thus Dan learned to fear nothing and have confidence in his master.

Then came the day when he was led out into an open field. A surcingle around his heart girth with two rings attached under his belly was his only harness. A running W was then fashioned at the end of a forty-foot rope in such a way that the trainer could pull up one or both front feet at the same time if he desired. The halter was removed and once again Dan thought for a moment he was a free horse. A careful step or two and then he broke for freedom – but no, a familiar voice called "Whoa" and both front feet were suddenly jerked out from under him and he went down in a heap. He got to his feet and obeyed the command to move forward again. Once more he tried

Dan would lie down on command for Sara, the city girl, to climb aboard.

to make a break for freedom but the same "Whoa" stopped him in his mighty lunge. Thus in a few days Dan learned to obey his master's commands and to have every confidence in him. When the saddle was finally thrown on Dan, he was unafraid of it or the man in the saddle. He was never given a chance to buck and to his last day Dan never tried to buck.

Red was ready to buck the second time, and every time he was ridden for months. He received some very rough handling during his first few months of captivity, and during that time he learned to fear man and anything in the hand of man. About that time Edwin purchased him. In his new home he was a stablemate for Dan.

Dan was now learning his gaits and was beginning to show the results of his education. Night after night, Gordon took him out to establish a good, fast, flat

Edwin has bagged some grouse on a trip into the Liumchen Mountain range.

walk. Then night after night, mile after mile, Dan was trained to singlefoot. He developed a tremendous speed in this gait and soon outclassed any other horse in the district. Red came in for a little training about the same time, but was unable to develop any gait worth mentioning except his already established dogtrot.

Jumping had always been Red's means of finding better pasture on the native reserves. But he liked to walk up to a fence, put his head over, then lift his front feet and bob up and over and down. He would easily clear a five-foot board fence in this way.

Dan was also showing possibilities as a jumper, and soon a little training had him clearing five feet in a long sweeping jump. Dan and Red became exceptionally good trail horses. The Hope-Princeton Trail, the Chilliwack River Trail, the Liumchen, Elk Mountain and dozens of other trails were regularly trod by both. They became good stock ponies and Red became a noted stock horse. He defeated all local horses in the stake races for years, turning around a stake on his hind legs and taking one jump on the back stretch before his front feet touched ground.

Dan became a trick horse. He'd lie down for a rider to mount or dismount, count very correctly, and answer yes or no as desired. With the kindest and most beautiful head a horse every had, Dan was taught to look mean on command, and the change that came over his face would strike terror into your heart as he came at you with ears back, teeth bared and eyes defiant. At another command he would stop and immediately be his docile self again.

Life had been very much a man's world at Edenbank with no sisters for the boys in the family. Even with Margaret's arrival, life went on very much the same as before. In the heat of the day, or when milking the cows at night, we boys would take off our shirts to keep cool. It was not something done in public very much in the 1920s, and when Margaret took a walk to see the cows being milked in the evening, there was a scramble to get shirts back on. It was therefore something of a shock to us boys when we learned one day in 1922 that a "girl!" – Margaret's young

Gordon and Oliver (wearing Stetson) in their special new Angora goat-hair chaps from Calgary, which made them sit tall in the saddle.

niece, Sara McKeil – was coming from Victoria to teach school in the valley and she would be boarding at Edenbank.

The day Sara arrived, we kept out of sight but we did see Edwin drive up to the front gate, let the pretty young teacher out of the car and escort her to the front door, to be met by Margaret. She looked "OK," was our general consensus, but we hated the thought of getting all dressed up to go in and meet her.

In due time, very quickly in fact, Sara became an accepted part of the household and soon won a place in the hearts of all. She had a new bicycle, sent to Edenbank from her home in Victoria, but had never learned to ride. For the few days before school started, and with the boys' help, she practised riding down the half-mile farm lane in preparation for her three-mile ride to school, going up the foothill at Promontory above the farm woodlot. Later Sara was able to drive Johnny Bang to Promontory school in the same cart we had used to go to school in Chilliwack. When she arrived, one of her pupils who was much taller than she (being only a diminutive five feet) would unhitch

A spectacular horse jump at an exhibition in New Westminster that must have astounded the young men. Oliver kept this photo in his own album.

the horse and tie him in the buggy shed out back.

The winters in those years were sometimes harsh, but the summers, though busy, were happy days for us and for our dad, especially when haying was finished. Edwin was always ready for a trip into the mountains. As a young man he had often gone into the hills with Chief Sepass, Harry Uslick or some other of his old native friends. Often he took Ray or the rest of us with him. Sometimes we took horses into mountains where the only trails were deer trails. To us this was the highlight of our summers.

In 1925, Edwin organized a large force of volunteer labour and established the Liumchen Trail into the beautiful parklands above the valley, at an elevation of between four thousand and five thousand feet. He and Chief Billy Sepass had scouted out and blazed this trail sometime before. Each year thereafter, parties large and small would leave Edenbank on horseback and head for Liumchen and a pleasant outing.[43]

From our meagre savings Gordon and I purchased Angora goat-hair chaps and Stetson hats. This was not too much appreciated by Edwin and Margaret, but while wearing these we felt very debonair. As well we felt very secure when we settled into the saddle. There was never any doubt when riding Dan and Red that our destination would be reached. The two of us had many wonderful rides together visiting friends, hunting in the foothills or just trail riding for pleasure.

Gordon, being an excellent horse trainer, had trained Dan to be a broad jumper. The old meadow, rough and rolling as

Good riding horses had their uses for recreation as well as for farm work and transportation. The polo team from Sardis, 1929. Left to right: Lorne Malcolm, Ron Wells, Oliver Wells, Ray Wells, Gordon Wells, Carl Wilson, Gordon Pearson, Scotty Redpath, George Martin, Tony Newby.

it was, was made into an arena where jumps were set up. We found our horses could jump about 4½ feet high. Dan proved to be a superior jumper – especially in the broad jump. Night after night during the summer, Gordon lengthened the span of the jump over rails lying on the ground. Later, when Charles Welch came to the Chilliwack Exhibition in 1926 with his group of champion jumping horses, he challenged local riders to compete with him. Gordon entered Dan in the broad jump. Dan was in his best form, and though carrying over two hundred pounds with Gordon in a western saddle, he finally outjumped the Calgary horses. Dan covered thirty-one feet for the winning jump. He became famous as a broad jumper.

When Gordon and I went to Vancouver in the fall of 1926 to take a vocational course in agriculture at the University of British Columbia, Dan was sold to the Point Grey Riding Academy. He was in the last Edenbank stock shipment to go down the Fraser River by boat. It was a sad day of farewell to a beautiful and faithful animal. Arriving in New Westminster, he was saddled and mounted by the new owner's jockey and ridden to Vancouver. Later we were told that Dan had covered the twelve-mile distance in less than two hours with his wonderful established singlefoot gait.

The mid-1920s were years of some of the greatest of all Calgary Stampedes. The riders were for the most part working cowboys, taking time off to ride in the stampede. Among the most famous riders of all time was Pete Knight, who rode such horses as Midnight to win the championship for three successive years. I watched the riding at the New Westminster Exhibition one time when the Calgary Stampede was brought to B.C. in the big oval at Queen's Park in New Westminster. Horses, steers and chuckwagons gave the grandstand great thrills. I had never tested my ability to ride a bucking horse. After watching the stampedes, all of us boys decided to try steer riding at the farm to test our skill and courage. One evening, three local native boys rode into Edenbank leading a grey horse. "Will you break him to ride for us?" they asked Gordon. "Sure," said Gordon. "Tie him up to that post in the barn there."

The boys did so and left. That night at suppertime, I ventured to say, "I've always wanted to try to ride a bucking horse; maybe I should try this one." It was a sure bet the grey would be a tough ride, or the native boys, who traditionally could handle just about anything, would not have brought him to Gordon.

Ray's wife, Alma, heard that I was going to ride a bronc after supper, and when the event was to take place, she sat on the fence waiting to see the fun. Gordon saddled Red and led the grey out into the old pasture field, while I donned my heavy chaps, took my saddle and followed. As I passed Alma, her only comment was "No pulling leather, remember!" – not too reassuring for me.

In the centre of the field, the grey was snubbed up close to the horn of Gordon's saddle with a blindfold fastened over his eyes. A saddle was gently let down from over Red's back. The cinch was tightened on the grey and everything was ready. There was no bridle. I was to have only a halter rope to hold.

I climbed up on the grey. Gordon handed me the halter rope, now loose from the saddlehorn, and quickly pulled the blindfold off the grey. For a second, the horse looked around, and then he snorted. As his head went down he let out a blood-curdling squeal of defiance. I had no time to feel fear, for the grey's head had gone out of sight between his front legs. I experienced a new feeling surprisingly different from the happy-go-lucky riding of a steer. I was high above ground and still in the saddle, but there was nothing in front.

For about six high stiff-legged bucks the grey fortunately kept a straight course. Then he started bucking in a tight circle. For a minute I seemed firm in the saddle, but each buck was throwing me out wide and I couldn't quite get back before the next pitch. Just as I felt the end was near, the grey changed course and came up under me. For another few bucks he kept his head right out of sight. Suddenly, to my great relief, he threw his head up and began to run. It was rough and fast, but what a relief! The grey was heading for a far fence when Gordon caught up and grabbed the rope. It was my first ride on a bucking bronc, and it would be my last.

By the time Gordon rode him back over to the reserve, he had made a good saddle horse out of the grey. The native boys admitted that the horse had bucked them all off and they'd all been afraid of him when they had brought him to Gordon. They'd known if anyone could break him in, Gordon could.

My brothers and I and a few friends formed a polo team, and for a time we gathered at Edenbank to learn to play polo. Fred Jubb was the instructor. Our team never made headlines but it was all great fun. Another pleasant diversion from regular riding was "Roman" riding, which was often an event at the exhibitions in competitive races. Rossy Redpath and I spent many evenings racing each other up the farm lane, Roman style. Each rider had two horses and rode with one foot on the back of each horse. Sometimes the horses had an English saddle tied together so they had to stay close. With two sets of lines and a surcingle around each horse, it was exciting to go flying up the half-mile lane. I used Red and a little horse by the name of Snap I had obtained as a colt out of an upper-country bunch. He was very fast – both he and Red were quick starters and became a good team for a quarter-mile race.

Rossy and I rode in a Roman race at the Chilliwack Exhibition that fall. Al Evans had a pair of thoroughbreds in a race with a rider from the Interior. Fortunately for Ross and I, the visitor on his fast thoroughbreds hadn't had a chance to practise enough with his team. Coming in on the home stretch, his faster horse crowded its mate into the rail and the thoroughbreds lost out. Rossy and I triumphed that day. ♒

CHAPTER 12

A Farm of Champions

In 1922, Edenbank began a livestock advertising campaign for the Ayrshire herd. This was to continue for forty years. An exhibition of good pure-bred stock was the foremost method of promoting a breed. All over western Canada, show circuits were so organized that a herd could continue, week after week, to travel to successive shows publicizing the cattle.

From the cover of an early-twentieth-century Canadian Ayrshire Review.

A natural showman himself and a keen exhibitor, Edwin encouraged me and my brother Gordon to exhibit the Ayrshire herd. Subsequently Ernest Farrow, who was in charge of the show herd, with our assistance, exhibited at Chilliwack, New Westminster, Vancouver and Victoria.[44] The sire of the Edenbank herd was Alta Crest Nonskid. For many years he was a champion bull and lived up to expectations. His female companions had pretty names – Nellie Burns, Evergreen Maid, Lady Nancy, Stately of Bonnie Doon and Coronation of Edenbank. Together they won a total of forty-seven first prizes in several different shows.

At the Vancouver Exhibition, the first-prize herd lined up for a photograph at the edge of the grounds, just beyond the old sheep barns. The picture taken shows a background of giant stumps and uncleared forest area. The Pacific National Exhibition is held at the same place now [in 1967] and there are stretches of only blacktop, which during exhibition time is covered with parked cars.

In production records too, Edenbank Ayrshires began making a mark. The animals Springhill White Beauty and Evergreen Maid of Beauty the 2nd set new Canadian records.

In 1923 Edenbank was again in show business.

Oliver and Gordon, in their late teens, are wearing Edenbank shirts as they tend to the show herd at the new exhibition barn at Vancouver's Hastings Park. For forty years the herd advertised the Ayrshire breed on the western show circuit and as far east as Toronto.

Early in the summer, a herd was fitted out for the Prairie circuit starting in July in Calgary. Springburn May Mischief, a top show cow, had been purchased from Gilbert McMillen, a famous eastern breeder. Before Calgary she was shown in Brandon, Manitoba, where her championship career began.

In June of that year, Bob Stewart, a husky Scot with years of experience in handling, feeding and fitting cattle, came to take charge of the show herd. His first undertaking of importance was to teach a new herd sire to lead and behave himself. Rena's Laddie of Elkhorn, a good-sized three-year-old bull, had come from California. He had been an expensive purchase because of the outstanding ancestry in his pedigree. However, Rena's Laddie had a mean disposition and had probably been mistreated in his earlier days. At least, he trusted no man and would crowd and crush his handler if he had a chance. Edwin and Gordon tried to lead him, but he was so fiery he could not be led safely, even with two handlers.

Bob Stewart had never known an Ayrshire bull he could not lead, so one day, with a stout staff fixed to a ring in the bull's nose and a light rope coiled in his hand, just in case he got into trouble, Bob started out alone to lead Laddie. The big bull moved along, behaving well, but was watching every move and waiting for an opportunity. (When leading a bull, it is necessary at all times to hold its head well up, otherwise one is immediately exposed to attack.)

Laddie began to exert heavy pressure to get his head down, but Bob held him firmly and never took his eye off that of the bull. Eventually when they were only a few yards from the barn door, Bob realized he was not going to be able to hold Laddie's head up much longer. The bull, sensing this, began to show signs of fight. Bob moved slowly back towards the barn. When he had about twenty feet more to travel, he turned his head slightly, perhaps to see how much farther he had to go. In that instant, Laddie dived at him and caught him with the point of one horn. Fortunately, the horn only creased the skin, but ripped the shirt off Bob's back. Bob gave the bull one final tremendous jerk on the nose and then leaped to the safety of the door, dropping the lead staff but still holding on to the light rope. Laddie had won for the time being but was kept home from future shows. He met his Waterloo only a few weeks later.

Well-groomed cattle, fitted with sack blankets for travel and grey flannelette blankets for washday, were a pretty sight as they were led out of the yard to be loaded into two boxcars for their big trip to Calgary. Gordon Wells, Archie McKenzie and Kenneth Atchison accompanied Bob Stewart with two carloads of thirty head of cattle to the Prairie circuit. This was a return engagement, to compete with the pioneer breeders from the Prairie provinces. They were the Mortsons of Fairlight, Saskatchewan; the Richardses of Red Deer, Alberta; and Roland Ness of Lakeview, Alberta.

Gordon thought Calgary was a highlight on the circuit. The stampede was everything that he dreamed it would be. The feature event of the parade was Slim Moorehouse and his big team. Moorehouse drove down Calgary's main street with seven loaded grain wagons in tandem. He held all the reins himself and drove his teams strung out in front of him the length of a city block – twelve horses of six teams in tandem hitch. Gordon was very impressed.

When Ayrshire show day was over, Gordon spent much time broadening his knowledge of western horsemanship. By the time he left Calgary he had determined to purchase those Angora goat-hair chaps and Stetsons from Riley and McCormick of Calgary. He came home with their catalogue and many other

Edwin and (left to right) Tom Bowers, Gordon, Ron and Oliver with their exhibition herd at Hastings Park, where the giant evergreens would soon fall to make room for expansion of the new fairgrounds, ca. 1923.

Some of the Ayrshire herd at Edenbank before leaving for the Prairie show circuit. The pure-bred cattle began winning prizes as early as 1907 and also set production records. This is the first field day sponsored by the Ayrshire Breeders' Association of B.C., in 1925.

ideas that he planned to try on his horse Dan. It was from that time that he and I started saving for our western outfits.

The Prairie circuit was a tough one on the cattle and on the young men in charge. Prairie heat and thunderstorms, alkali water and vast open cowsheds were long remembered. Cramped boxcars were not the ideal place for either cattle or crew to travel, eat and rest. Despite all the hardships, the results of the trips were excellent. From the Edenbank herd, Bonalee's Lassie, a home-bred cow, was reserve champion to Springburn May Mischief, grand champion female, while Alta Crest Nonskid continued to be grand champion sire.

When the herds returned for the British Columbia show circuit, the entire Mortson family, being involved in the competitions, came and camped on the fairgrounds in true western style. They did this wherever they went following the different circuits. At the West Coast fairs in New Westminster, the herds of Shannon Brothers, pioneer Ayrshire breeders of Cloverdale, B.C., and of E.W. Van Tassel, a leading Ayrshire breeder of Wenatchee, Washington, made competition very keen. In nine exhibitions, the Edenbank herd won a total of $3,000 in prize money, most of which was used for expenses. The exhibition herd did much to popularize Ayrshire cattle and stimulate sales. That fall, a sale of pure-bred Ayrshire cattle was held at Edenbank and many new Ayrshire breeders attended, buying their foundation cattle.

In January 1925, Edwin left home to attend meetings of the Canadian Ayrshire breeders' association in eastern Canada. Gordon accompanied him and together they visited many outstanding herds in Ontario and Quebec. On the way home, they visited Strathglass and the 250-head herd at Alta Crest, the two leading American herds. There they arranged the purchase of Alta Crest Spicy Sam, to be delivered in the fall.

The year 1925 was to be a banner year for Edwin and his Ayrshires. Since he had been elected president of the Ayrshire Breeders' Association of Canada, it seemed fitting that Edenbank should present a good showing at the leading exhibitions. Edwin therefore arranged for Ken Hay, an experienced agriculturist, to come and prepare the show herd and be in charge during the year. Ken came with the highest recommendation that leading Ayrshire breeders in eastern Canada could give. He was from Howick, Quebec, the breed's stronghold. Ken arrived in mid-May following his graduation from the University of British Columbia.

The cattle were soon selected, and Ken busied himself with making rope halters and a new set of sack blankets. He mixed what he considered a suitable ration for the herd and tied each animal separately in comfortable stalls. They were kept well bedded and clean. As the weeks went by, the cattle were trained to lead and stand correctly. Their hides were softened with daily brushing, and blanketing protected them from adverse weather conditions and the ever-present flies, at the same time retaining the natural oil of the skin. By late June, the herd was in peak condition. Before leaving for the Prairie circuit, the herd was the feature of the program for the first field day sponsored by the Ayrshire Breeders' Association of B.C., held at Edenbank Farm.

The competition was heavy that year and a feeling of excitement was felt by all as sixteen animals left

By winning ribbons (and prize money) at livestock exhibitions across the West, the Ayrshire herd increased cattle sales and gained Edenbank a national reputation.

Edenbank under Ken Hay's supervision. During the season the herd set an unprecedented record. At four major Prairie shows, they won sixteen first prizes, fifteen seconds and three grand championships. Again, Alta Crest Nonskid maintained his title of grand champion bull of the West, defeating McDonald Competitor three times out of four. Back in B.C., Spicy Sam, even as a senior calf, made Nonskid strive to hold his championship honours. The young bull was first in his class, being junior champion and reserve grand champion.

Altogether, at twelve major exhibitions, the herd won seventy-nine firsts, seventy-nine seconds, fifty-eight thirds and twenty-six fourth prizes. Ken Hay had proven his ability not only to fit out a show herd of Ayrshires, but also to maintain the animals in peak condition over a long season of steady travel and exhibiting, which didn't conclude until October.

British Columbia was planning to send an exhibit of livestock to the Royal Winter Fair in Toronto. Ken was willing to take the Edenbank herd to the fair in Toronto and to enter them in the greatest of all Ayrshire shows. At eighteen years of age, I was more than pleased to accompany him on this great adventure. Preparations for the trip included the refitting of the herd with blankets and nice new leather show halters. The CPR was asked to supply a fifty-foot automobile car, which provided added width and greater headroom. Decks built into this car were strongly reinforced to carry the weight of hay and grain necessary for a ten-day trip. Barrels for drinking water

for the cattle had to be located near the doors for easy filling at divisional points. Living accommodation for the handlers – a place to sleep and room to cook and eat – was located on a deck above the cattle. The Ayrshire herd was selected from the cattle that had been on the summer circuit. To these were added six Guernsey cows, which were also part of the B.C. exhibit.

The cattle in the car were tied to a rail, which was securely fastened to the wall of the boxcar about sixteen inches from the floor. In this way, the cattle could lie or stand comfortably, and during the shunting of cars back and forth nothing projected to hurt the animals. The bull was enclosed securely at the end of the car, where he stood crosswise behind planks. On the deck above, the men slept as comfortably as the weather permitted, the cattle providing some warmth for their comfort.

On the trip, a daily routine of work left little time for leisure. Feeding and watering three times each day was in itself a chore, as everything had to be carried along behind the cattle and then up beside their heads. Regularly, several times a day, manure was cleared away and thrown out, provided the train was travelling in open country.

There were nine cows to be milked by hand, three times a day. Two cows that had calved on the circuit during the fall had been trained to drink their own milk while it was warm and fresh. I would milk a pailful and then give it back to the cow just milked. Each day, for ten days, about fifty gallons of milk were thrown out the door, and every day the cattle's blankets were removed and the animals thoroughly brushed.

Leaving home at six o'clock on October 26, the cattle arrived in Toronto in good condition on November 5 and had a couple of weeks to rest up and prepare for the great day. As show day approached, the cattle's heads, necks, tails and udders were clipped. Horns were polished until they shone like wax. Washday preceded show day. As each cow came out of the wash rack, she was blanketed, first in clean flannelette and then with a heavier blanket. These blankets remained on until just prior to the animal's appearance in the show ring on judging day. Then they were removed and the cow quickly rubbed down with a clean, lightly oiled cloth. This gave the coat of clean hair a soft, bright appearance. The animals were carefully fed, neither too much nor too little, and before they left their stall for the show ring, their flanks were levelled with water to a smooth, graceful blending with their ribs in order that a general symmetry of conformation be exemplified.

To enter the ring at the Royal Winter Fair is a never-to-be-forgotten experience, known to few stockmen. There, in 1925, at the Ayrshire breed's greatest show of the period, Ken Hay exhibited the Edenbank Ayrshires before the Ayrshire world's renowned and keenest judge, Adam Montgomery, a famous Scottish breeder of Ayrshires.

Edenbank Ayrshires brought back high honours to British Columbia, and Edenbank was forever indebted to Ken Hay, whose skill and endeavour wrought wonders with good cattle. During the wintry trip home, we had no problem en route with the cattle but we did have difficulty keeping warm.

When the ribbons were emptied out of the trunk that winter, Margaret immediately set to work to make each of us boys a quilt cover composed of closely quilted winning silk ribbons of red, blue, yellow, green and gold. The blues and reds represented first and second prizes. The greens and golds were usually championship ribbons.

While I was away from home on the trip to the Royal Winter Fair in late 1925, my place at the farm was taken by Bill McFaul, a neighbour's boy, who was later to take the Edenbank herd on one of its greatest adventures. Bill was just thirteen when he first came to Edenbank in his first year of high school. Each day he would come to the farm before he headed to school in Chilliwack. His chores included milking twelve cows (by hand), helping to turn the cream separator, and feeding calves and pigs.

Sheep too had always been part of the livestock family at Edenbank. First it was the long-wool breeds, whose wool was so desirable in pioneer days. Later, when the grounds at Edenbank had been landscaped by Edwin, he sought out park sheep, to pasture on the parkland slopes along the Luckakuck and surrounding the house. The Cheviot breed seemed to be ideally suited, being of medium size, beautifully proportioned, alert and active, and having a princely

Lunch is being hosted at the 1925 Ayrshire field day by the Wells family. Margaret is standing at the left, Edwin is carving at the head of the table, Oliver and Gordon wear caps and white shirts and are helping to serve.

carriage. The first ewes came from the Summerland Experimental Farm in 1923. Two years later, Edwin, following the line of his basic flock-improvement policy, purchased a top-quality ram and a show ewe from Macdonald College in Quebec and from A. Ayre of Hampton, Ontario.

Leonard Higginson, a friend, neighbour and school chum of mine, offered to take the Cheviots to the exhibitions along with his Southdowns. Thus Edenbank's Cheviots were introduced to the show ring and distinguished themselves, winning many awards under Leonard's expert

The parkland around the farmhouse was kept "mowed" by a flock of Border Cheviot sheep specially purchased and bred by Edwin. Later Oliver raised North Country Cheviots.

ability. Forty years later, Bill Higginson, son of Leonard, was responsible for the showing of Edenbank's North Country Cheviots. When Bob Sibbald, a young Scot from the Scottish border country, walked into Edenbank in 1926 to buy cattle, his old loves, the "Chee-ve-ots" as he called them, reminded him of his flock back home. Bob ended up buying Cheviots that day instead of Ayrshires.

Bob, along with his well-trained border collie dog and flock of Edenbank's Cheviot sheep, frequently represented Edenbank in the show circuits of the West during the next ten years. Bob knew Cheviots. He had been born and raised with them in the Cheviot Hills of Scotland. When war broke out in 1914, he, like so many of his kind, left his native land and enlisted. Following the armistice, he came to Canada to live in Matsqui.

Each year he would come to Edenbank to pick out a show flock. As he and I walked out into the field among the Cheviots, I would hear him say, "That is the good ewe I had last year" or "There is the lamb I had two years ago." And he was always right. When you asked him how he knew (for the sheep looked very much alike), he would say, "When I was a boy, we had tae learn to ken sheep. There would be competitions for the boys. You would be shown the head of a sheep for a minute only – the head being pushed through a hole in a curtain. The sheep would then be turned into a pen with twenty others and you had to pick out the ewe you had seen."

Bob would select his show flock early and take them to his home. When next seen at the shows they were elegantly presented, with snow-white heads and legs, black noses and hooves, and fleeces washed and trimmed to present a superb form. The competition was keen, but always the thrifty Scot ended up the year with a few dollars in his pockets and a few dollars for Edenbank. He was able to relive those glorious memories of old Scotland in those shows, and the Cheviots returned home quiet and well mannered, carrying their heads high.

When the Cheviots had grown in numbers to a beautiful flock of thirty to forty ewes, the old enemies began night raids. Sheep-killing dogs marauded the flocks. The only solution was to sit up all night and wait for them with gun and spotlight.

One night, I was perched in a big walnut tree overlooking a small field where the sheep were bedded down for the night. All was quiet, and staying awake was the only problem. Suddenly I heard the sound of dogs. Their running barks came from far away, beyond the barn, where another small flock was pasturing near the river. I scrambled down and made my way past the barn to a gate, where I stopped to listen. I was not able to see well but heard the savage barking of the dogs, their barks intermingling with the splashing of water, indicating they had driven a sheep into the shallow stream and were mauling it. With gun loaded and flashlight ready to turn on, I made my way quietly in the pitch dark to the bank of the stream.

Because of the poor visibility and the excitement of the kill, the dogs had not detected my approach. When I was ready, I flashed the light on the dogs, at the same time holding it along the lower side of the shotgun barrel. A big red Irish setter was startled into plunging straight towards me. Waiting till he neared, I took careful aim and pulled the trigger. At the moment the flash of the gun broke the darkness, the Irish setter, a hunting dog and sheep-killer, died instantly. The other killer dog escaped across the stream. A second shot failed to stop him, and luckily for him he never returned. ௮

CHAPTER 13

Memorable Hands

*I*t always seemed to be a signal for the north wind to start to blow and the temperature to drop when Edwin left for the east in mid-winter to attend the annual meetings of the Ayrshire Breeders' Association of Canada. And so it had been in January 1923. For days, the northeast wind howled around the buildings. In spite of every effort, the frost was getting inside buildings, freezing water bowls, taps and pipes and causing much extra work. Then  snow started and came with the wind. For two days it snowed – fine, powdery snow, which formed into great drifts at the back door of the house, across the yard towards the barn, up over the board fences and gates. Behind the barn, the big drifts on the approaches to the haymows and at the creamery hill were nearly eight feet deep. Through these drifts, the milk had to be taken to the platform of the B.C. Electric Railway in Sardis.

Already short-handed, with 108 head of cattle and 20 horses to feed and care for, Gordon was greatly relieved one day when a middle-aged man, in western dress, walked into the barn and asked for a job. He was tall, well-built and wore a good Stetson, close-fitting mackinaw coat and, over his breeches, fine leather leggings. To protect his face and ears from the wind and snow he wore only a set of earmuffs. He gave his name as Hughie Humble. No one ever knew for sure whether it was his real name, and no one ever asked. Gordon discussed the work required and took him to the house to speak favourably for him when he asked Margaret for a job. He was polite and frequently addressed Margaret as "Ma'am." His accent

The hay coils have been carefully built by experts with hand-held forks, and the crew has managed to heave the hay high up onto the wagon. The teamster wrapping his reins around the rack has expertly stacked the load, and soon the horses will pull the wagon down the lane, through the barnyard and up into the loft of the barn. The newly built Fraser Valley Milk Producers' Association plant is in the background. Photo ca. 1945.

THE ROOT HOUSE   MWeeden/74

The old root cellar sketched by Marie Weeden in 1974. The farm bell that called the workers is mounted at the top back. In the 1920s, one of the first farm cars, a Studebaker, was kept in the root cellar, which by that time had become a garage.

was slightly Southern. He got the job.

Hughie was a godsend that winter to Gordon and the family. He understood and could handle horses. He spoke of having been a mule skinner, which accounted for his ability to use the blacksnake (a long leather whip with a short, heavy, loaded stock, which was used in the West to drive long freight teams). With a sixteen-foot blacksnake, Hughie could snap a match out of your fingers without harming you. His ability to take horses through snowdrifts with sleighs or wagons, his knowledge of livestock and his apparent immunity to cold were a veritable blessing in that storm that lasted for weeks.

Before Edwin returned, Gordon had warned Hughie that he would get fired if his dad heard him swearing,

as Hughie sometimes did unconsciously and with vehemence. Hughie had said, "He won't hear me swearing," and he never did.

Hughie had a wonderful voice, was a fast milker and seemed to enjoy milking cows. Invariably he would sing while he milked and often he would sing hymns. Somewhere, sometime in his younger days, he must have had a home life similar to that at Edenbank. He did thoroughly enjoy the home that winter. One of his favourite hymns, which was often sung at his request, was the "Glory Song." Around the piano at home, or in Carman Methodist Church, which he attended with the family each Sunday, dressed in his western best, his clear, strong voice would boom out, "O that will be glory for me, / Glory for me, glory for me, / When by His grace I shall look on His face, / That will be glory, be glory for me."

Wing, the cook, was the only one at Edenbank who tangled with Hughie. Hughie Humble liked his coffee strong, very strong. He continually chided Wing for his weak coffee. He asked Wing to leave the pot on the stove and just add more coffee each time. Wing stood it for a time, but he was accustomed to having people eat what was placed before them. Finally, one day, Hughie chided Wing once too often by asking for "more of that dishwater." Wing obliged and actually brought him a cup . . . of dishwater. That ended the feud!

Edwin was away quite some time. Soon after he came home, spring work started and Hughie and Gordon were in the fields ploughing every fine day. When they came together at the end of the field, they would often let their horses rest a spell and have a short visit. "I guess I'll be moving on," Hughie said one day. "What's the matter?" came Gordon's surprised query. "Oh, just an itchy foot, I guess," replied Hughie. At the end of the month Hughie did walk away, just as mysteriously as he had come. No one knew to or from where.

Wing – the wonderful man who helped Mrs. Bradshaw mother the boys after Gertie was gone. He prepared their favourite raisin pies and survived all the boys' pranks.

ﷺ

Each spring, young stock were usually put out to pasture, driven down to the big commonage on Sumas Prairie near the lake. They were cared for by a cowboy who usually tented at the upper end of the prairie where the Vedder River entered Sumas Lake. In later years, stock were driven out to the Big Prairie to the east, where the cattle would be enclosed in a large fenced pasture.

Edwin realized that the pasturing of young cattle on Sumas Prairie or the Big Prairie was soon going to be a thing of the past, because of advancing settlement. He therefore purchased about thirty acres of wooded foothill property on Promontory Heights, about 2½ miles from the farm. He took us boys there to clear land, burn brush piles or slash, and sow grass seed. The acreage was soon turned into a good rough pasture area for young stock.[45]

Orion Bowman leased a few acres there and established a mill on the land. He operated the mill for about twenty years, until all the local timber was cut. In the lease agreement, Edwin made provision for Edenbank Farm to get all the slab wood it needed for domestic use, without cost.

Both Gordon and I in later years hauled heavy slab wood home with team and wagon, during all kinds of weather. We piled it in a long, neat pile near the six-foot circular saw in the barnyard. Each Saturday during the winter months, Edwin, Gordon, Ronald and I would cut this wood, using the big saw powered by electricity and driven by long belts from high in the loft. Usually the wood was dried in a big pile and made fairly good firewood, but old Wing came close to cursing sometimes when the basement of the big house sometimes was filled with wet and green wood from the mill.

For years, Edwin had taken care of the veterinary work on the farm. Occasionally, he would call Ed Chadsey, Aunt Alma's husband, who had taken some veterinary training. He was pleased when Dr. Milton arrived in the valley in 1922 and became Edenbank's veterinarian. During the succeeding twenty years he gave generously of his time and energy. During the Depression years in the 1930s, he provided regular weekly service calls for a monthly fee equal to less than one call at 1967 rates.

He was a progressive vet, always searching for the most up-to-date information on those diseases that still baffled the veterinary profession at the time. In the treatment of "milk fever," the use of calcium, pumped slowly into the bloodstream, was recognized as a new treatment. Dr. Milton was one of the first to venture beyond a single dose in cases of relapse. In fact, he treated one cow for five consecutive mornings, not knowing whether each succeeding dose would be an overdose. The cow recovered.

For abortion prevention, Dr. Milton early recognized the value of "Strain 19," a vaccine then in use in Washington State to immunize cattle against milk fever. He imported this serum before it was marketed in Canada and began vaccinating the Edenbank herd, giving it protection for several years. He was very much a dedicated professional. One night, in order to treat a sick cow, Dr. Milton walked the three miles from Chilliwack on the B.C. Electric Railway right-of-way when all roads were blocked during a severe snowstorm.

During the early '20s, Jack Wood worked at Edenbank. Jack was a good stockman and all of us boys enjoyed working with him. During his stay, the brothers Ed and Ora Canfield also worked on the farm through the summer months. About thirty years before, the Canfields' father, as a young man, had come from Ontario to British Columbia and married into the Wells family. Ed Canfield was a welcome visitor each summer during the haying season. In his summer vacations from his vocation as a schoolteacher, he blistered his hands on the fork handle and was a very dedicated worker.

In 1925, Herb Martin, a neighbour's son, came to work at Edenbank along with David McLeod. Herb was a good milker but one day was almost killed by a cow that began kicking at a cat running under while Herb was milking her. The milk spilled but Herb survived. When Herb moved on from Edenbank, he eventually became herdsman of the great Holstein herd owned by the provincial government at Colony Farm of Essondale.

As I have been thinking back to all the men over the years who have worked here at the farm, I have made a list of those men who would have been called to work and to dinner by the old farm bell on top of the old root cellar.[46]

The Fraser Valley Milk Producers' Association purchased seven acres of land from Edwin in 1925, in preparation for the erection of their utility plant. Again Edenbank became the base for an enlarged dairy operation. The piece of land, lying beside the B.C. Electric Railway, sold at $600 per acre, which was then a noteworthy price.

The farm then comprised 160 acres and had taxes each year amounting to $500. The animal count was 90 Ayrshires, 15 Cheviots and 5 brood sows. There were also three teams and two saddle horses. The farming operation required about 35 acres in grain for home use and about 35 acres of hay, with 10 acres of corn for silage and as much as 10 acres planted to mangels and turnips. Often, over 300 tons of mangels were placed in pits for winter use.

When the grain was ready to be cut, Edwin would have Gordon start the binder and others would stook

Evidently Oliver persuaded Sara to at least sit on the binder behind the Clydesdale team – an adventurous task for her.

Bringing in a heavy oat crop to be threshed by the noisy steam thresher. In the foreground is a woodpile to "keep up the steam," and a chute conveys the separated straw into the barn. Sacks would be filled with the grain as the oats were threshed.

up the sheaves. When well stooked, the sheaves would stand against rain and wind until dry. If the thresher, Herbert Cartmell, was not able to come when the grain was dry enough to thresh, Edwin would start us boys and several men hauling in and stacking the sheaves in tall stacks which measured thirty feet in diameter. In this manner, the sheaves were safe against bad weather and could be threshed in almost any weather conditions.

One year, Gordon, Ronald, Sid Plevy and I were put to work demolishing the old hay barn that had stood in the big meadow for fifty years. It was one of the first hay barns built on the farm. The frame was of squared timbers, hewn with a broadaxe. The joints were mortise and tenon, pinned together with wooden pins. The walls were covered by one-by-ten-inch No. 1 rough lumber standing vertically and secured by nailing with squared iron nails to horizontal beams, which ran along the walls.

The boards were first stripped off the framework and the next job was to take the roof apart. We decided it would be much easier to do this if the barn were collapsed and the roof lay on the ground. The framework was loose and swayed easily, and it looked as if it would be easy to pull it over sideways. Gordon

went back to the horse barn to get a team and a cable and blocks for pulling.

When the proper hitch had been secured and the team gave a good pull, the barn's frame started to go as planned, then stopped and could not be moved. We decided that a main crossbeam of the end of the barn should be cut off just where it was joined into the corner post. Ronald, who had no fear of heights, went up with a heavy crosscut saw to do the job, while Gordon made ready for the next pull.

As Ronald worked, he stood on a beam about twenty feet aboveground that joined the corner post at right angles to the beam he was sawing. He was leaning over a heavy brace as he worked. I stood watching on the ground below. Sid was with Gordon on the other side, expecting to help Gordon when the team pulled again after Ronald had cut the beam. The ridgepole of the roof ran the full length of the barn, which had a high gable roof.

When Ron cut through the beam, everything broke loose with a great crash. The unexpected happened – the roof collapsed, forcing the sides of the barn out. The whole barn began crashing to the earth with a terrific force.

I was looking up, just in time to see one high beam

of the outside wall arching down on me, with Ron standing on it high in the air, holding on to the brace in front of him as he flew backwards. I ran hard and fast, turning to look as soon as I was clear. At the last moment I saw Ron jump free of the cascading beam just before it smashed to the ground. A cool presence of mind had saved him from certain death. As he was hurled backwards on the beam, he had swung under the brace and righted himself on the other side with barely time to jump off the beam before it struck.

That day Ronald probably started his lifetime flying career. The cool-headed manner in which he saved himself would in future be a great boon to him in his years of commercial flying. His flying career would take him into some of the most challenging flying conditions in all of western North America, from the Cascades to the D.E.W. line. While flying he has lost engines several times, but his confidence and ability to keep calm have allowed him to land his craft safely each time, just as he landed from the barn that day.

Ron and the Eagle Rock, 1938. He learned to fly in one of these aircraft and was the first to sneak in a landing at the then new airport where Lansdowne Park shopping mall is now. Ron was the manager of the Chilliwack Flying Club in 1946 and before that a flight instructor during World War II.

In order to maintain and increase the family's interest in the Ayrshire herd, in 1926 Edwin began to register the cattle under the name of Edwin A. Wells & Sons. That fall, Gordon and I enrolled at the University of British Columbia to take a short occupational course in agriculture. Dean Frederick M. Clement, then head of the Faculty of Agriculture at UBC, had on his staff Professors H.M. King and Davis in the Department of Livestock; Mr. Blythe Eagles in the Dairy Research Laboratory; Professor Paul Boving in Agronomy; Professors Buck and Alden F. Barss in Horticulture; and Professor Hare, head of Agricultural Economics. While these men were taking a keen interest in individual members of the then small classes in agriculture, they were at the same time establishing the foundation of every department of the Faculty of Agriculture.

Dean Clement undertook a survey of the dairy farms in thelower Fraser Valley under the direction of Professor Hare, who compiled some very interesting results. Among the general findings of the survey, in which Edenbank Farm participated, was the observation that a forty-acre farm was an ideal size for a one-man operation. Larger farms showed a wider variation in net profit. The figures revealed that the net income of the dairy farmer at that time was very low. For his labour, the average dairy farmer received six cents per hour.

While Gordon and I were away at college, Ronald took on the added responsibility of milking the cows with newcomer Sid Plevy. Employment was hard to come by at the time, and Sid had walked into the Chilliwack Valley on old Yale Road. He was fortunate in that he was given a buggy ride by a Mr. Trott, who was pleased to learn that Sid was a fellow countryman of his, having come from the same town in England.

When Mr. Trott phoned Edwin, asking for a job for Sid, it turned out to be an opportune time and Sid was hired. Edwin always refrained from hiring men who drank, smoked or used rough language. But now Sid arrived smoking. Edwin compromised and Sid said he would quit smoking. He tried to stop more than once, but it always got the better of him. He even spent $10 on a cure, which was a third of a month's wages. He kept on trying, so Edwin didn't bother him and Sid stayed on. He was a good worker and we boys enjoyed his company. His father had been a "master of the hounds" in England, and with that background, Sid was quite at home riding a horse.

One evening Gordon was riding on the Big Prairie with Normy Nowell. Normy for years had been driving wild horses from Interior ranges to Chilliwack. They made a deal to trade saddle horses, Gord getting Normy's big, powerful horse, known as Goldie. When they parted, Normy cautioned Gordon, "Always keep your hat tied when you ride him."

Gordon got along well with Goldie, always riding him with a saddle. Yet Normy's was good advice,

City girls and starlit nights. Songs around the campfire and long, long remembered days of bliss. These young women, all friends, wrote a booklet about this trip to Liumchen Mountain in 1928. Christie Harris wrote poetry, Ada Currie penned the delightful illustrations, and Joy Rickaby recorded the daily diary of their rides over Liumchen's flowered meadows and hills. Gordon and Joy fell in love – another Liumchen romance. Left to right: Christie (Irwin) Harris, Ada Currie, Ernest Farrow (chaperone), Joy Rickaby, Leslie Young. PHOTO BY GORDON WELLS

because Gordon knew the horse would run away with him if given the chance. We learned later that Normy had been running wild horses with Goldie, and Goldie had been allowed to run as wild in the chase as the wild horses themselves.

One day, when Gordon was ploughing, Sid went into the horse barn to get a saddle horse to ride down to the back of the farm. I was in the barn getting a big Clydesdale mare, Nellie, harnessed for work with the dump cart. To my surprise, Sid put a bridle on Goldie and jumped on bareback. "You'd better put a saddle on," I commented. "I'll be all right," said Sid and rode out. "I bet I'll see daylight under you before you get halfway," I forecast, as Sid rode off towards the lane holding Goldie to a canter.

Having experienced riding Goldie myself, I stood holding Nellie at the door . . . watching. As I expected, the horse gradually increased its speed. Sid realized he had better slow him down and checked him with a jerk. Goldie then played his trump card. Stiff-legged for a second, he broke his speed so suddenly Sid was bounced into the air and his lines slackened. When he came down, he was still on Goldie, but the horse was now running wildly at a terrifying speed, impossible to check. Where the B.C. Electric Railway crossed the farm lane, there was a graded rise of two or three feet in the laneway with heavy planks between the rails to form a road crossing. The pair flew down

the laneway at breakneck speed, towards a railway section gang repairing the crossing. They had all the planks torn up and lying upside down with the great spikes pointing up.

From the horse barn, I could only see that the crewmen appeared to have backed away as the galloping horse approached. I saw the horse and rider rise in a tremendous jump and then disappear. For a moment, the men seemed petrified – but then they went on with their work, so I knew that Sid must have survived.

It transpired that when Sid saw the railway crossing, he knew the horse would take it in one great jump, and of this he was not afraid. But about twenty yards beyond the tracks, a high board gate was closed across the laneway. Sid decided to dismount before the horse crashed the gate, as he would not be able to gather himself for a jump before he was into it. In England, his father had taught him how to get off a runaway horse: "Bring your right leg around and over as you let yourself down on the left side, with the horse's withers under your right arm, then let your feet touch the ground and let go of the withers."

Sid had made up his mind to do this, but the horse on landing veered to the side, deciding to try to jump the rail fence panel next to the gate. Sid's leg was just over the horse's back when he left it, head first, landing upside down on his shoulders against the bottom board of the gate.

Yale Road East with Mount Cheam as backdrop.
PHOTO BY WILSON STUDIO

As he himself flew through the air, he had a glimpse of Goldie going through the fence and a rail flying high in the air. He picked himself up and with a stout heart walked back down into the field, caught Goldie and, with trembling hand, got back on.

Gordon had been watching from his seat on a plough in a nearby field. Sid rode Goldie over at a walk to have a talk with him. When he started away, Gordon cautioned, "Now don't try to lope him home." After leaving the ploughed field, Sid, anxious to prove that he could ride Goldie bareback, started the horse off again on an easy lope. There was only a quarter of a mile distance left to the barn when Goldie again got the upper hand. Sid again was almost unloaded as Goldie stretched out and broke into another wild run.

Quickly I turned the Clydesdale mare broadside to the doorway of the horse barn to prevent Goldie turning in at top speed. Sid smartly decided to get off and

this time he made it, with his horse running full-speed past the barn. He didn't let go of his lines and ended up in the middle of the yard, under the horse's front legs, but unhurt. When he walked back to the barn, trembling like a leaf, he looked at Goldie, then turned to me and said, "Jesus, can't that horse run, Master!"

Sid slept alone in the men's room above the kitchen. He had become quite one of the family when one morning sometime later, he did not turn up at the barn. A check of his room revealed that he had departed in the night, leaving a simple note: "Won't be back." Several years later, the records of production testers reported seeing him at the big CPR farm in Alberta. Then, after years of silence, a letter came from the Near East. Sid had become a mechanic with the Royal Air Force in Egypt during the Second World War. After more years of silence, another letter arrived, addressed to Ronald, c/o Edenbank Farm. It was a request from Sid for cigarettes. He was in a convalescent home in England, broke and in poor health. By return post, two cartons of cigarettes were sent back to Sid. He was never heard from again.

In 1928, some major changes were made to the established routine at Edenbank. Edwin purchased a milking machine for use at the farm. While this labour-saving device was not exactly an innovation, this machine was the first of its kind to come to Edenbank. With it, the heavy morning and evening chores of milking cows by hand became a thing of the past. Fewer men were needed to do daily chores. The farmland clearing and much of the drainage had also been completed by this time. The workload was somewhat eased.

During one summer in the late 1920s, a party of young people went together on a horse trip into the beautiful Liumchen range. Ernest Farrow was their chaperone. Included in this group were Gordon Wells and Joy Rickaby. The two were immediately attracted to each other, and subsequently Gordon and Joy were engaged and married in 1929. Two other young people in that group were Ada Currie and Christie (Irwin) Harris.[47] After the outing, the latter put together a trip diary with illustrations by Ada and poems by Christie. Along with the diary was a photo album of the holiday, a copy of which was presented to Edwin and Margaret, who were hosts to the party during the preparations for the trip.

CHAPTER 14

The Hungry Thirties

Captain J.C. Dunwaters by 1909 had established Fintry, a beautiful 2,500-acre estate on the shores of Okanagan Lake. He was a wealthy Scot who, for a period of years, did much to promote the Ayrshire breed in British Columbia and brought to Fintry the best Ayrshires he could buy in America and Scotland. In his enthusiasm for the breed he sponsored the importation of three shipments of Ayrshire cattle, two of which he sold in the Okanagan Valley at auction. The other herd he gave as a gift to the Province of British Columbia, for use at the University of B.C. From these cattle, Edenbank would one day purchase an outstanding herd sire and UBC would develop many outstanding animals.

When the UBC Ayrshire herd arrived from Scotland, their beautiful upturned horns gave them a very regal look as they paraded into their new home. Although the B.C. Ayrshire breeders

Marie and Betty Wells ca. 1939.

found it difficult to make the decision, after several years of debate, they unanimously agreed that their herds would be dehorned in the interests of the welfare of their cattle. To John Young, the Scotsman who accompanied the herd to B.C., it was little short of sacrilege to do such a terrible thing to the "bonnie Scotch coo." Young, who came with his family to UBC, where he stayed on until his retirement, raised his family there in an idyllic setting of farmland in the centre of the developing university.[48]

Edenbank aquired a dehorning crate made in preparation for the big job of dehorning sixty-five mature Ayrshires. Arrangements were made for Arthur Zink to come and help with the work that day. Mr. Zink was experienced in the use of a Keystone dehorner, a giant scissor-like instrument that could cut through the base of the hardest horns, using his powerful hands.

A cool day in early spring was selected, in order that the cows might be turned loose in the yard as usual after the dehorning. One by one they were led or driven into the crate and made fast with the use of two squeeze bars. A strong string was made taut around the base of the horns to prevent excessive bleeding. The dehorners were used quickly on each horn and the animal was released.

After dehorning, that "Scottish beauty" wasn't then able to rip open another beast's bowels, as one cow had done to her stablemate the year before. By evening of that memorable day, sixty-five head had lost their horns, with no serious consequence. Two of the old cows, whose horns were hard as iron, dropped as if they had been felled with a poleaxe when the dehorners snapped through their horns. They also quickly recovered. On the third day after dehorning, strings around the base of the horns were cut and all was well. Thereafter, horns were removed from the young calves by the use of caustic, a more gentle method.

In 1930, Ken Hay again took charge of the Edenbank show herd and made a sweep of championships at Calgary, Edmonton, Saskatoon and Regina. At the Armstrong show Noble Betsy Wylie, shown by Fintry, was grand champion bull, defeating Edenbank Robinhood 30. The latter bull had been purchased from William Higginson and was son of old Willowmoor Robinhood 18F, whose daughters would be mated with him.

Robinhood 30 was the first bull to give me a lesson on the need for caution in handling mature bulls. I did not know that Ronald and his pals Cecil Shaw and Bill McFaul had been doing a little "bull-baiting," as boys would do. Bill McFaul, quite unintentionally perhaps, had teased Robinhood to take after him when he went into his paddock to catch a cow. Ronald and Cecil, however, had simply baited the bull, and when he charged them they would jump a fence to safety – sometimes with only a second to spare.

Unaware of these happenings, one day I put a staff on Robinhood and led him out into a little paddock behind the barn, expecting to take the bull for a walk in preparation for exhibition. Robinhood stopped moving forward and tried to get his head down and back up. I held him, but could not move him except to allow the bull to move sideways. Robinhood then got down on his knees and began to roar in defiance. I was alone, with no help within calling. My only hope was to keep control until he was close enough to a fence.

After what seemed a very long struggle, I undertook to do what Bob Stewart had done to get away from the bull Laddie. My only escape was to jump the high board fence in one great leap. When close enough, I gave Robinhood a tremendous jerk on the ring to divert his attention momentarily. I then dropped the staff and took a flying leap, just barely making the fence. Robinhood's head crashed between my legs as I was going over. Surprisingly, I still had the lead rope in my hand, so I quickly tied the bull's head up high to the limb of a tree near the fence. Then I went for my father and together, one on either side, and each with a long rope, we gave Robinhood a lesson in behaviour. Before leading him again, Edwin wrapped the bull's ring with galvanized wire. The roughness of the wire on the ring made the nose quite painful when any pressure was exerted. The bull soon learned to respect the guiding staff in his master's hands. Continuous handling eventually made a quiet bull out of Robinhood. By the time he returned from the show circuit he had forgotten those early tauntings by the bull baiters.

While cattle were making the farm famous as a livestock breeding establishment during the late 1920s, there was also a fairly buoyant export market for Edenbank. Pure-bred cattle were exported to Washington and Oregon, and trade had developed with China and Malaysia. The export firm Kirkland & Rose of Vancouver handled the shipments.

The introduction of milking machines had greatly

For years after, this dehorning crate stood behind the barn. In its day it expedited a monumental task. Arthur Zink managed to dehorn sixty-one of Edenbank's mature Ayrshire cattle one spring day in 1927. He was paid 20 cents per head, for a total of $12.20. Many of the cows lost an average of one hundred pounds from the shock. From then on calves had their heads treated with a chemical so no horns would develop.

Daughters of Willowmoor Robinhood 18F. Fourteen of his daughters had production records exceeding five hundred pounds butterfat. The daughters established a long list of wins at exhibition, culminating in many ribbons at the Royal Winter Fair in Toronto.

reduced the labour involved in milking the herd. An electrically driven separator was in use now and the cream shipped brought 50 cents per pound butterfat. Skim milk was fed to the pigs, and market hogs sold at 12¼ cents per pound.

The farm records regularly compiled by Margaret were continually being used to determine selections in breeding stock and to eliminate unprofitable producers. The daughters of Willowmoor Robinhood 18F proved to be heavy producers of milk, with over 4% test. At the exhibitions, Edwin's Get of Sire became the outstanding group in the herd classes and were much admired.

As Edwin became more active in community affairs, I took over herd management entirely. I tried to increase milk production by milking three times daily. One spring, seven cows produced five hundred pounds of milk a day (seventy pounds each, a record at the time).

In 1930, Edenbank's summary of listed assets recorded 160 acres, valued at $150 per acre. Equipment included wagons and accessories, bobsleighs and cutters, gang ploughs and mowers. Receipts for the year 1930 were $12,900 and expenses $10,300, giving a net income of $2,531. One of the new farm machinery inventions of the period was an improved manure spreader. Purchased at $228, this implement required a heavy team to draw, but eliminated much arduous labour involved in cleaning out gutters in the cow barn. For years the same job had been done with the use of a wagon with a watertight box. The load on the new machine was hauled out into the field as with the wagon, but the implement did the spreading instead of hand spreading several tons of manure each day by a manure fork!

Soon after returning to the farm from my studies at UBC, I was asked by the Canadian Broadcasting Corporation to take part with Professor King in a radio farm broadcast program. The subject was mixed farming. This method was then the most economical type of farm operation.

A typical operation on a forty-acre farm consisted of fifteen milking cows plus young stock, a team of horses, some pigs and chickens. Only the owner and his family were the workers. A few acres of grain were usually grown to supplement the mangels. Corn and hay were fed to stock and straw provided necessary bedding. At threshing time, the farmer helped his neighbour, who in turn returned the favour when requested. Almost everything that was consumed was grown on the farm. The net income from such a farm was never large, but farm life gave the family a sense of independence and satisfaction.

So it was at Edenbank. The family, with some assistance, operated the farm. The boarding house for hired help became a home for a married man to live in with his family. Single men often lived in our home with the family, and young men of the community were employed on a part-time basis.

In haying season there were sore muscles from long days of work but always pleasant recollections. Many times the wagon stacker would get half buried by great forkfuls of loose hay thrown onto the load from the forks of the pitchers. There would be great merriment when this happened.

Oliver driving a team and wagon with his nephew Blaine aboard, ca. 1945.

Haying meant sweat and toil in the summer heat. But when the load was on and during the drive up the lane to the barn, the well-earned rest riding atop the load brought about a pleasant sense of relaxation. On occasion, when three or more teams were hauling, there was a brief stop for a breather in the shade of a big maple or birch whose great limbs fanned over the laneway, the same lane Allen had cut through the forest several decades earlier. Each of the lane trees he had planted grew into beautiful specimens, with limbs spreading out thirty feet in every direction.

Often, as one left the shade and went further along the lane, from atop a load of loose hay, one had a splendid vantage point to view the flight of an osprey, or fish hawk. An osprey for many years had an established line of flight crossing the lane at right angles as it flew over the farm to its nest of young in the Chilliwack River valley. It regularly caught its fish in the Fraser River, north of the farm. When the southwest wind was blowing strongly, the bird would fly low enough to give an exhibition of its fine catch and the manner in which it held the fish. The fish appeared to act as a keel to steady the bird's flight.

Sara McKeil and I were married in the spring of 1931. On our honeymoon, we had a wonderful holiday. We drove south to California in the family car, a 1930 Chevrolet sedan purchased by Edwin for $1,089. It had been bought with a small cash down payment, the balance being a trade-in of two older vehicles, a Studebaker touring car for $467 and a Ford for $250. There was a gas price war raging then and the Great Depression was striking America. Gasoline in California was only eight cents a gallon. Little did we realize that at home, milk prices had dropped as well to a new low. We were happy, however, that the fuel bill for the trip was quite modest.

Further bad economic news was discovered when we arrived back at Edenbank. Butterfat – the farm's main source of income – had fallen from 50 to 28 cents a pound and the price of beef cows from $150 to $30. Sara and I, as newlyweds, were not thinking much then of depressed farm prices, and our joy managed to inspire the farm staff for a few weeks. That summer when haying was over, we went alone by horseback up into the mountains of Liumchen Park with Dan and Red to enjoy one of the most beautiful landscapes in all of the Cascades. This was a place that held romantic memories for both of us.

In 1931, Edenbank forgot about the Depression long enough to entertain royalty. The Chilliwack Board of Trade requested that Edenbank be a point of call during the visit of the king and queen of Siam. It was

Sara McKeil and Oliver Wells married in spring 1931 and enjoyed a California road trip before returning to face the economic realities of the Depression.

hoped they would be entertained at the pioneer farm. The king and queen accepted the invitation and visited Edenbank. The ladies of Carman United Church acted as caterers.

As reported in the *Chilliwack Progress*:

> Lovely flowers graced the tables and the choicest of roses made into corsage bouquets for the ladies and button-holes for the gentlemen marked each place. These were the gift of the B.C. Nurseries of Sardis. It was altogether a luncheon fit for a King and Queen, though entirely informal in character.
>
> In addition to the royal party, there were present – Reeve and Mrs. Wells, the former sitting on the left of the Queen and the latter on the right of the King; Mayor and Mrs. E. Manuel; Pres. T.P. Knight of the Board of Trade and Mrs. Knight; Mr. W.J. Park, of the F.V.M.P.A.;

The king of Siam and his entourage leaving Edenbank on his Canadian tour, 1931. Their visit included a demonstration of the new-fangled milking machines.

E.H. Barton, Sec. of the Board of Trade, and Mrs. C.A. Barber.

The royal party inspected the Ayrshire herd and were particularly interested in the demonstration put on for them of machine-milking of the cows – the first they had seen. Oliver had the nerve to suggest to them that they could feel the action of the machine by placing a thumb into the teat-cup. This the king and two princes, as well as the lady-in-waiting did and laughed happily at the result.

During the next two or three years, a deep economic depression settled over the entire nation. It was felt in every phase of life at Edenbank. The milk cheque – the basic income of the farm – dropped to a net return of $164 per month. Men were laid off. Having started married life on a wage of $45 per month, I soon had to accept $35, with $3 subtracted for electricity. This gave Sara and me $32 per month, plus living quarters and unlimited farm produce. Strangely enough, the circumstances of many others always seemed harder.

Gordon, also newly married, had homesteaded in the Peace River country and barely established when the crash of '29 came. There was no market for his oats and barley. Edwin generously purchased a forty-ton carload of feed grain from Gordon at 11 cents a bushel f.o.b. Peace River. The freight charges were the same, which brought the cost of grain delivered to

Sardis to 22 cents a bushel. Gordon was delighted to sell it, and Edwin and I were glad to have extra grain.

During the Depression, hungry men by the hundreds were looking for employment. Many would call at the farm, asking for a sandwich and work. There was no farm income to hire and pay anyone. A couple with a large family occupied the hired man's house. Edwin asked for $6 a month rent and gave them a chance to work to pay for it.

Ben Von Niessen came as another immigrant worker to the farm. He was a big, strong man who had escaped from Russia. His wages were $35 a month and he "batched" in the house that Old Wing had used. By this time Wing had returned to China. Wing wished to go back home to die, as all the old Chinese then wished. He had been a good and faithful employee for fifteen years. After Wing's departure Sara and Margaret together worked out an amicable agreement for managing the household.[49]

Edwin was highly involved in municipal affairs, most of which related to the Depression. He had a feeling of respect and sympathy for families who were on the foothill farms trying desperately to make a living without going on relief.

The export to China of two- and three-year-old bred heifers became a major item in the farm economy. In 1932, eleven head sold at an average of $130. When the cheque came in, Margaret had dozens of cheques made out ready for delivery to pay long-overdue accounts. Edwin was finally forced to take out a loan from the Canadian Farm Loan Board in order to clear off $6,000 indebtedness.

Because there were so many men on the move through the valley, there was always a fear that some night a barn might be burned accidentally by men sleeping in a haymow. Occasionally, permission was given for men to sleep in a stall in the horse barn, but never in the dry mows filled with loose hay.

One morning, as I was feeding the stock, I noticed by the behaviour of the calves that someone must be in the pen with them, trying to keep out of sight. I passed along, giving no sign of recognition that anything might be wrong. On the other side of the barn Ben Von Niessen was milking cows. I told him that someone was hiding in the calf pen and asked him to come up on one side while I went in to flush out the intruder. The man hiding proved to be only a harmless hungry wanderer, seeking a warm place to sleep among the cattle. He was taken up to breakfast, after which he trudged away in his endless search for work and lodging.

Only once was Sara badly frightened during those dark days when men walked the roads in despair.

Unshaven and grimy-looking men, often full of malice and desperation, would sometimes arrive. Sara was alone one day in the downstairs kitchen when suddenly a rough-looking man appeared in the passage between the dining room and the kitchen. He had walked in the unlocked front door. Sara could see that he was drunk and also a very frightening-looking character. Trying to keep calm, she offered him a chair and said she would get him a cup of tea. She then slipped out and called me, fortunately nearby. It was evening and the man said he was looking for the road to Vancouver. We had tea and a sandwich with him and then I offered to walk with him until he was on the right road. It was a relief for Sara when I returned after escorting the visitor away. Even after that incident no doors were ever locked at Edenbank, nor for many years to come.

In the hungry thirties, Edenbank continued with the exhibition of pure-bred livestock. It was a common sight, during those years, to see dozens of vagrant men riding the freight trains on which the exhibition stock travelled during summer months. I frequently took a flock of Cheviot sheep down into Washington State. Cattlemen with exhibition stock often found it necessary to fit their cars with what were called "hobo gates." These were slatted gates that allowed the fresh air to get into the car to keep the livestock cool and fresh and at the same time prevented others from getting into the warm shelter. I had a money pocket sewn into the inside of my undershirt, as I sometimes carried $100 or more en route between fairs, and there was plenty of chance of being robbed.

One night, Leonard Higginson and I were in our exhibition car, keeping watch on the sheep. When all seemed safe and the train had started, we climbed to the deck above to get some sleep. I always slept with a pitchfork beside me, just in case. During the night I was awakened by Leonard, who was busy trying to persuade an intoxicated hobo from coming into the car over the low gate. The man was in a bad mood and kept on coming. He got into the car and was on his way to the ladder to come up on the deck. I remained quiet in the dark, wondering what success Leonard would have with gentle persuasion. When it proved of no avail, I turned a flashlight onto the pitchfork and shoved it out in front, letting out a shout in no uncertain voice: "Get out of here!!" The man quickly changed his tune and started for the door.

Later that night, again I awoke and felt something was wrong. The train was rolling along full speed. When a glimmer of light came into the car, I could see a man sitting on the deck not six feet from me. I gave no sign that would let the intruder know I was

ter. She was a beautiful curly-haired darling and was immediately loved by all. We named her Margaret Marie and called her "Marie."

In the mid-thirties, a young couple, Norman and Ethel Bell, were married in Manitoba and started west on their honeymoon. Norman had been raised in the mixed farming area of Manitoba, but decided to head west with his bride to get away from farm work and the milking of cows. In high hopes, they turned their eyes to the west for a start in a new life. The country was still in the midst of the Depression, but the Bells did not realize to what extent this would affect them until they drove to B.C. They came upon great camps of unemployed men working on forestry projects in return for government assistance. It wouldn't be long before thousands of these men marched in angry protest.

When the Bells arrived in Chilliwack, their inquiries brought no hope of employment. After renting a small cabin at Vedder Crossing, Norman stopped in at Edenbank one day in his search for work. When he returned to their cabin that night, Ethel asked him the usual question: "Did you find a job?"

"No," he replied, "but I met a nice man." The next Sunday the couples met again at church. Afterwards when they were staying near Cottonwood Corner, Edwin visited Norman and Ethel. Later the Bells reminisced and told of Edwin's kindness and his interest in their plight. Still later Ethel recalled her first visit to the Edenbank home in 1935.[50]

> While we were enjoying a cup of tea a young woman came in carrying a beautiful baby about six months of age. It was Sara and her daughter, Marie. I held out my arms and Marie came to me with her beautiful smile. Betty was outside with her dad and I met her later. I was very lonely then being so far from home, and separated from Mother, Dad and my five brothers. Sara and Ollie became our dearest friends.

A few days after their first meeting, on Edwin's invitation Norman started work at Edenbank. On that first day he was given a four-horse team, Nig and Prince with Jip and Red, and asked to start ploughing with a two-bottom gang plough. That evening, after he came in from the field at four o'clock and had a cup of tea, he went into the barn to milk cows. This was the farm work he had driven hundreds miles to get away from! However, now it was a job much appreciated. He and Ethel soon moved into the old creamery, which was now the hired man's house, and

Oliver with his daughter Betty on his shoulders, 1935.

aware of his presence, deciding to wait until the train stopped. I could then wake Leonard and together we could put the stranger off, if necessary. I must have been very weary that night. After watching for a time and being lulled by the swaying of the car, I fell asleep. When I awoke the stranger had gone. My money was safe, and only a little food had been taken from the grub box.

There was little that could be done to relieve the hardships of those difficult times, so the Wells family worked and waited, worked and planned for the day when things would be better again.

On March 7, 1933, a baby girl, Sara Elizabeth (to become known as Betty) was born to Sara. We experienced a new-found happiness as parents, which neither long hours of work nor scarcity of money could detract from. In 1935, Sara and I had a second daugh-

became great friends of Sara and mine. The Bells were happy in the old house and soon became well known and a welcome part of the community. Norman's starting wage was a whopping $25 a month for the winter months, with house and milk provided. In the spring his wages increased to $35.

Norman stayed almost two years at Edenbank. Ethel would often care for Betty and Marie while Sara helped with the farm work, driving horses or operating the hoist in the barn loft. My brother Casey, who was very innovative, put together the hoist from parts he obtained at an old mill. A power-driven clutch, with a steel drum for the cable, proved to be a handy and more efficient method of unloading hay wagons than the old horse-drawn

Edwin loved his grandchildren. Here he is visiting with Betty and Marie in 1935.

method. Sara sometimes had the job of standing near the loft door and handling the gears.

Work on the farm as usual was heavy that autumn. The corn was cut by hand. Day after day, the men bent to their tasks. Rain or shine, the left arm encircled a hill of corn that stood eight or ten feet tall, while the right lifted a heavy, short-handled hoe to bring it down in a heavy blow that would cut off five or six stalks. The armful was dropped on the ground crosswise to the rows that had been hilled by a horse-drawn cultivator. Two or three more armloads were cut and dropped onto the first, to form a bundle weighing fifty to seventy-five pounds.

When hauling-in started, bundles of two low-slung corn racks would be lifted by men bending over and slipping one arm underneath and the other overtop. They were then carried and dropped onto the wagon to build piles several feet deep. The wagonload weighed possibly one and a half tons. A team of horses pulled the wagon to the barn – up into the upper driveway, where the corn bundles were again lifted off in armfuls and thrown onto the table of a cutting box. Machine power came in at this point. A power-driven four-bladed corn cutter cut the stalks into short lengths, which were blown into the silo. The silage was there spread out evenly and trampled to exclude

air pockets and prevent spoilage. It was heavy work for team and men. Many times the work had to proceed in mud and rain to get everything harvested before winter set in.

Edwin had passed his sixty-sixth birthday but still loved a fine-looking horse. One particular day he had an urge to buy some good horses he knew were being sold cheaply. After three years on the Prairies and cowboying at the '76 Ranch, Ray had returned to Chilliwack and undertaken to halter-break about twenty horses being offered for sale. They were "stampede" horses, which had known no life except to be driven in from the range during the stampede season, to be used in corrals and bucking competitions. They were big, strong, medium-weight horses, which Edwin felt would sell well below what he was sure they were worth. When the sale was over, Edwin had purchased four of these horses for $175. He asked Ray to lead them the three miles out to the farm from Chilliwack.

It was wintertime and dark. The road was covered with hard-packed ice and snow. Ray tied the horses head to tail, which was customary when trailing several horses behind a saddle horse. He tied the lead rope securely to the horn of his saddle, as was his custom. Unfortunately, on the way home from Chilliwack, Ray and his four trailing horses met a bus at a curve in the road. As the lights of the bus swung in on the horses, they jumped away from the light and directly in front of the bus. The driver applied the brakes, but the bus simply slid on unchecked, striking and killing one horse. The others, being tied together, were snapped around and carried along by the bus. Ray's horse was also swept by the bus, but never lost its feet. It was quite a disaster. Eventually Ray arrived home with only three horses.

Edwin had no trouble breaking two of them to drive but the third had a wicked disposition. It would strike, bite or kick when handled. For the first time, a heavy plank on the side of a stall in the horse barn had to be removed so a harness could be put on the horse from overtop. I worked with my

Oliver on Marie's saddle horse, Flash, bringing in the cattle at milking time, ca. 1950.

father for days but we made no progress in handling this horse and finally gave up. Then we turned to Gordon for help. After four years in the Peace River, Gordon had returned to the Chilliwack Valley and was farming on his own. Edwin offered him the use of the difficult horse if he could break it to drive. Gordon had been breaking and training horses almost continuously in the Peace country. He had seen the natives there master a horse of this type. Their method of breaking a horse too dangerous to handle was very simple. The horse was tied to a tree where it would be entirely alone. The only person it ever had contact with was the person who fed and watered it. Feed and water were reduced to a starvation diet, until the horse was so glad to see its master come with food it would forget to try to kick, strike or bite. Gradually the feed and water were increased again, but not until the horse had been ridden or driven each day, while it lacked strength to resist effectively. When all else failed, Gordon tried the native way. The method worked and Gordon finally had the horse driving in a team. When he returned the horse to Edenbank at the end of the season and began driving his own team

of quiet Clydesdales, he admitted that it was quite a relief.

For a few of the worst years of the Depression, Edenbank Ayrshires did not compete on the distant Prairie circuit. Don Richardson, a neighbour, came to Edenbank from his father's farm to show the herd at local fairs.

With two daughters now to look after, naturally Sara was a bit busier but she always rose to the task. Hot summer days would find her either hoeing in Wing's big garden or running the fork lift for haying. By 1937, economic times had improved somewhat in the valley. Sara and I made some alterations to the upstairs apartment to make it more comfortable for our family. Downstairs, Edwin and Margaret had a sawdust burner installed in their old wood stove to provide more efficient heating, and the dumb waiter was remodelled to bring up two rectangular boxes of fuel from the basement.

During that same year, Edenbank purchased Fintry Ringleader, a son of Captain J.C. Dunwaters' world record producer Fintry Honeysuckle. When the animal was two years old, he headed the Edenbank Ayrshire herd on the western show circuits. ༄

CHAPTER 15

Edenbank under the Third Generation

The year 1939 brought the third generation of the Wells family into full control of the management of Edenbank. In that year, I rented the farm as a going concern from Edwin, who retired from active farming.

I was an ardent admirer of the Ayrshire cow and had a love for show ring competitions just as had my father. There, an animal could be displayed in perfect form, and always the herdsman with each successive exhibition would set new goals for himself, for rarely could one make a clean sweep of all major prizes.

Don Richardson had responded to my request that he take the Edenbank herd again to the western Prairie circuit in 1939. A new lot of cows, daughters of Edenbank Robinhood 30, were brought to calving at the right time to show at their best. Don, with his nephew Bruce Richardson, established new records for the Edenbank herd in those shows. Edenbank Robin's Maid, destined to be the cow to symbolize breed perfection for the next few years, was

grand champion wherever shown. Grouped with two other daughters of Robinhood, they became the undefeated Get of Sire at Calgary, Edmonton, Saskatoon, Regina, Vancouver and Victoria. They were a snow-white trio.[51]

Always endeavouring to beautify the farm further, Edwin added to the original landscaping with young oaks and sycamore maples he had grown from seed. He planted and protected each young tree in a fence corner of the farm fields. He also set out a line of trees along the Evans Road end of the farm and lined the right-of-way of the B.C. Electric with young trees. He lived to see them grow into beautiful specimens. The year that B.C. Nurseries sold their tree stock, I went to the nursery and brought home a wagonload of young trees at $1 apiece. These were planted along the riverbank area at the front of the farm. This area eventually became a parklike setting of weeping willows, silver maple, copper beech, golden willows, green beech, weeping birch and a wide variety of maples.[52]

A special group of prize animals, daughters of Edenbank Robinhood 30th, the Get of Sire entry for exhibition in 1944. Oliver Wells is standing on the left, Bruce Richardson centre and Don Richardson on the right. The cows from left to right are Edenbank Robin's Maid, Crummies Snowball and Nellie's Ella 4th.

Edenbank Royal Nugget heads this group at the Victoria Exhibition. The old exhibition buildings are well shown. This group won first prize Aged Herd.

As I took over farm management, my interest in natural history led me to do more work on the river-bottom area. I was able to establish some trout ponds. Often working late into the evenings, using a team and scraper I dug out ponds and established control gates and screens for young trout. When farm responsibilities increased, I gave up the arduous hobby of trout rearing and released the fish. I later obtained Canada geese and mallard ducks for the ponds. To give added protection to wildlife and to further improve the area, I undertook to landscape four acres of river bottom, located at the northeastern corner of the farm along Vedder Road. One year, I planted over seven hundred trees and shrubs. At about this time, between us, my father and I purchased a few acres across Vedder Road from Edenbank. That land, too, we set about draining and landscaping in an effort to bring it into residential use and beautify the entire area.

During the war years, 1939–45, farm labour was "frozen" by government order in an effort to assure a constant supply of food for the war effort. I had young Henry Pauls working with me, a married man who came to Canada with his family after having escaped from Russia and Stalin. His family had been well-to-do farmers prior to the Revolution, in which they lost everything. Henry was a good worker and remained at Edenbank long enough to father two or three more children before he left. Henry and I both worked hard from 5:00 A.M. to 7:00 P.M. each day except Sundays,

when necessary work required only about five hours.

After the war, when Henry asked to leave, he said he was sorry but he had to get away to a change of work. A young neighbour, Art Steffen, worked by the day and at times filled in when I was away with an Ayrshire exhibit at the fairs. Four young men, sons of the natives who had helped A.C. Wells during those early years, now came again to assist when help was scarce during the haying season. The four were Harvey Sepass, son of the old Chief Sepass; Paul Tommie; Oliver Uslick, son of Harry Uslick, who so often went into the mountains with Edwin; and Richard Malloway, son of Julius Malloway, one of the oldest families of the Chilliwack natives.

During the latter part of 1941, Edwin became seriously ill and was not expected to live. He chose to stay home in his final illness to be nursed by Margaret and Sara. He was able to enjoy the fine vista of the Cascade Mountains from his window in the dining room, where he was made comfortable. Edwin died in his home at Edenbank in January 1942. To the last, he always had his mind on the future, and it was nearly impossible to get him to write or even talk very much about early history. Not long before his death, he looked out over the parklands that he had created at Edenbank and said, "It is beautiful, Oliver, but there is another place even more beautiful." His Christian faith in the existence of a heaven, in which the soul of man would live in a land where all was beauty, was very real.

The Ayrshire herd at Edenbank had always depended on the selection and use of outstanding sires. From the beginning of the records of production (ROP) testing of dairy cattle by the federal government, the Edenbank cows had been continually on test. ROP inspectors called at the farm at unheralded times to weigh and test milk and check record production figures. They were always welcomed at Edenbank. One of these men, who was among the first to do this work in western Canada, was affectionately known by the Wells boys at Edenbank as "Daddy" Watson. We boys were then raising rabbits. Daddy Watson showed us how to skin a rabbit and butcher it ready for cooking. Mr. Wiltshire, another inspector, like Daddy Watson, always brought a fishing rod and a shotgun with him in the fall. Both were men of the great outdoors.

In those early days, the visiting milk "tester" stayed for two days at the farm home, recording four or more milkings. The third tester we had was a former cowboy of the West before there were any fences on the range. This man, Edgerton, came originally from England, and had come west to be free and live the life of a cowhand. In 1906–07, when the worst blizzard in the memory of the men of the range drove the cattle from Canada down into the States, Edgerton had been there. He had seen cattle carcasses piled deep in the ravines, frozen to death by the thousands, but he spoke very little of his range life. His dress was a combination of an English gentleman and a western plainsman.

In 1939, when the Ayrshire Breeders' Association of Canada herd test report was published, Edenbank was in eighth place in all of Canada, with twenty-two cows on test.

When the daughters of Fintry Ringleader came into production, it was evident to me that they would improve the herd for both type and production. I therefore repurchased a few that I had sold and also repurchased Edenbank Ringleader and Edenbank Ringleader 27, two good sons of Fintry Ringleader.

During 1945, the Ayrshire Breeders' Association of Canada provided for "type" classification of herds.

I immediately made application for the Edenbank herd to be included. Professor H.M. King made the first official type classification of the herd, and his report follows:

Score	Rating	Edenbank herd	Year	Overall %
90+ points	Excellent	6 cows	1945	84.89
85–90	Very good	14		
80–84	Good	19		
75–79	Fair	5		

The herd was classified for the third time in November 1947, by which time it had improved to eight excellent cows and had an overall average of 86.64%.

In preparation for sending another show herd from Edenbank to the Prairie circuit in 1946, cows were bred to calve during the summer and early fall. These were daughters of Fintry Ringleader. During this period of pure-bred livestock promotion in western Canada, the Class A fairs, at the request of various breed associations, set up prize lists that gave a breeder a chance to exhibit about fifteen animals. These animals, apart from showing in their respective individual classes, could also be shown in groups. The winning of first place in group classes was considered by the exhibitors to be of the greatest importance, because they gave recognition to the fact that such a herd was a desirable place to go to purchase breeding stock. These group classes included Breeders Herd, Dairy Herd, Senior Herd, Get of Sire and Progeny of Dam.

Three Ayrshiremen – Jock McBryde, Oliver Wells and Archie Stevenson – at the "Red and White" Ayrshire breeders' show at Edenbank, 1948. Oliver, who almost never imbibed, told with an amused smile of the camaraderie amongst the old Scots who were showmen and fellow breeders of Ayrshires. When they all gathered at the exhibition each fall and the evenings progressed after chores, many had a "wee nip" or two. It then became very difficult for Oliver to understand their thick Scottish accent as they told stories.

Bill McFaul agreed to prepare the show herd for the 1946 circuit, which began in Calgary in July. A fifty-foot automobile car from the CPR was spotted on the siding of the B.C. Electric at Sardis, where it was made ready for the trip. Edenbank Ringleader, five years old, was to head the herd. The cows Edenbank White Beauty 2nd, Edenbank Ella 3rd and Edenbank Rosebud 2nd were chosen. In all, nineteen head were made ready for the trip, and when Bill herded them down Vedder Road to be loaded into the car, they were beautifully fitted out for the first show.

It was known that competition would be stronger

Bill McFaul (right) and assistant loading a boxcar at the B.C. Electric Sardis station in preparation for a rail trip to the western show circuit. The Edenbank boxcar would be transferred if necessary to another rail line depending on the destination.

than in previous years and that Calgary would be the hardest show at which to win. Hodgson & Borett, of Forest Lawn, Alberta, had purchased several daughters of Fintry Ringleader from Edenbank in 1944, and they were to match against their own kin. The judge at Calgary would be John Young, the well-respected herdsman from Scotland who the reader will recall was in charge of the Ayrshire herd at UBC. John was recognized as an outstanding authority on the Ayrshire type and a man whose final judgement was made only after careful appraisal.

Professor Grant MacEwan was to act as judge at the Edmonton Exhibition and was widely known in western Canada as a most competent judge of livestock. Press reports covering the 1946 show season wrote of the triumphant tour that the Edenbank Ayrshires made that year.

Commenting on the exhibit of Ayrshires at Calgary, John Young called it "The biggest and best show of Ayrshires I've seen yet in western Canada." Of the dry cow class (in which Edenbank White Beauty 2nd took first place and Edenbank Ella 3rd was second), he declared it was "The best class I have ever had the opportunity of placing." In Edmonton, Regina, Saskatoon and the state of Montana, the herd continued to do well.

After a successful showing at these larger fairs, the herd returned home to rest a spell and prepare to go farther east to compete at the Royal Winter Fair in Toronto. When a list of all western winners was published in the fall of 1946, Edenbank Ayrshires were winners in seven out of eight classifications, a notable record.

Bill McFaul continued in charge of the show herd that left for the huge Royal Winter Fair in November via the CPR. I accompanied Bill and we took fourteen head. Edenbank Ringleader 8 had been sold, but during the summer, I had fitted and trained the bull Edenbank Ringleader 27, who traditionally had been difficult to handle alone and thus show to advantage. However, he did respond to my training and was now ready to stand up and show off his 2,000 pounds of good quality and character in no uncertain manner.

The trip east was very cold. At times it was 20 to 30 degrees below zero outside the cars as we travelled over the Prairies and through Ontario, but it was mild weather when we reached Toronto. To keep warm at night, Bill and I heated large stones on our Coleman heater we used for cooking, then put them into our beds to warm them before crawling up onto the deck to retire.

Oliver Wells and Jack Fotheringham holding two of their favourites, Edenbank Ringleader and Ella 3rd. In 1947, the last year Oliver exhibited the Ayrshires, the Ayrshire Breeders' Association of Canada classified the Edenbank herd as having eight "excellent" cows and an overall average of 86.64%. PHOTO BY JAMES E. ROSE, TORONTO

"The Royal" that year of 1946 was the first post-war show. Three hundred and fifty Ayrshires of the best herds in Canada and the U.S.A. competed. Of the Canadian herds, two that impressed me the most were those of Burnside (R.R. Ness & Sons) and P.D. McArthur & Sons, both of Howick, Quebec. I observed in those herds a quality of refinement that few western herds possessed. Uniformity of type was similar for each herd. These were examples of what could be accomplished by breeders with a fine eye and an ability to produce superior livestock as models of the breed.

Ella's pride. The photo demonstrates an "excellent udder."

In the show ring, Edenbank Ringleader 27 distinguished himself by placing second in a large class of mature bulls. His son, Robin Beauty, who had been junior and reserve grand champion in the West, won first place as a yearling. The Edenbank females stood up well in their classes, but the cows that had won on the western circuit and were producing fifty to sixty pounds of milk a day had lost too much of their "bloom" to win. All told it was a most worthwhile trip and gave recognition to the Edenbank herd, which retained a high reputation for years to come.

On the return trip, the temperature had dropped to 30 degrees below zero when I got out of the car to go to a store at White River, Ontario.[53] Bill, not realizing the actual outside temperature, complained about the chill when he left the car for a hose to fill the water barrels. It continued cold as the car rolled west day after day. Ice formed on the metal roof inside the car as moisture from the air condensed and froze. By the time we reached the Rockies, the car had become an ice igloo. Overhead, the ice and frost was six inches deep. The water barrels froze every night, but otherwise no damage was done. When the car started warming up west of the Rockies, the thaw set in overhead and special sleeping quarters had to be roofed in so we could keep dry. It was a long, uncomfortable trip of seven days and seven nights, but men and cattle all survived and arrived home feeling a bit weary but quite fit.

The last exhibits to which I took the show herd were the B.C. Class A fairs in 1947. I was helped by a young neighbour, Jack Fotheringham. As my assistant, Jack helped at Edenbank for several years and knew the cattle well. He was also a keen exhibitor and junior showman. White Beauty 2nd and Ella 3rd swept the championships on this occasion. Edenbank Ringleader 27 defeated a new rival, shown by Shannon Brothers, and retained his position as champion. This bull continued to be difficult to handle, always watching for a chance to "get" me, so I kept the nose ring wrapped with wire and tied him carefully each time I entered the stall. Remembering my earlier experiences with bulls, I kept the animal's nose high up and away from me so I could get a halter rope securely fastened before the bull could get into a position to charge.

Trouble did come one day when I had gone home for the day and Jack Enoch, who was herdsman at home at Edenbank, took my place at the exhibition. A parade of champions was called, and Jack took Ringleader 27 out to the ring. He behaved well until, back in his stall, Jack bent over to tie him up without first making sure the bull could not get to him. Quick as a flash the bull caught him on his head. Fortunately, the animal had been dehorned. He rubbed Jack up and down the wall and as he was going up the next time, Archie Stevenson, who was close behind the bull, struck the animal a blow on the rump. This apparently speeded up the lift of his head enough to throw Jack clear out over a four-inch pipe, which acted as a guardrail. Jack was taken to hospital by ambulance, but was later released when it was found he was not seriously crushed. He was, however, very badly bruised.

I admit I was shaking at the knees a bit the next day when I had to take Ringleader 27 out again on parade. Before going out alone with the bull, I asked Bill Child, a long-time herdsman, to be ready to give me a hand if necessary. The bull behaved well, but somehow he was so much like a cat ready to pounce that this was his last trip to the shows. Following these two banner years, the Edenbank herd depended more on its herd-classification excellence along with publicity and advertising, and less on exhibitions, which had, in past years, been so essential for herd and breed recognition. And so the years of the show circuits came to a close. ♋

CHAPTER 16

The Great Fraternity

As someone wise once said, "One cannot build alone. There must be others of like mind or what is built is never great; for there are none to recognize its greatness." So it is with the building of a herd, or of a breed of cattle.

In the nineteenth century, there arose in Great Britain a group of men who established the basic breeds of livestock and the principles of breeding by which they could be improved. Some of the greatest of these men were in Scotland, where many of the world's foremost breeds of livestock were born. From Scotland, the Ayrshire cow came to America, and with her came the Scotsmen to care for her. They formed the Society for the Importation of Ayrshire Cattle and also the Society for the Registration of Pedigrees.

At about the same time these two societies united and became the Ayrshire Breeders' Association of Canada, A.C. Wells became a vice-president of the association. Later Edwin continued the tradition and served terms as director and president. Visiting the great herds of Canada and the U.S.A., Edwin made personal friends of many of the founders, and recognized their ability and good judgement in herd management. Still later, in 1947, I became a director of the same association,

The annual meeting of the Ayrshire Breeders' Association of Canada, late 1940s. This photo shows the executive and directors of the association in one of the years when Oliver was western representative. Oliver is seated fifth from the right end of the table. Others pictured are J.R. Pelletier, George Sheah, William Hunter, James Betne, J.S. McKecknie, Alex McGillvary, Gus Topain, Ronald Pidgeon, J.J. Joubert, Stan Chagyon, Alex Summerland, Rene Trepanier, J.S. Hyde, Doug Ness, Urskin Rogers, P.E. McArther and Professor Alec Ness. PHOTO BY JEAN BISSON, ABC NEWS PICTURES, MONTREAL

A typical junior-class judging at the Chilliwack fair – lots of Ayrshires in the 1940s. Betty Wells in left foreground, Rob McBlain second from right, Jim Stevenson hatless in the second row with ribbon in his pocket.

representing B.C. and Alberta, a capacity in which I served consecutive two-year terms.

At both directors' and annual meetings, I met with breeders from all parts of Canada and enjoyed the hospitality of Quebec and Ontario directors. I was driven to farms to see many of the leading Ayrshire herds and their owners, who shared their experiences and knowledge. All seemed sincere in a common cause, which was simply the elevation of the Ayrshire breed to prominence in Canadian agriculture.

During my term of office, some of the promotional activity included classification for type, approval of sires relating to the production records of their daughters, and the introduction of herd testing programs.

Provincially, Edenbank supported the Ayrshire Breeders' Association of B.C.. Edwin was the group's first president and later I served in the same office. In 1939, together with a number of local breeders, we formed the Chilliwack Ayrshire Breeders' Club. I became the club president, with Bill McFaul acting as secretary.

In 1925, Edenbank was host to the first Ayrshire breeders' field day held in B.C. News reports of the event in the *Chilliwack Progress* indicate it was a successful gathering and a great benefit to the breed as well as a pleasant social event. The Ayrshire herd being fitted by Ken Hay for the Prairie circuit that year was the feature attraction of the day. It included two recently imported herd sires, which had come from the eastern United States.

In 1938, the Edenbank home and gardens again hosted the Ayrshire breeders in what was described as "the largest gathering on record." By this time, the Scotsmen of this great fraternity were beginning to influence proceedings, which was in keeping with the Ayrshire cow's Scottish ancestry. The report of the day, carried by the *Family Herald and Weekly Star*, began: "The Pipers H.M. Eddie, of Sumas, and James Duncan, of Langley, in full Highland costume, marched up and down, playing lively Scottish airs on the bagpipes."

Betty, our five-year-old daughter, had her picture taken holding an Ayrshire cow. She represented the fourth generation at Edenbank to hold the lead on an Ayrshire. Her upbringing, however, had been a little sheltered so far as kilts and bagpipes were concerned. When the pipers marched by too closely for her young ears, she said to her mother, "I don't like the noise those ladies with the funny skirts are making."

Guests at the event included Mayor Charles Barber of Chilliwack and Reeve W.T. Richardson of the Municipality. Sam Shannon, of the famous Grandview herd of Cloverdale, placed the Get of Sire groups, which were judged by the "guests." Don and Bruce Richardson and George Challenger gave demonstrations relating to model Ayrshire type.

Many field days followed during succeeding years as the breed gained recognition and support from more young men from Scotland. Edenbank remained an important centre for breed publicity and activity. Junior Farmers, the forerunner of the 4-H clubs, were given recognition and a chance to increase their interest in the Ayrshire cow. Among the winners of the judging contests at the 1938 field day was David Young, son of John Young from the University of B.C. Thirty years later, Dave was to hold one of the top positions at Ottawa in the federal Department of Agriculture.

At the 1940 field day, Dr. J.C. Berry of the Department of Animal Husbandry at UBC assigned official placing in classes judged by the Junior Farmers. Dr. Berry himself, as a teammate on the UBC team that won first place in judging at Portland, Oregon, had gained some of his judging experience at Edenbank in earlier years. Violet Paton, daughter of one of Scotland's sons, John Paton, won the judging competition in 1940, and Fred Bryant, of the Chilliwack Calf Club, won the showmanship competition for juniors. Twenty-six years later, Fred was to be secretary of the Ayrshire Breeders' Association of B.C. and one of the breed's most enthusiastic supporters and promoters.

Like his father, George, who had come from Great Britain years before, he retained a close relationship with the family at Edenbank.

I was re-elected president of the Ayrshire Breeders' Association of B.C. in 1943. In my report at the annual meeting of that year, I referred to the work being carried on by the junior calf clubs. I stated that "the future of agriculture depends largely on the membership of these clubs."

Junior Farmers clubs of all breeds soon became organized in B.C. under the provincial government programs as 4-H clubs and worked in co-operation with Future Farmer clubs of the western United States. For many years, Edenbank acted as host each year to a large group of 4-H and Future Farmer boys and girls from Washington State schools who came to judge livestock. At the same time, the 4-H movement in the Chilliwack Valley gathered momentum with enrolment of a hundred members. Each year, boys and

Ayrshire men of Chilliwack and the Fraser Valley with "twa wee Scottish lassies," 1948. Standing in photo, left to right: Andy McFarlane, Oliver Wells, Hugh Bone, Gordon Stewart, Mr. Newton, James Ross, Dave Young, John Young. Kneeling beside the dancers, on the left, Tommy McBlain, and right, Johnny Paton.

Dr. J.C. Berry gives a demonstration of horse judging at the Agassiz experimental farm, ca. 1945.

girls came to Edenbank to judge both cattle and sheep. The family enjoyed hosting literally thousands of these young farmers-to-be. The older generation sensed that the gatherings provided a wonderful stimulation and encouragement for these youngsters.

At Edenbank, many of the budding young farmers learned to recognize that breeding of cattle is a creative art, based on an animal's pedigree, conformation and performance. The ideal animal exists only in the mind of a breeder and must also be established in the mind of each individual who wishes to excel in the art.

At the 1944 Ayrshire gathering at Edenbank, a calf was donated for auction by UBC to raise funds for the wartime "Milk for Britain" fund. It was purchased for $210 by Harold Young, a Sardis breeder and long-time friend of the family.

Archie Stevenson became president of the Ayrshire Breeders' Association of B.C. in 1947. I was enjoying my work with the executive, as they were all keen and dedicated breeders. I found them forthright and honest in criticisms and always aware of their role in the great fraternity of Ayrshire breeders. It was my privilege to associate with such veteran and enthusiastic breeders as the Shannon Brothers, Hugh Davidson, George Bryant, H. Dawson & Son, Captain and Mrs. J.C. Dunwaters, Richard Brothers, Andy Young, Roland Ness and E.W. Van Tassel. In more recent years, Archie Stevenson, John Young, J.C. Berry, T.R. McBlain, John Paton, Hodgson & Borrett, Don Morton and Jock McBryde, Fred Bryant and Bill McFaul were among my many friends and associates at Edenbank.

CHAPTER 17

Irrigation and the Flood of '48

In 1944, the five sons of Edwin Wells met together at Gordon Wells's home, Edenlea Farm, and formed the Wells Family Society. By order of our ages we were Ray, Casey, Gordon, Oliver and Ronald. The written objectives were:

1. To strengthen family ties.
2. To provide recreation facilities for the use and pleasure of the members.
3. To carry out such projects as would perpetuate the conservation of natural history as would be in keeping with the ideals of E.A. Wells.

The financial structure of the society was based on the value of a woodlot property at the north end of Cultus Lake, formerly owned by E.A. Wells and Ronald. This would be taken over by the society members, with each assuming equal financial responsibility. Over the next nearly twenty-five years, there was a continuation of family gatherings and social evenings, which for the most part centred on meetings of society members. Many of the gatherings were held at the old farm. The property at Cultus Lake was later sold and during the war years, while Ronald was away serving in the RCAF, a property at Loon Lake in the Interior of B.C. was purchased in his name. After that time, many of the family enjoyed summer holidays and fall hunting of big game at the comfortable log cabin at Loon Lake. The cabin was

This photo captures the dyke on the Fraser River breaking at Hatzic during the '48 flood. Ron Wells tells of how he and friend Reg Taylor, when the river was at its peak, flew out over the Greendale area and were just above the Zink farm when a small break appeared in the dyke. In no time there was an opening as wide as a house and the water beneath them raged through the break in a small tidal wave.

built with the expert help and supervision of Ed Dougherty, who had hunted there for years with Ray, Gordon and Ron.

The telephone rang one evening in the spring of 1947. "Hello, Oliver, it's George Challenger speaking." George always had something in mind when he phoned, and generally it had to do with some aspect of agriculture, dairy cattle or Junior Farmers work and gardening. This time, however, he sounded very mysterious. "Can Ralph Gram and I come in to see you in the morning?" was all he said. "Sure, be glad to see you," I volunteered. It was the briefest call I remembered between the two of us.

I was still wondering what Ralph Gram and George could be wanting to talk about when they called the next morning. Ralph was editor of *Farming News* and agricultural representative for the B.C. Electric Railway Company. George was a dairy farmer and had a beautiful herd of pure-bred Jerseys. He was also a local representative of the railway company. George came straight to the subject at hand after we sat down together in the farm office. "You'll remember, Oliver, we were talking last summer about the possibility of irrigating pasture land, here in the valley – like they are doing a bit on the dry land in Washington State."

I said I remembered, and Ralph exclaimed, "George and I were wondering if you would be interested in a project in which we might do a little experimenting to determine if it would pay to irrigate pasture land here?" I had already been attempting to grow even larger grass crops and was therefore quite willing to co-operate in this trial.

Ralph came back a few days later with promised co-operation from the B.C. Electric Railway Company and the Dominion Experimental Farm Service at Agassiz. Farm superintendent Harold Hicks had offered to place Mills Clarke in charge of the project.

Thus Edenbank became the site of the first large-scale experimental irrigation project for dairy farms in the Chilliwack Valley. I agreed to the installation of an irrigation system by Pumps & Power of Vancouver and said I would do some necessary physical work. B.C. Electric agreed to establish power con-

Gulls following the plough. They were always close by to find worms in the fresh soil turned over by the machine.

nections and supply electricity without charge for one year. The experimental farm would keep records concerning the application of water and fertilizers, and records of relative yields. At the end of one year, I was to have the option of purchasing the system if I desired. The cost would be $2,500. It was capable of irrigating thirty-three acres by sprinkler.

I purchased the system after receiving a detailed analysis of the first year's operation. The net gain from irrigation on the thirty acres was $640. The experiment continued for five years, with conclusive results in favour of irrigation.

The Chilliwack Valley has an annual rainfall of fifty inches, but sparse amounts during the growing season. With irrigation, I found I was assured of a heavy yield every year. I could produce thirty tons of green grass per acre and could pasture up to two cows per acre instead of one. The growing season was lengthened and the cows could spend more of the year on pasture. One of the greatest advantages was to be able to spread commercial fertilizers at any time during the growing season. To me, irrigation was a means to an end. I was able to produce more milk from the daughters and granddaughters of Fintry Ringleader, using less land.

Then came the flood year of 1948. Fifty-four years had passed since the great flood of '94. To me, the flood of '94 was something that had happened to the pioneers, certainly a terrible event and something to be remembered, but nothing more. Another major flood was not anticipated. Was 1948 to be another '94? No one knew the answer as the month of May slowly drew to a close. The Fraser River level rose higher than it had since that flood year so long ago.

On the night of June 2, Percy Evans drove into the yard at Edenbank and asked me if he could bring some seed oats for storage in the granary, where they would be safe above high water, "just in case a dyke breaks." If this were to happen, Percy's farm would be ten feet under water. "Sure," I said, "and don't you think you had better move your cows out too? What *are* you going to do if a dyke breaks?" Percy's farm was on the Old Yale Road near the Vedder Canal.

Percy, a son of Al Evans and grandson of Jane Evans, the late A.C. Wells's sister, was his usual casual self, in spite of the fact that his farm was in an area bounded by two dykes, the Fraser River on the north and the Vedder River on the west. Behind these dykes, the water was standing eighteen feet above the ground level within. The dykes had been softening for days and seepage was bubbling up out of the sandy subsoil in dozens of boils. All along the miles of dykes, hundreds of volunteer workers were labouring night and day, sandbagging soft places in the hope that the Fraser would be contained until it stopped its steady rise. Dykes in the Lower Mainland had already broken in many places, causing much flooding.

The cabin at Loon Lake, B.C., owned by the Wells Family Society and built by the Wells brothers with much help from Ed Dougherty. Sara at the front door, ca. 1945.

"What *are* you going to do if a dyke breaks?" I asked Percy again that night. He replied: "If it breaks on the Fraser's side, we'll go like hell over the canal bridge, over the Vedder. If it breaks on the Vedder side, we'll go like hell up the highway." My only comment was, "Well, if you need a place to put your cattle, don't be afraid to bring them here."

At 5:00 P.M. on the evening of June 3, Percy was milking cows and watching the cars pass on the adjacent highway. He noticed two cars pass by with wet wheels. He rushed outside and looked towards the Fraser dyke. It had broken in a low draw! A wall of water barely half a mile away and five feet high was rushing straight towards him. One shout from Percy and his sons began turning the cows loose into the barnyard. Quickly, they drove them out onto the road west over the canal bridge to safety, as the flood waters lapped at their heels.

By ten o'clock that night, truckloads of Percy's cows began arriving at Edenbank. It was already dark when the first of the cattle were unloaded into the corral between the barns. The men returned via Vedder Mountain Road to the west of the canal for another load. Both Percy's sons-in-law, Ray McDaniels and Walter Moore, escorted the cattle. I made the horse barn available for use as a milking barn and provided a six-acre field for their herd to pasture in.

The Wells brothers loved to get together at their family society meetings and swap stories, especially about horses and the old days. They all had the ability to relate colourful tales. Here they are at the original meeting of the Wells Family Society, ca. 1944. Left to right: Ron, Gordon, Ray, Oliver and Casey.

Ray Wells, Edwin and Gertrude's oldest son, was born the year of the great flood of '94. He always loved a good horse and entered his last race in a sulky at the age of ninety-six – and won! When he lost his driver's licence he bought a new driving horse and buggy and added even more than his usual colour to the character of Chilliwack. Ray spent some time living and riding on ranches, from B.C. to the famous " '76" on the Prairies.

Again as in '94 a huge flood had covered a large portion of the valley, but this time because of a tremendous volunteer effort of sandbagging to reinforce them, dykes around Chilliwack held. For a few days, until they could find other accommodation, the two boys looking after Percy's herd ate with the family at Edenbank and slept in the attic. Soon a routine was established and after the first week of disruption, the summer days got back to some degree of normality at Edenbank.

Percy's farm was one of the last to be pumped dry after the river dropped to lower levels and the breach in the dyke was repaired. It was early September before his cattle could go back to their own barn. The government and a flood relief fund assisted those who were flooded out and paid for feed consumed away from home farms. The Evans family sent grateful acknowledgements of the hospitality accorded them at our farm.

At the farm, recollections of mud and the inconvenience caused by extra cattle and heavy rain were soon almost forgotten. The family remembered the many pleasant times of those days when everyone worked so well together. At breakfast time, the young men who had looked after Percy's herd would slip off their gumboots as they came in from the back door veranda. Laddie, a four-month-old collie pup, would entertain them by the table. He would vanish under the table regularly, trying to plague them by wrestling with their woollen socks, as they tried to use their feet to subdue him.

One night, after the young men had gone to bed in the attic, another son-in-law of Percy's came to visit and inquire whether he could help out. I showed him up to the attic. The two long flights of stairs opened out into the large attic, with plastered walls and ceiling. The boys had comfortable beds there and lots of space. It was Ken Kiernan who bunked in with them that night and who lived near Percy on the Old Yale highway near the Vedder Canal. Ken years later would be elected to the provincial legislature in the W.A.C. Bennett government and would hold several different portfolios, including minister of Agriculture, minister of Parks and Recreation, and minister of Mines. ✍

CHAPTER 18

A New Sire

The visit to the Royal Winter Fair in 1946 had given me an insight into the calibre of the men who were most successful nationally in the fine art of cattle breeding. I befriended herdsmen whose family names had become synonymous with Ayrshire cattle of distinction. The veteran breeders there were friends of the earlier generations: R.R. Ness of Burnside; P.D. McArthur of Cherrybank; Jack Black of Willowhaugh; Cummings of Glengary; Gilbert McMillan of Springburn. All were familiar names.

I had been privileged to be an invited guest at their various farms and homes, and to view herds of good cattle during visits east from 1947 to 1950. A particular visit to Burnside was to have a lasting influence on the development of the Edenbank herd. Douglas Ness took me to the home of his father, R.R. Ness, who had been the founder of the famous Burnside herd and was then retired, but still a dynamic force in the prominence of Burnside. His herd was an example of what could be done by continual careful breeding

Carnell Standard Bearer was a successful herd sire purchased by Oliver from the Templeton farm in Scotland through the assistance of Doug Ness of Burnside Farms, Quebec. This photo shows him as a calf, before he was imported from Scotland. He grew into an impressive herd sire, and his daughters were excellent producers. PHOTO BY TEMPLETON FARMS, SCOTLAND

A winter scene along Vedder Road after a heavy snowfall, ca. 1950. Folks had to walk for groceries, and milk delivery was by sleigh from the Fraser Valley Milk Producers' Association.

of an established type and the use of carefully selected sires. His sires were usually purchased in Scotland.

These pleasant visits were followed by a trip to the eastern States to see the Strathglass herd. Here in 1944, I purchased a young herd sire, Strathglass Brown Form. For several years, I aspired to bring imported blood such as this into the Edenbank herd. In the days of Edwin Wells, the Scottish herds of prominence had been Lessnessock, Auchinbrain, Bargenoch, Howies, Garclaugh, Dunlop, Hobsland, Nethercraig, Castle Douglas and Barcheskie. They too were all very familiar names.

In more recent years, I had been subscribing to the Scottish publications *Farming News* and the *Ayrshire Cattle Society's Journal* and watched with interest the rise to prominence of certain herds, whose cattle were also combining type and production.

In the very early development of the breed there had been two lines of thought in the minds of the Scottish breeders. What was supreme in the Ayrshire type? The "vessel" breeders put great importance on the perfect udder with small, evenly placed teats. The "yield" breeders tended to lay the greatest stress on heavy production, with less stress on the model udders.

Leading breeders who rose to the top of the ladder in that great society of breeders during the latter 1940s were the men who gave recognition to production and were not averse to introducing the "vessel" blood into their herds if necessary, to improve the cows' udders.

During the summer of 1948, Edenbank was visited by Hugh Bone, secretary of the Ayrshire Cattle

Society of Scotland, a distinguished authority on the breed. His efforts had been responsible for much of the breed's advancement. It was my good fortune to be able to entertain this gentleman at Edenbank. In the fall of the same year, Edenbank Farm donated a silver trophy to the Chilliwack Ayrshire Breeders' Club, to be known as the Edenbank Challenge Trophy. It was to be competed for annually, with production records and conformation being the criteria.

The sire Strathglass Brown Form had not given the Edenbank herd results as good as I had expected. Therefore, I was anxious to import a herd sire directly from Scotland. With this in mind, I wrote to the Templetons of Carnell. My research indicated that this herd was leading all Scotland in production and was also distinguishing itself at regular shows and sales. After corresponding with George Templeton of Carnell Home Farm in Hurlford, Scotland, regarding the bloodlines I was interested in and the price of a young herd sire, I asked Douglas Ness, of Burnside Farms, to make the final selection and arrangements for the importation of a young herd sire.

Edenbank purchased Carnell Standard Bearer for $1,500. The calf was sent in a larger importation of stock being arranged by Burnside. After six weeks in quarantine in Quebec, Standard Bearer travelled west by express train, arriving at Edenbank in August 1949. He was the most expensive herd sire ever brought to Edenbank. I often reflected later that I ordered the bull when my bank account was already in the red the same amount as the price of the bull. However, sales of pure-bred Ayrshires were brisk at the time, and a planned shipment of cattle to a sale in northern Idaho brought prices up to $750 for young cows from the Edenbank herd.

The use of Standard Bearer on the daughters of Fintry Ringleader was one day to be recognized as the breeding program that lifted the Edenbank herd to a top place among Canada's leading herds. I was delighted when the first crop of bull calves, sired by Standard Bearer and out of the best daughters of Fintry Ringleader, brought in money enough to pay for the bull and the cost of his importation.

One of the first sons, Edenbank Standard Bearer, was out of Edenbank Ella 3rd, an "excellent" grand champion daughter of Fintry Ringleader with high production records. This bull calf was exported to New Zealand. The purchaser, Mr. Hutchings of Dalemere Farms, Rotorua, visited Edenbank and saw the dam and sire before he made the purchase. Edenbank Standard Bearer, purchased at $500, had a one-month voyage in a heavy plank box stall, which had been built on the deck of a freighter at a cost of $700. He arrived in New Zealand in good condition and was indeed a good Edenbank standard-bearer.

Oliver's three North Country ewes imported from Scotland. The upright silo can be seen in the background.

The year 1949 was a boom year for the farm. Sales were easily made at the highest prices ever received. The only sombre news was the death of Fintry Ringleader at twelve years of age. I took advantage of the better times to make repairs and improvements to the big barn. Edwin had installed Louden stanchions, but as yet the floors were of wood, the original cedar blocks were still in the aisles and there was planking under the cows. With the help of Mr. Edstrom and Dave Kirkness, local builders, I took out all the wooden floors in the dairy barn and put down concrete. At the same time we changed the stanchions to chain ties for the comfort of the cattle. A total floor area of 100 feet by 60 feet was laid in concrete and the dairy barn took on a neat, modern look, showing off the herd to better advantage. The roof of the big barn was also in need of repairs. At a cost of $2,000, equal to half the original cost of the barn, a new roof of Duroid-Barrett shingles was put on.

Very cold weather came the following winter. For a week the temperature was around freezing with a cold northeast wind blowing. Snow fell to a depth of two feet. The wind velocity at times was seventy miles an hour. For three weeks roads were blocked and most water systems froze solid. Horses and sleighs brought out from storage were the only conveyances by which milk could be hauled. Power failed and the milking machine at Edenbank had to be operated from the vacuum on the tractor's engine. Spring arrived quite late and the cows were not out to graze until April 23.

After about twenty-five years of breeding beautiful park sheep, I decided it would be more profitable to establish a flock of North Country Cheviots. I therefore sold the farm flock of Border Cheviots. The North Countries were larger animals that I considered superior to the Border Cheviots. In 1950 I ordered three ewes, which were to come directly from Scotland as part of a shipment arranged to come to Alberta. They arrived at Edenbank on March 27, 1951, and gave birth to lambs in April. They were the first North Country Cheviots to be imported into B.C. and were an especially good trio of ewes with true Scottish names, Knockglass, Borgie Mains and Spittal Mains, their flock names in Scotland. These sheep did well at Edenbank and for the next ten years their progeny sold at high prices and their popularity spread rapidly.

The year 1950 came to a close with more vicious cold and snowstorms, as in the previous January. Rarely did the Wells family go out for Christmas dinner, but they did go to the Fotheringhams that year in spite of snow and a sub-zero temperature.

As the reader again will recall, young Jack Fotheringham had been working with me for some time and was often at the farm to help prepare cattle for exhibition. When the Fotheringham family came west from Alberta during the war years to live close to their father Douglas, then stationed at the Royal Canadian Engineers Camp, the family stayed first at the Edenbank home. Later they moved into the old boarding house on the farm. They had expected to get away from cold Prairie winters, but in fact that first winter at Edenbank the winds blew bitterly cold and snowdrifts engulfed cars on the main road to the engineers' camp.

Another storm broke loose again in greater fury. It closed the new Chilliwack High School, which could not be kept heated. Snow blocked most roads and young people were unable to attend school that winter for a full month. The main Vedder Road was closed for many days and huge drifts built up along the banks of the Luckakuck. A family friendship with the Fotheringhams developed as years went by and at the Christmas dinner reunion in 1950, memories of Christmas dinners at Edenbank were recalled during the time Doug was overseas.

Midway through the twentieth century Edenbank made the change from horsepower to tractor. Jack Enoch had come to the farm in 1944 and became herdsman during the years I was attending Ayrshire Breeders' Association meetings in eastern Canada. I had originally interviewed Jack at the Armstrong Exhibition. He was a native of the Okanagan Valley and was very capable with horses and tractor. When I purchased a Cockshutt 30 tractor in 1950, I depended on Jack's help and knowledge of tractor implements. Jack's wife, Amy Enoch, became an enthusiastic member of the Sardis community and generously shared her natural gift of music. Before switching to the tractor, I had made up my mind to specialize in grassland farming and to limit the farm's overhead to what was required for that type

Over the years this scale weighed hundreds of thousands of pounds of milk in the old cow barn.

of farming. Jack had had some experience in putting up hay with a sweep on the front of a tractor. Plans were therefore made to put up the hay at Edenbank using the new method.

The sweep was a contrivance hinging on the tractor arms. Metal teeth projected forward for about five feet. After the sweep was loaded with hay especially coiled for it, it would be lifted and the hay carried to the barn or stacked on the lift of the tractor. For two years, Edenbank hay was all hauled in on this sweep, a single tractor bringing in over one hundred tons each season. This proved to be a very economical method of putting up hay, the cost being $2.50 per ton for hauling. A crew of only three men was required.

The Enoch family lived in the old boarding house and became close friends of ours. They too were raising a young family. When they came to Edenbank, their first Christmas was upstairs, where our family had set up a Christmas tree and an improvised fireplace for Santa Claus. Mrs. Enoch, a teacher and Sunday school worker, was a happy companion for Sara, and the two families shared many moments together.

During Jack's five years at Edenbank he assisted the

Edenbank show herd in making the greatest publicity drive ever. The show cow Edenbank White Beauty 2nd, often grand champion, was on occasion defeated by her own stablemate, Ella 3rd. Both were cows that had been classified "excellent," and for two years they took grand and reserve grand championships. The full brother of Ella 3rd, Edenbank Ringleader 27, was grand champion bull. Strangely enough, these two famous cows were both defeated at the Chilliwack Exhibition one year by Edenbank May, with John Young as judge. He knew he was placing a cow that had been classified as "excellent." No one doubted John Young's decision – he was one of those grand Scottish stockmen who had a feeling for the good ones. Of Edenbank May that day he said, "It is 'her' day, like a bride on her wedding day." Edenbank May proved John Young had an eye for a good cow. Her many descendants, which were sired by Carnell Standard Bearer, were the best ever produced at Edenbank.

A letter had come to the farm from Scotland in 1945 inquiring about the prices of Ayrshire cattle. As a result of subsequent correspondence, two young men, Tony and David Way, immigrated to Canada. They purchased a jeep in eastern Canada and drove west until one day they drove into the yard and up to the back door at Edenbank. It was near lunchtime and Sara invited them in. Their broad accent was in keeping with their English clothes. Their manner was gentlemanly, yet full of a zest for living that reflected a will to establish themselves in the West.

The following year, the Ways began their own heavy task of making a farm out of a partially cleared piece of land up in the Chilliwack River valley. They bought Ayrshires at Edenbank and came often to discuss everyday challenges that confronted them. Their parents joined them later and together they worked to establish a new home at a time when it was difficult if not impossible to get capital out of Britain.

With no sons to help me, I often turned to my girls for assistance. They were trained early in the handling of livestock and became professional "showmen." During the haying season, they did the raking and tedding and operated the hoist when hay was being hauled in. ௸

CHAPTER 19

Prominent Guests
and a New Resident Breed

Guests at Edenbank had, from the earliest pioneer days, contributed much to the broadening of interests and cultural development of the family. Visitors to the pioneer home of A.C. Wells included missionaries and ordained ministers, early legislative members and the first organizers of agricultural associations. To Edwin's home also had come leaders of church and civic organizations, agricultural associations, conservation and parkland development, and leaders in Ayrshire cattle breeding. Men and women arrived and in conversation shared common interests and goals. In doing so both hosts and guests were left with a feeling of enrichment and fulfilment.

And so it was in our home. While Sara and I lived in the apartment upstairs, we hosted and entertained many prominent guests from many walks of life. Early in the 1940s, it was our pleasure to entertain three of

Quebec's foremost agriculturists. Dr. G. Toupin, of Oka Agricultural Institute, where one of the famous old Ayrshire herds of Quebec originated, came to Edenbank for a short visit with René Trépanier. René was later to become deputy minister of Agriculture for the province of Quebec. Both men held terms of office as president of the Ayrshire Breeders' Association of Canada at the time I was serving for several years as a director. Two years later, Mr. J.R. Pelletier, of Sainte-Anne-de-la-Pocatière, Quebec, visited Edenbank. He was superintendent of the experimental station there and in charge of the oldest Ayrshire herd in Canada. Mr. Pelletier served not only as president of the Ayrshire Breeders' Association of Canada but also as an advisor to the Food and Agriculture Organization of the United Nations.

The year 1948 is remembered as the year when Hugh Bone, secretary of the Ayrshire Cattle Society

Blaine Wells, Oliver's nephew, assisted Oliver with the Angus show herd during the 1950s.

of Great Britain, accompanied by his wife, visited the farm. It was the same year as the auctioneer J.K. Kirkwood first visited (the latter gentleman being a member of the firm of Thimberley & Shoreland Auctioneers, of Reading in the county of Berkshire, England). An auctioneer of exceptional ability, he would raise the prices for the best of all breeds to new highs during the years 1948–52. After his visit to Edenbank, he wrote to me and Sara expressing his appreciation of the kindness shown to him and referred especially to Marie, who acted as hostess in Sara's absence.

From Rotorua, New Zealand, an airmail letter arrived dated January 1950. It was from Fred Hutchings and began: "I am taking the liberty of writing to you as my son, Don, is leaving for Canada on the *Aorangi* on the 31st of this month. He will be coming with the idea of having a look at as many Ayrshires as possible, with the object of importing our next bulls." Don arrived and he was enjoyed as a guest at Edenbank for a week. He then travelled east to see more herds. When he wrote from home, after a three-month stay in Canada, he referred to his visit to Edenbank. "It was just like being home, staying with you."

The former Lord Mayor of London, T.S. Bennett, who maintained a fine Ayrshire herd at Manor House,

Lower Wick, Worcestershire, England, visited Edenbank in 1950. He, along with his wife, Dorothy, were most appreciative guests. Their departure from the Wellses' summer home at Cultus Lake was long remembered. There, in jolly good humour, the ex–Lord Mayor extended his hand and said, "Shake the hand that shook the hand of Sir Winston Churchill." And for many years afterwards his parting comment was a source of fun between us and family friends Wilf and Elsie Graham.

The London Dairy Show was world-famous as the scene of great competitions between Ayrshire and Holstein dairy cows. In 1947, the champion Ayrshire and reserve champion were both owned by W.H. Slater of Eyton Farm in Shropshire, England. For several years, Mr. Slater was the major winner of this great show. It was therefore with a great deal of pleasure that I joined with other B.C. Ayrshire breeders in extending a hearty welcome to Mr. and Mrs. Slater, who visited B.C. in 1951.

When an Ayrshire herd was given to the University of B.C. through the courtesy of Captain Dunwaters and the established Ayrshire breeders in Scotland, at least one of the cows, Lochinoch Lassie, came to B.C. from the herd of the earl of Stair, of

The dining room at Edenbank showing the high oak wainscoting and cabinetry done by Charles Davis. He later told Oliver that as they had run out of oak wood, Edwin had suggested using an old oak bedstead from the attic, with which they made the cupboard to the left of the dining-room fireplace. Photo from the Chilliwack Progress, *ca. 1970s.*

The living room at the farm, where many guests were entertained and family gatherings took place for five generations. CHILLIWACK PROGRESS PHOTO

Lochinoch Castle. A press photograph of some of the animals at Lochinoch was published in Canada at the time of the importation, and I kept the clipping in my scrapbook of the Ayrshire breed.

One of the most pleasant memories of the year 1951 was a visit to Edenbank of Lady Marion Phillips and her husband, Mr. Hanning Phillips. A brother-in-law of Lady Phillips, Colonel Niall Rankin, had been at Edenbank the previous year and had suggested the visit. Lady Phillips had written to me on August 2, saying they were going to be in Vancouver in September on a business trip, that they were starting a farm in Sussex and establishing an Ayrshire herd. "It would be particularly nice if we could come to see you."

A most charming person, Lady Phillips brought with her the Ayrshire pedigrees that were of particular interest to us both. I recall we sat on the piano bench comparing knowledge of Scottish Ayrshire bloodlines. She was thrilled when I produced a picture of the Ayrshires at Lochinoch Castle, the home of her father, the earl of Stair. She was able to identify herself in the photo as the young lady holding one of the cows. Her husband did not share the enthusiasm of his good lady for the Ayrshire, but he did enjoy the drive down the farm lane to the open land-

scape. They were both captivated by the panoramic view of the mountain ranges surrounding the valley.

I remember 1954 as the year of the visit of the Scottish lassies with their proud escorts and kinfolk: Jessie Young (accompanied by her husband, John Young, and their son Dave), from Carnell Home Farm, Kilmarnock; Jean Barr, of Hobsland, Ayrshire; and Grace Templeton, of Well Park, Kilmarnock, Ayrshire. They were a fine trio, whose families were so deeply imbued in the history of the Ayrshire breed that they were known by their herd name almost as well as by their surname. We all enjoyed a heart-warming visit over a good cup of tea.

When I had developed a grassland farming plan sufficient to carry a larger herd of Ayrshires, I began to plan for the day when I might wish to farm without having to keep up the heavy work and long hours necessary in dairy farming. I studied the possibility of producing beef on grass and decided to start breeding a small herd of Aberdeen Angus cattle. Prices were high in 1951, as high as they had ever been, and so I contented myself with the purchase of twelve Aberdeen Angus heifer calves and a small well-bred bull calf, obtained from the herd of J.A. McDonald of Bellingham, Washington. In 1952, I added four cows from an Okanagan herd and thus was finally launched into Aberdeen Angus breeding along with the Ayrshire business.

The Angus were used as "followers" during the pasture season. As the dairy herd was rotated in the pasture management program, the Angus followed behind, getting what was left in the fields after the dairy cows had taken the best of the pasture. This system worked well – the Ayrshires made higher production records, and the Angus, thrifty by nature, kept the after-grass mowed off clean so that when they left a field, the clipped pasture later grew into a field of fine-quality grass.

A selection of the entries from the daybook I kept in 1953 gives a good indication of the farm's activities during that period.

January 1
Weather mild – put 4 Angus cows
in loose-box, their feed to be hay,
straw, silage.

January 6
First cold snow and storm – temperature
16 degrees above 0 (F).

January 15
Finished top-dressing (stable manure)
No. 1 Field at 8 tons per acre.

January 20
Finished top-dressing (stable manure)
No. 3 Field at 8 tons per acre.
Hauling manure from box-stalls –
Fred Van Winkle helping in afternoon.

January 28
Col. Rutherford and Mr. Pearse
– Vet[erans] Land Act head men, called to
see dairy and farm 'sweep' used for hay
and silage. Col. R. considered sweep best
of hundreds he had seen.
Ordered grass seed from Buckerfields –
named varieties for 20 acres.

February 21
Aunt Jessie Knight (oldest daughter of
Pioneer Isaac Kipp) was buried today –
weather mild.

February 22
Large numbers of birds in the Sanctuary.

February 25
Charley Finney bull-dozing on river front.

February 26
Re-landscaping Sanctuary – changed river
in front of house.

February 27
Finished manuring No. 4 pasture field.

February 28
Jack Scott (with wife and baby) arrived
from Vancouver to start work on farm.

March 1
Weather fine and mild.

March 9
Jack and I to McDonald herd of
A. Angus Cattle – picked out two bull
calves at $150 each.

March 12
Went up to Kamloops Bull Sale –
bulls to sell to good advantage must be
2 years old, plenty of size and bone and
be well fitted.
Weather cold and wet.

April 1
Vern Dickie purchased lot on Spruce Drive
at $750.

April 3
Cows out to grass, daytime only.

April 5
Finished plowing 20 acres.

April 6
Cleared out fence bottom along lane.

April 11
Marie off to Calgary (with Flash) to ride
with Chilliwack Drill Team at Calgary
Stampede.

April 12
Sunday – light snowfall.

April 16
Cows out at night.

This aerial photo of the farm, looking west, shows the open fields, the farm lane (upper right) and the mature landscaping that Allen, Edwin and Oliver had planted over the years. The buildings are the farm home (left), the horse barn and granary (centre), and the cow barn (right).
PHOTO BY CASEY WELLS

April 18
Finished seeding 20 acres to
mixed grain.
'Curlew' [a rare bird] in field for a week.

April 25
Finished seeding 20 acres to grass and
clover seed.

April 30
Beef Growers (Coast Cattlemen's Assoc.)
organizational meeting at Abbotsford.

June 22
Cows finished first round of pasture fields,
having been one week on each pasture.
Thirty dairy cows, followed by sixteen
Angus cows with calves.

June 30
Re-building barn-yard and
paddock fences.

July 7
Sara, Betty and I to Calgary
[Oliver judging Ayrshire cattle].

July 17
Started cutting hay. Cutting and coiling
until 24th.

July 25
Started hauling hay, John McFaul, Jack and
I. Hauled 7 days, 12 ton per day.

August 3
Finished hauling, except for 15 large (700 lb.)
coils. Hay yields – 32 acres yielded 95 tons.

August 10
Blaine [young son of Ronald] helping from
1–4 in afternoons, working on Show cattle.

August 10
Reid Bros. started combining grain
12 acres.Started irrigating pastures.

August 24
Sold Angus steer to Henry's Meat Market
@ 34 cents per lb. dressed weight. Sold 2 lambs
to Henry's @ 46 cents per lb. dressed = $46.92.

September 18 to 20
Sara and I to Naramata (Okanagan) to
visit Marie.

September 23
Sold 4 A. Angus cows to
Neil McGregor – $900.

September 24
Receipts – Exhibition cheques –
Chilliwack $92.00 Pac. Nat. Exh. $407.55.

September 28
Sent certified cheque of ($27.00) to W.G.
MacPherson, Mulben Mains, Mulben,
Scotland, for two Aberdeen Angus-bred
heifers; for late October shipment.

October 1
New bird in Sanctuary – Green heron
(a rare bird in B.C.). Cows on corn silage
and grass.

October 15
Cows off grass, on to silage, grain and hay.
Angus still on late pasture.

October 16
Letter from MacPherson – heifers gone into
quarantine at Glasgow Quarantine Station,
in preparation for shipment.

October 17
Green heron still in Sanctuary.

October 21
Morning frost.
Imported six steers from J. McDonald.

October 27
Received M.O. $50 from M. A. Piel,
Pritchard, B.C., for Ram lamb.

November 1
Weather mild and wet. Ayrshire heifers into
barn. Angus on to old pastures.
Bought new Manure Spreader, price
$440 – $200 allowance on old spreader.

November 25
Obtained farm-loan, $1,140 to cover cost of

importing 2 A. Angus heifers.
Sent cheque to British Livestock Exports
Agent in Montreal – $493.00
Sent cheque to E.J. Cammaret, Rothford,
Alta., to cover cost of Quarantine and
Transportation to Alta., $320.00.
Express charges Alta. to Edenbank, $166.00

November 30
Rain during November = 12 inches.

December 5
Stormy, cold rain – Angus cows into shed.
Fred Van Winkle helped hauling out
manure, covered pasture fields (1) and (3)
in November and December.

December 23
Angus heifers arrived from Scotland.
Extremely good heifers.

December 25
Xmas – Betty and Marie home –
weather mild.
Xmas dinner at Fotheringhams'.

December 31
Pair of Canada Geese arrived (by Express)
from R. Steuch, Abernethy, Sask. Geese are
known as Jacob and Rachael. Total rain
during 1953 was 94 inches.

In March 1954, I returned to Kamloops with Angus
bulls for the Kamloops sale. It was my first attempt
to compete in the beef world, where the B.C. beef
cattlemen were in control of the judging and the sale.
Three Edenbank bulls made a good mark. Edenbank
Prince was reserve grand champion and sold at $450.
Edenbank King and Edenbank Baron were sold at
$380 and $350. Up to this time, Angus cattle
were not well known, nor had they been well represented at Kamloops. I was of a like mind with other
Angus breeders. While in Kamloops we got together
and formed the B.C. Aberdeen Angus Association,
whose purpose was to promote the breed in B.C. I was
elected president.

CHAPTER 20

Years of Celebration and Recognition

At this time, Albert Card was acting herdsman at Edenbank. Albert spent several years with us and then moved on to become farm manager for a hobby farmer. He was paid $150 per month, plus house and milk, which was then as high as any self-sufficient farm could pay. Every year, the difficulty of obtaining good hired help grew more acute for the dairy farms in the Fraser Valley. Good men stayed four or five years and inevitably were taken by wealthy men who farmed as a hobby and could pay higher wages.

I decided to keep the dairy herd at a size I could milk and handle myself. With publication of type classification and herd-average records,

it was no longer necessary to show an exhibition herd for publicity reasons. I therefore concentrated on increasing the production of the Ayrshire herd and on keeping up a steady advertisement in the *Canadian Ayrshire Review,* the breed's monthly publication. Late in 1956, I imported Carnell White Star, a young bull of similar breeding to Standard Bearer, for the purpose of "line-breeding." The daughters of Carnell came into full production during the late 1950s, and the reports of their success individually and as a herd read like a herdsman's dream.

Artificial breeding was becoming more extensively used all the time and the federal Department of Agriculture purchased two sons

This photo shows the main platform used at the 1958 field day, with many friends and Ayrshire breeders and their families in attendance.

of Standard Bearer for use in artificial breeding units in B.C. They were sons of Edenbank Ella 2nd and Edenbank Ella 3rd. In 1957, the herd average was about 30% above breed average. By 1959, the herd average had risen to nearly 50% above breed average. Carnell Standard Bearer became recognized as an Approved Sire in both Canada and the U.S.A. because of the high production of his daughters. In 1958, an Ayrshire Breeders' Association of Canada press release noted that the Edenbank herd of Sardis was leader in production of all Ayrshire herds in Canada of similar size.

The year 1958 was British Columbia's centennial, and to celebrate this event, the Ayrshire Breeders' Association of B.C. accepted my invitation to stage a Centennial Field Day at Edenbank – one of B.C.'s centennial farms and also the site of the first B.C. Ayrshire breeders' field day. Points of historic interest about the farm were identified and tape recordings were broadcast periodically throughout the day to give historical accounts of the farm and its Ayrshire cattle. A thousand visitors came that day to Edenbank, many pioneers of the valley who spoke about their first visits to Edenbank. Fred Bryant and George Cruikshank looked after judging competi-

tions and platform entertainment. Scottish pipers and Highland dancers entertained during the afternoon. Children had canoe rides on the river. Following the official ceremonies, the Ayrshire Breeders' Association of B.C. presented a silver cup to Elizabeth, Betty's daughter, representing the fifth generation at Edenbank. It was fitting that the Edenbank herd won the B.C. Ayrshire Breeders' production trophy for 1958–59.

In 1959, the Ayrshire Breeders' Association of Canada inaugurated a competition. The objective was to give recognition to the contribution made to the advancement of the breed by breeders of outstanding animals. In the competition I nominated cows in five categories. These included seven cows that had produced more than 100,000 pounds of milk in eight lactations; two "excellent" cows; and fifteen "very good" cows, with at least 130% of the breed average. I was fortunate to be one of seventeen breeders across Canada to receive a national Superior Breeder Award. In 1959, the herd averaged 525 pounds of butterfat per cow. This was the highest herd average in Canada for Ayrshires. For years, the slogan on all Edenbank Farm achievements for Ayrshire cattle had been "Utility and Beauty Combined."

This photo was labelled "Introducing a new generation." Oliver is holding Elizabeth Purkiss, his first grandchild.

Oliver receiving a hand-tooled leather citation from the Ayrshire Breeders' Association of B.C. on the occasion of his retirement as an active breeder of Ayrshires in 1963. Presenting the award is Ron Robson, B.C. director of the Ayrshire Breeders' Association of Canada.
PHOTO BY RODGERS STUDIO

On receiving this award, I certainly felt a humble sense of gratitude and a strong feeling of success.

The North Country Cheviot sheep also held up the slogan that year, with three ewes selling at public auction for an average of $108, the highest of all breeds in B.C. It seems that Scottish livestock breeders never miss an opportunity to see the fine animals that they had exported. The animals were considered as ambassadors of goodwill. So it was with Mr. and Mrs. D.H. Macadie, who came to Edenbank to see the North Country Cheviot flock. I had raised the flock from three ewes imported in 1951 from the Macadies of Thurso, Caithness. Their farm was in the far northern county of Scotland, where the North Country Cheviot was developed originally from stock derived from the Cheviot Hills of the south Border Country. Sara and I enjoyed this visit immensely and were pleased to have this personal contact.

In 1962, Alister Clyne, a North Country Cheviot sheep breeder from Field of Noss, Wick, Scotland, came to Canada to judge the breed exhibit at Brandon, Manitoba. Later Ted Townsend of Brandon brought him west to see the various flocks in western Canada. It was a great pleasure and privilege for me to discuss the breed with Mr. Clyne at Edenbank, where he spoke highly of the growing flock. In the past Sara and I had been invited to visit the Clynes' old country home in Scotland.[54]

I continued to take great pleasure in the stock and field work. I was still working from twelve to fifteen hours a day, but noticed with regret that my health was beginning to suffer. Provincial regulations regarding barns, dairies and equipment used in the production of retail milk were becoming more rigid and demanding. If I were to continue dairying at Edenbank, it would be necessary to lay out immense sums of money to modernize buildings and equipment. Houses were being built closer and closer to Edenbank, and neighbours were complaining of the aroma

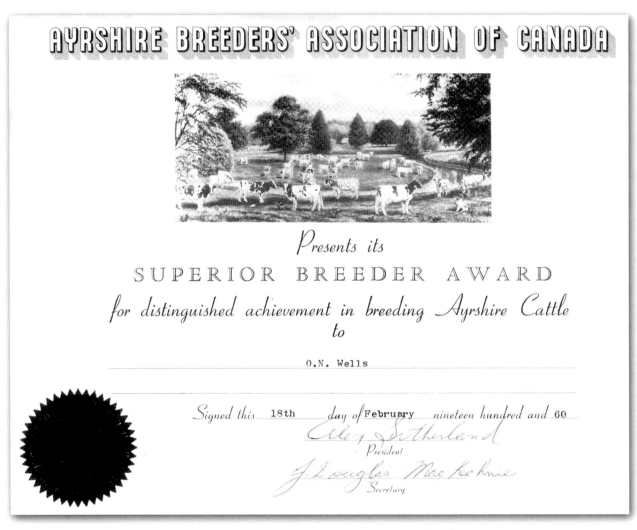

A Superior Breeder Award presented to Oliver by the Ayrshire Breeders' Association of Canada, February 18, 1960.

of silage. There was also the necessity of building a suitable home for a hired man.

With no sons to follow into the dairying business or to possibly continue with the Ayrshire herd, I pondered the wisdom of selling the Ayrshire herd while it was "on top." I might then turn my efforts to the less arduous tasks of breeding Aberdeen Angus beef cattle and growing cash crops. The difficult decision was made with regret, and in the spring of 1962 I sold the

Ayrshire herd to Harold Bailey of Ryder Lake Farms. Harold, a businessman, had proven himself an enthusiast in Ayrshire cattle breeding, and he had a beautiful farm for the herd on the foothills above the valley.

Subsequently, I was very fortunate to be honoured by the Ayrshire Breeders' Association of Canada with a life membership in the association, "in recognition of valuable and devoted service to the Ayrshire Breed of Cattle in Canada."[55] ⟡

CHAPTER 21

Bringing Nature Back

*D*uring the passage of one hundred years, 1867–1967, the natural history associated with Edenbank underwent even more extreme change than the changes associated with agricultural development. When Allen Wells left his canoe and walked over the area that was to become Edenbank Farm, he was in wilderness. In places, the forest of spruce and cedar, hemlock and fir was thick enough to exclude the light of the sun. The little prairies were covered with wild grasses and wildflowers, with clumps of willow, vine maple and cranberry bushes. The banks of the streams, sloughs and beaver ponds were lined with alder, birch, red osier, dogwood, maple, cottonwood and poplar.

To Allen, bears were all too numerous. They killed the pigs and therefore had to be shot or trapped. Beaver were a nuisance, for their dams flooded the fields, which had to be drained. The natives were invited to take the pelts. Deer were abundant in the valley and venison was a welcome change of diet during winter. The deer were therefore occasionally killed for food, but not for sport.

During the summer months one might see golden eagles soaring high over the valley. Most of the time they stayed back in the mountains, taking their food nearer their nesting sites. Turkey vultures were abundant, and often spiralled down in their wide circles to come to rest in a newly cut hay field to pick up some carrion flesh. The crow was common, and occasionally a pair of ravens with their family of young birds from their moun-

Two hungry birds in their nest, a photo no doubt taken from one of the blinds that were built to observe and photograph birds in the sanctuary.

tain breeding grounds would visit the pioneer's cleared fields in search of food.

Overhead, huge sandhill cranes or wild turkeys, as the pioneers called them, could be seen regularly as they flew to the marshland at the eastern end of the valley from nesting grounds on Sumas Prairie. The pioneer thought favourably of them, for they bothered no one and were good eating.

The lowly weasel was a plague about the chicken house. When young chickens were penned for the night, a weasel occasionally would get in and kill a dozen or more, not bothering to eat the carcass, but preferring simply to suck out the blood.

When Edwin was a young lad, he watched for coyotes, and sometimes a wolf that might try to steal a lamb or calf. When fall came, the pioneer hung up his winter supply of wild fowl outdoors to freeze. Great flocks of Canada geese and occasionally large flocks of white-fronts would settle into a grain stubble field. Edwin, or one of the men, would use a horse and cart for camouflage and walk up close enough to shoot and bag one, never for sport, but to supplement the food supply. From the rafters in the woodshed would hang rows of mallard ducks and Canada geese. During the late fall and winter, Allen and Edwin would often kill a beef and the carcass would be left to cool overnight, hanging in a shed or barn. They always took care to close the doors securely to keep out predators. Magpies would come by the dozen to a feast so provided if it was left unprotected.

In the evening, thrushes would fill the air with their sweet, melodious song, welcoming the night. And at night, the great horned owl was always lurking near the poultry yard, hoping to pick up a fresh fowl for breakfast. Its *hoo-hoo-hoo, hoo, hoo* call would come from one bird and be answered immediately by its mate. The sound was weird, yet fascinating on a dark night when heard in the clearing in the forest.

On a clear summer night, the constant droning of diving nighthawks would keep the listener and watcher searching the sky, hoping to see the next one make his dive to scoop up insects in his wide-open beak. The little pygmy owl was the one owl that often could be seen in the evening just before dusk. Natives feared that evil spirits were associated with this bird. To hear one cry under certain conditions meant to them that death or sorrow in the family was foretold.

In 1887, a young man by the name of Allan Brooks walked the banks of the Luckakuck along the front of Edenbank Farm. He crossed the farm often in the years to follow on his long walks in search of wildlife specimens, many of them recorded for the first time. He was a collector in those early years, and most of the specimens he sent east to the William Brewster Museum. In later years Allan made his home in the Interior of B.C. but always had fond memories of his days in the Fraser Valley collecting specimens, farming and shooting.

The sweep of the Chilliwack River crossing the front of the farm in 1875–94 created a new environment for wildlife. Salmon and trout of all species came in a year-round rush of spawning runs. January and February brought the steelhead, March and April the cutthroat, and early summer, the spring salmon. Then there would be a summer run of sockeye before the dog salmon came in the fall. These were followed by coho and humpbacks, which lasted into December, when the steelhead again began another cycle. Salmon by the thousands rushed up the stream in their given season, so many that their spawning holes would change the course of the river at times, undermining bridges and fences. In the fall of the year, the carcasses of the spent fish, which die soon after spawning, were so numerous along the riverbank and gravel bars that they were hauled away in wagonloads, taken out into the hop fields to be ploughed in for fertilizer.

A.C. Wells once made an effort to stop the salmon at a point in the river near Coqualeetza. There he built a salmon fence across the river on a platform, but the salmon dug under and bypassed the fence.

Bald eagles came in great numbers to feast on the salmon runs. Along the river, the kingfishers chattered as they fought over nesting areas in the steep earth banks where small round openings were evidence of homesites. Striking harlequin ducks and wood ducks, the most beautiful of all, were numerous along the river, the former nesting in the mountainous region upstream and the latter in the old cottonwood trees, where nesting cavities could be found in rotten or broken-off tree tops. The dipper bird was fascinating to watch in October. He jumped right from water-washed boulders into the torrent, submerged in a search for the eggs of the dog salmon in the gravel. He would soon appear again, "dipping" his body as if bowing in recognition of his own performance.

Over the river, during the summer months, cedar waxwings darted out to select favourite insects and return to their perches on the overhanging trees, whether evergreen or alder, nesting often in the boughs of spruce trees growing nearby. In the winter months, when bird food was scarce, it was a common sight to see the ruffed grouse "budding" in the wild crabapple trees along the river. With them might be the Bohemian waxwings, dapper crested birds with a dark fawn colouring and red waxlike spots on their wing coverlets. The waxwings would feed on the fruit of the tree rather than the buds, as did the grouse.

After 1895, the Chilliwack River no longer flowed in the channel now known as the Luckakuck. The spring water stream remained, with abundant runs of salmon. The gravel bars and pools teemed with shorebirds. On the Luckakuck in 1902, a white-faced glossy ibis was spotted, the only record of this bird in the area.

On the partially cleared farm, woodpeckers were numerous. The great pileated woodpecker, the largest of the species, left his mark very clearly when he searched for his meal of grubs in a dead stump. The red-headed woodpecker was common and not to be confused with the Lewis' woodpecker, which came during the fall when fruit was ripe. Downie woodpeckers and sapsuckers were common, ringing the tree trunks with little holes in perfect circles, sometimes causing damage to trees.

In some fields small stumps were left in rough pasture to rot out and there many interesting species of birds could be seen regularly. The yellow-breasted western meadowlarks, with their lovely song, were numerous. Their nests were undisturbed by man and their natural enemy, the crow, did not fare well when the western kingbirds set upon him to drive him out of the area. When severe snowstorms came during winter months, it was quite common to see dozens

The restful view out the kitchen nook window, where one could admire the trees and lawn and, in the distance, the sanctuary. A wonderfully tranquil place for a cup of Sara's tea. Oliver and his native friends sat here at the table as the stories of their heritage were recalled and recorded.

of meadowlarks searching out food on the piles of manure behind the barns.

The wild band-tailed pigeons, with their soft-toned beauty, came in great flocks to the newly planted grain fields. They had but few enemies and at times their numbers were sufficient to devastate a whole corner of a grain field. At evening, they flew to their nesting sites in the big timber at the base of the mountains.

By the time the third generation of the Wells family was old enough to carry a gun, the Chilliwack Valley was at its peak as a hunter's paradise. For weeks in the spring and fall the whirr of wings never ceased. To the west, Sumas Lake, containing 10,000 acres of water and 20,000 acres of marginal lands and sloughs, was resting place and feeding grounds for millions of ducks and geese. To the east was the big native prairie, thousands of acres of swampy land, feeding grounds for countless swarms of migrating waterfowl. Looking up from Edenbank one could watch the night flight – or the morning flight, it mattered not – but for hours at a time great flocks filled the sky as they winged back and forth from one feeding ground to another. For weeks the valley was full of migrating birds.

Then followed those years when farm produce was in great demand. Lands were cleared and cultivated. The long-cherished woodlots became pastures and

the valley fast became a dairying centre. Pheasants were introduced at this time, and while agricultural lands still carried considerable marginal uncleared areas, pheasants multiplied rapidly and hunting was very attractive. Ducks were still numerous and hunters too multiplied.

Then up went the cry for more drainage and more land. The whole of Sumas Lake was drained and the big native prairie slowly dried out. Farmers demanded even better drainage, and existing farms were cleared of woods and brush. Thus the "hunter's paradise" started its decline. Yet hunters still became more numerous. The kill was heavy and the protection afforded by water and cover fast faded away. The results were soon drastic.

As the fourth generation took up the gun, the valley was a changed scene – a valley of homes and settlement. Farms were clean and well kept, with only the old riverbed channels uncultivated. In the fall, the skies were no longer filled with great flocks of ducks and geese. Strict game regulations were enacted to control the killing of birds. Hunting was still considered fair, but only if there were some place a fellow could hunt.

At Edenbank, until the late fall of 1937, no one ever saw a "No Hunting" sign. Everyone was free to hunt over the farm just as they had been since 1867. But we boys suddenly decided something had to be done. Ducks and geese had long ago become only a memory at Edenbank. There were a few pheasants, but not enough for the Wells family and their neighbours, let alone the odd dozen hunters who had been forced off Sumas Prairie and were in quest of more birds and unprotected land.

And so the signs went up: "Game Restoration Area," "No Hunting," "Bird Sanctuary." And strange as it may seem after this brief history, scarcely a shot has since broken the tranquility and peace for birds on the farm. A large block of the farm had signs posted between Vedder and Evans Roads and between Stevenson and Wells Roads.

Welcome visitors to the new sanctuary.

On January 1, 1938, an inventory was taken of game birds on the farm, revealing about sixteen hens and four cock pheasants. Years before, the blue grouse had taken to the high hills, and the willow grouse and bear and deer had all sought shelter in the foothills. Fortunately over the years a love of trees and of natural beauty had been passed down from one generation to another in the family. Therefore a foundation was laid for more intensive work in the re-establishment of wildlife at Edenbank.

The protection given the pheasants on the farm, in three years, justified the belief that refuge areas of as little as 160 acres, scattered over the valley, would provide a definite increase in number of birds available for shooting in the surrounding lands. My fondest hope was to increase the number of migrating birds in the district and to attract them to remain in the valley for longer periods.

In the spring of 1938, I obtained a few eggs from a breeder and raised my first mallards to act as decoys. By fall I had a small number of wild mallards visiting regularly. The following spring, under permit, I raised about thirty mallards and soon had buffleheads, butterballs, hooded mergansers and wood ducks to join them regularly at the sanctuary. I kept a diary of visiting and returning birds.

The creek was partially diverted to create ponds and marshlands. Protective trees and shrubbery were set out and hedges planted to screen buildings and roads. The cattle were fenced back off the river bottomlands, allowing protective slough and marsh grasses, willows and vines to grow and make attractive nesting cover. Soon twenty acres of riverbed was a secluded sanctuary for birds of all kinds.

Wood ducks came in the spring in increasing numbers. Each morning the cry of the female could be heard as, coming from her nest, she swept overhead to join her brilliantly coloured mate on the pool. Wild mallards nested outside, but came each morning to feed. Then finally in September and early October of 1939, ducks began to come in numbers.

Mallards and teal, about sixty birds, came regularly before the season opened. Then a few widgeon started coming. I remember watching one bird that had several feathers shot out of one wing. At first he came alone, then with half a dozen, and soon he brought a flock of twenty or more. By early November, widgeons were flying in flocks of one hundred, an unusual sight, over Edenbank. The mallards and teal increased. A few spoonbills found the sanctuary, and when an additional two acres was flooded, the birds swung in low over the farm and dropped down onto the water. To me it was a splendid and rewarding sight. In two years, Edenbank had reverted to a farm stocked heavily enough with pheasants to supply the surrounding lands with good shooting and had become a resting place for hundreds of migrating ducks. A few Canada geese arrived each spring to join the geese bred and raised on the farm as decoys, however, for years it had been unusual to see or hear many geese except passing high overhead.[56]

Snipe and plover also rapidly increased in these congenial surroundings. In the spring of 1940, mallards, buffleheads, goldeneyes, teal, hooded merganser, scaup ducks and wood ducks were all visitors to the sanctuary. Newcomers that summer were greater yellowlegs, sandpipers and cinnamon teal. The fall of 1940 brought flocks of ducks into the skies over Edenbank such as had not been seen for years. At times, 1,500 ducks were in the sanctuary, resting through the day and leaving in the evening to return again late next morning. To have the ducks circle over my head within easy range or to see half a dozen cock pheasants on the fence in the garden as I went in for breakfast were the moments that made the sanctuary worthwhile. ❧

CHAPTER 22

An Avian and Artistic Legacy

arly in the years of bird sanctuary development, Sara and I obtained a permit to carry out bird-bandings. We received a supply of bands and report forms and operated a trap for small birds at the feeding tray by our kitchen bay windowsill. There juncos, song sparrows, chickadees and kinglets were caught and banded with tiny, numbered aluminum bands. It was interesting each winter to watch for birds to return with a record of a previous visit. An old canary cage was used for the trap, and held the birds without injuring them. I was able to gently lift them out to secure a tiny leg band, then open my hand to let them fly away.

Oliver Wells Slough

Ducks to be banded were caught in a trap shaped like a water lily leaf. A funnel-shaped entrance allowed them to enter to take food, but they were never able to find their way out again. Ducks banded at Edenbank were later shot at points as distant as Alaska and Fort McLeod in Alberta. In one period of nine months after banding at Edenbank, a mallard flew south and then back north on another flyway to Fort McLeod.

Sara and I looked forward each year to the coming seasons, which brought back to Edenbank some of the wildlife it had known in the days when the farm was a paradise for birds. The curlew, once common on the farm but long since forgotten, reappeared. The bittern

Bird-banding was undertaken in the sanctuary's early years to keep track of feathered visitors and to trace their migration routes. This canary cage sat on a platform outside Sara and Oliver's upstairs kitchen window, from where they were able to reach out to gently bring in birds to be banded.

A red-winged blackbird pair and western yellowthroat in the Edenbank sanctuary. Painted for Oliver by Allan Brooks.

It read in part, "I know your place well. As a youngster, I used to visit it often, from 1887 on. It is an excellent place for a Sanctuary." The letter was dated May 4, 1939. His last paragraph was an invitation: "If you can come up to Okanagan in July or August, I can show you the best example of protection as applied to ducks and water-fowl, where we have raised the increase from 5% to 85% by controlling the crow."

There followed several years of most interesting correspondence and visits back and forth with Allan Brooks, his wife and son, both at their home in the Okanagan and at Edenbank. Major Brooks was particularly interested in the Bullock's orioles nesting at the farm, for they were very rare in the area in early days.

In 1941, I was raising Canada geese under permit from the federal government and had obtained a pure strain of the western (as it was then called) Canada goose, which migrates only along the Pacific coast. Allan Brooks saw the birds when he was a guest in our home that year. He spoke of their rarity in captivity and mentioned that their offspring would be in great demand where wildfowl are bred under permit. He predicted that someday, the little green heron and the night heron would appear in the sanctuary at Edenbank – birds almost unknown in the area. If a downy young gosling of the western Canada goose ever died, he wanted it sent to him, preserved in formalin, in order that he might make his bird-skin collection more complete. His amazing collection of eight thousand skins was preserved in his own museum for use in his illustrative work. One of his many contracts, then recently completed, was for the National Geographic *Book of Birds*, for which he illustrated twelve hundred birds of America.

I searched out the National Geographic magazines and books. In 1942, I commissioned two original watercolour paintings from Allan Brooks, which later graced the walls at Edenbank. One was a Bullock's oriole at the nest and the other the yellowthroat and red-winged blackbird, regular visitors to the Edenbank sanctuary.[57]

A great friendship sprang up between the Brooks family, myself, Sara and our daughters, Betty and Marie. It was a wonderful occasion in the summer of 1945 when we visited them at Okanagan Landing. The following years at Edenbank were greatly influenced by this visit. I tramped the hillsides with Allan observing hundreds of birds in their natural settings, and the girls and Sara canoed and relaxed by the lake. They were able to watch in fascination as Brooks painted in his studio.

In November 1945, I shot a horned owl, which I believed was harmful at Edenbank. It was a light-

returned and a rail nested in the marsh. A northern phalarope paid a call on its way south one fall. A Canada goose stayed the summer. In the springtime, a shining pair of blue-winged teal made their home on the stream in front of the house until they decided that the marsh was the safest place for their brood. Here they had the company of the first brood of wood ducks to stay the summer in the sanctuary.

Again the snipe were cutting the air in flocks of fifty as they gathered in the marsh. The killdeer gathered in the fields in flocks of a hundred birds, their silvery streaks cutting the air in playful frolic as they seemed to try out their wings for the long flight south. Soon the ducks came in and once again Edenbank enjoyed the sound of whirring wings.

Establishing the Edenbank bird sanctuary was not accomplished without some discouraging moments. When searching for support for the idea, I had read that Ernest Thompson Seton had thought favourably of small sanctuary areas. I learned also the mailing address of the great Canadian artist-naturalist Allan Brooks and sent a letter to him in his home at Okanagan Landing, B.C. To my surprise and delight, an answer quickly came back from Brooks, who was out doing fieldwork in Madera Canyon in the Santa Rita Mountains of Arizona. His reply was most encouraging.

coloured bird, and I sent it to Brooks in order that it might become a specimen of value. A letter of acknowledgement from him indicated the bird was an Arctic horned owl, not the ordinary type, but a migrant from Alaska or Yukon. He knew of only one other having been shot in the Chilliwack Valley, in 1888 by John Nowell.

I had also asked Brooks to do a painting of the mountain blue-birds on Liumchen Mountain. His November letter in reply indicated he would make the painting about January 20, when he had completed a set of game bird paintings for the University of Washington. Very sadly, Allan Brooks was stricken with cancer and died quite suddenly, soon after his last letter to me.

Allan Brooks came to the Chilliwack area in 1887 as a boy of eighteen. He roamed the nearby mountains and hills, spending his free hours in the outdoors sketching and collecting specimens of bird and animal life. This photo of the renowned wildlife artist in his studio was taken during the summer of 1945 when Oliver and family were visiting Brooks in the Okanagan.

Believing that there might never again be an illustrator of birds of the calibre of Allan Brooks, I set about gathering a collection of paintings representative of his work. Within a few years our walls were covered with some of the finest pieces of Brooks's artwork. In all, we assembled forty-five paintings and drawings from all over America.

Mr. J.W. Winson, of Huntingdon, B.C., a well-known naturalist and writer, visited Edenbank often after the sanctuary was established and the paintings hung. "Oliver," he said one day, "people have come for years to see your cattle; now you will be having people come to see your birds and beautiful Brooks paintings."

A little green heron, the second one recorded in B.C., came to Edenbank and Mr. Winson, who came to see it, remarked, "And to think so rare a bird was seen and not taken." His conservationist mind was on the right track, for by 1967, the little green herons were nesting and raising young at Edenbank and I saw a mature bird the last day that this was written, December 31, 1967.

Mr. Winson was also right in his prediction, for people came from far and near to see the sanctuary and Allan Brooks's paintings. In 1948, I answered a request from Peter Scott, which had been published in the Audubon Society's magazine. Scott asked that anyone who had geese of special interest get in touch with him. Thus began a correspondence

with the son of the world-famous explorer and one of the world's best-known ornithologists and illustrators of waterfowl.

Peter Scott's first letter to Edenbank is still on file, dated January 5, 1948. It read, in part, "Dear Mr. Wells, I was most interested to receive your letter and to know of your association with Allan Brooks, whose work I have always admired so much. I shall be delighted to exchange a pair of Barnacle Geese for a pair of your Western Canadas." It was signed Peter Scott – Director, The Severn Wildfowl Trust, Slimbridge, England.

As it turned out, a fox killed the barnacle geese that he planned to send to me. However, in a letter of September 20, 1948, concerning the western Canadas, Peter Scott wrote: "You will be glad to know that the geese arrived safely in excellent condition. I am more than delighted with them."

That was the beginning of a long and interesting correspondence and goose exchange with Peter Scott. At first, his letters were written in his own hand in great detail, and occasionally asking advice as he was getting under way the building of the greatest waterfowl collection in the world. In later years, he was very busy in public speaking tours and television programs, apart from his tremendous task of illustrating *Waterfowl of the World*, three volumes of which were given to the library at Edenbank.

Another most interesting contact, which I established through my interest in western Canada geese,

Golden Eagle & Canada Goose –
A. Brooks –

Edenbank had a long history of exporting livestock to far-flung destinations. In the 1940s, Oliver began to ship wildfowl and eggs to interested breeders. Niall Rankin, of Antarctic fame, requested that Oliver incubate wild duck and goose eggs for him, which he would first gather in the Arctic. Oliver gladly complied.

came in a letter from Colonel Niall Rankin, writing from the Waterfowl Research Station at Delta, Manitoba. He wrote in May 1948: "Your name has been given me by Peter Scott as possibly having some Western Canadas. I lost my collection of Waterfowl in Scotland during the war, and am much hoping to take back the foundation of a breeding stock with me in September."

Subsequently, I shipped birds to Halifax, where Rankin gathered the shipment with his own to cross the Atlantic. After arriving in Great Britain, Niall Rankin wrote from his home at House of Treshnish, Calgary, Isle of Mull, Argyle, Scotland. Of the trip with the birds he wrote: "They seemed to experience no ill effects from their journey across the Atlantic, although by the time they got here they had been in their crates a full two weeks."

The next year, Rankin had completed plans for a 1950 trip to Alaska and asked me if I would undertake to hatch wild duck and goose eggs of several species, which would be shipped to Edenbank by air from Alaska. I happily agreed and followed detailed instruc-

tions in making preparations for this unusual undertaking. Rankin was so confident of the entire project that he had two large crates especially constructed and shipped by sea from Scotland to Edenbank, in readiness for shipment of the birds, which were to be hatched from eggs sent down by plane from Alaska.

On June 10, 1950, Rankin was at Hooper Bay, Alaska, to send a shipment of wild goose and duck eggs out by air. They arrived in Vancouver, where I picked up the crates containing the precious cargo, all neatly packed in foam rubber cases to prevent injury to the eggs. That summer at Edenbank, six borrowed Rhode Island Red clucky hens sat contentedly on wild emperor, white-front, cackling goose and black brant eggs, all taken in the wild on the Alaskan coast.

Late in July, Rankin arrived at Edenbank from Alaska with his seventeen-year-old son Ian. He brought with him a large shipment of young goslings and ducklings, mostly rare in captivity and requiring special feed. Rankin almost immediately went to the butcher shop in Sardis and bought several pounds of ground beef to feed his diving ducks.

Niall and his son were an enjoyable pair to have as guests for a week or so at Edenbank. During this time I learned a little of the greatness of this modest man, whose hobby was building up a collection of the waterfowl of the world on his spacious estate. A letter from him dated January 30, 1952, indicated that he had had a wonderful summer trip in 1951 to the western Arctic, to Southampton Island, where he spent five weeks. In the letter he also made reference to the fact that they had just experienced the worst gale ever to strike their isle in Scotland, with winds of 120 miles an hour. He noted: "At the same time, the wire fencing of one of my goose enclosures was flattened and my Western Canadas (from Edenbank) walked out on to the sea and have never been heard of since."

It was with a feeling of loss and sorrow that Sara and I learned of the sudden death of Colonel Rankin in 1965 while he was on an expedition in Kalahari, South Africa.

Geese again left Edenbank in 1961 en route to Peter Scott's Severn Wildfowl Trust. This time, they flew via Trans-Canada Air Lines over the polar route, landed at Rotterdam, Holland, and from there were reshipped by air to England, where they were received in excellent condition.

I had gathered the collection of Allan Brooks paintings at Edenbank in the hope that a collection of this great Canadian's work would be preserved in Canada and that his work would receive just recognition. In 1949, I offered the loan of the Brooks paintings to the Vancouver Art Gallery. The loan was gratefully accepted and a three-week exhibition was presented as a memorial show. Included was an exhibit of the many extraordinary bird books that Allan Brooks had illustrated.

In 1952, Dr. Alden H. Miller of the University of California, editor of *The Condor*, indicated that the journal of the Cooper Ornithological Club would appreciate the opportunity of reproducing an Allan Brooks painting in a special issue being published to pay tribute to Lee Chambers, late business manager of the club and long-time friend of Allan Brooks. As Lee Chambers had done much to assist in the gathering of the Brooks paintings, I was pleased to send them *Wardens of the Arctic*, an exciting gyrfalcon picture, which had been purchased from Mrs. Brooks. Later, in 1957, it was purchased from me by Allan Cecil Brooks, who was increasing his own collection of his father's works.

The year 1956 saw the Brooks paintings on show in the Seattle Art Museum, where a special exhibition of bird art was displayed in conjunction with the annual meeting of the Cooper Ornithological Club of California. I attended the show and, apart from enjoying the wonderful exhibition of paintings of America's leading artist-naturalists, I met and enjoyed a discussion with Jean de Lacure, author of *Waterfowl of the World* and the greatest living authority on the subject.

Then came a letter from the Glenbow Foundation of Calgary asking for an opportunity to discuss the

The sanctuary in late afternoon from the western bank. PHOTO BY MRS. R. NIXON. COURTESY OF EDNA FOTHERINGHAM

purchase of some of the Brooks paintings. The foundation wished to enhance their collection of Western Canadiana. J.G. Cathcart, then curator of the museum, called at Edenbank just before Christmas 1956 to see the paintings. Mr. Cathcart, a born Westerner of pleasant good humour and personality, left me with a feeling of confidence in the Glenbow Foundation. He asked for first opportunity on their behalf to purchase the paintings. In due course, seven pictures were sold to the Glenbow.

In late June 1957, I was invited to make an expense-free trip to Calgary and Banff to see the Glenbow Foundation collections and to meet Eric Harvie, its president. I enjoyed his kind hospitality in Calgary and was allowed to listen in on a telephone conversation when Mr. Harvie was called to discuss oil-drilling

operations in the Arctic. These drillings were the first attempted by leading oil producers of Alberta.

From Calgary, I was driven to Banff by Andy Russell, western Canada's most outstanding big game guide, who operated in the Waterton Lakes area. Andy was in Calgary establishing a contract with the Glenbow Foundation to photograph in colour the alpine flowers of the Rockies. He had spent his lifetime in grizzly bear country and eventually published many books about the grizzly and Canada's Rockies. At Banff, I met the legendary Norman Luxton, a dynamic elderly gentleman of boundless energy and enthusiasm. As a young man, Luxton had spanned the continent on canoe trips, starting from Banff, where the headwaters of mighty rivers begin their flow to the west, north and east. Not content with that, Luxton had taken a

Oliver answered British ornithologist Peter Scott's request for information about "geese of special interest" and subsequently shipped him western Canada geese in 1948 and 1961. Here he is at Trans-Canada Air Lines, delivering his western Canada geese for transport to Holland. They were then sent on to Peter Scott in England.

trip with a retired seaman, Captain John C. Voss, from Victoria to Fiji in a Nootka Indian dugout canoe, the *Tilikum*, which is now preserved at Victoria, B.C. He helped put Banff "on the map."

Luxton's old "Sign of the Goat Trading Post, Taxidermy and Museum" at Banff was a centre of pioneer interest. The collection included many interesting pictures, among them original paintings done for him by Allan Brooks. The most unusual painting was of a prairie grass fire – a night scene, in which two cowboys are depicted dragging a freshly killed half-carcass of beef along the line of fire to extinguish it – their horse straining with the weight of

George Lodge, a well-known artist and naturalist whom Allan Brooks had visited in England, was commissioned by Oliver to paint The Stag at Eve. *The work was done when Lodge was quite elderly but still very talented.*

the load at the end of a lariat as they plunge wildly along on the frightening task.

Also in Banff, I met Charles Biel, noted cowboy sculptor, who for years produced under his skilled hands the bronze sculptures of the chuckwagon races. His elegant trophy went to the race winner. Born a western cowboy, Charlie Biel had received instruction in art from the West's great Charles Russell. Biel had been a friend of Russell's and had led his empty-saddled horse at the time of Russell's funeral. I requested from Charlie that he do a bronze of Dan, the much-loved horse of Edenbank. Yes, Charlie would do it! But some artists work only when the spirit moves them. I had to later remind him of the commission. I had already supplied Charlie with several pictures and all pertinent information, and Charlie's Christmas greetings for 1967 came back with a note from Mrs. Biel, whose father was Norman Luxton, "Charlie says he hasn't forgotten and will get at it if you remind him."

At the request of Mr. Harvie, I sent some of my Brooks paintings to the Glenbow Foundation in Calgary for inspection and display. At that time, agreement on their value was not reached, and the pictures were returned to Edenbank. I had pressed for publication of a biography of Allan Brooks as part of any agreement of sale. When this fell through, a writing of his biography on my recommendation was started by Hamilton M. Laing of Comox, a fellow naturalist of Allan Brooks. I had met Laing in the mountains above Chilliwack in 1927. Laing visited Edenbank to see the Brooks pictures in 1957 and went ahead with the writing of the biography.[58]

In the spring of 1958, the Vancouver Art Gallery was preparing for its summer exhibition called *100 Years of B.C. Art*. R.M. Hume, the curator, asked if he might come to Edenbank and select two Brooks paintings for the show. This he did, and also requested a Thomas Fripp watercolour painting then hanging at Edenbank, *Cherry Creek Ranch*.

The following year, a letter came from Albert Hochbaum, director of the Waterfowl Research Station in Delta, Manitoba, who was making arrangements for an exhibit of the work of Canadian bird artists. He worked to mount a comprehensive display of the works of Allan Brooks, a retrospective display. I crated forty-five pieces of Brooks's art and shipped them again, this time to Regina, where they went on display in the Norman Mackenzie Art Gallery as a special feature in connection with the annual meeting of the American Ornithologists' Union, which was taking place in that city. I visited the show and met many of America's leading artists whose paintings were on exhibition in the new Regina museum. At that time I arranged for a picture to come to Edenbank from Hochbaum, himself a capable artist whose book *The Canvasback on a Prairie Marsh* is considered a classic in ornithological literature.

Another of Canada's most famous wildlife artists, Clarence Tellenius, of Winnipeg, Manitoba, was already a corresponding acquaintance of mine. Tellenius created the background for the wildlife exhibits in Ottawa's new museum and also created the dioramas at the new provincial museum in Victoria. I purchased Tellenius's *Black Bear at Jessica Lake*, which also hung in our home at Edenbank.[59]

In 1961, a request came from the director of the Charles W. Bowers Memorial Museum in California asking for an opportunity to exhibit the Allan Brooks paintings. By this time, I had given two of the better pictures to Betty and two to Marie. They agreed to allow their pictures to be included and so a fine display again crossed into the U.S.A. for an extended tour of museums in Santa Barbara, Los Angeles and San Francisco during the early part of 1961.

In February 1962, the Allan Brooks paintings were once again gathered together and delivered to the Vancouver City Museum, where they went on display

An oil painting by Shelley Weeden, daughter of Dick and Marie, of the Luckakuck and sanctuary.

to preserve the dignity of Canada's native people by painting life portraits of many of their leaders. She visited Edenbank in 1963 in response to Sara's invitation and while she was our guest painted a portrait of Bob Joe, a local native historian. She also painted two beautiful landscapes. Joining them on our walls were original watercolour paintings of totem poles by Ruth Harvey. Of special interest are *The Eagle of Yan, Hole in the Sky* and *Last of Totems on the Skeena.* Also hung were two lovely originals in oil by Lynn Bogue Hunt, a famous wildfowl artist of the United States, plus two original paintings by George E. Lodge, friend of the late Allan Brooks and noted British artist-naturalist. Lodge had painted *The Stag at Eve* at my request.

My love of alpine flowers had prompted me to take many colour photos of wildflowers in the parklands of Liumchen and Elk Mountains. In my library of natural history was one book entitled *Old Man's Garden* by Annora Brown of Fort McLeod, Alberta. Correspondence with Annora Brown resulted in her undertaking a commission for me. The result of her work is a vivid watercolour painting of alpine flowers, set in a natural background of mountains and meadows, reminiscent of the trips Sara and I made into the alpine meadows of Liumchen. The picture hung in the bedroom at Edenbank, where it was much enjoyed.

The works of the great artist-naturalists that decorated the home at Edenbank were symbolic of an atmosphere that extended beyond its walls, where Canada geese and mallard ducks provided an ever-pleasant focal point in a landscape of natural beauty. At the feeding tray near the window, during winter months, the presence of chickadees, juncos, song sparrows, house finches, golden-crowned kinglets and many other birds signified the reassurance that wildlife had come to associate with Edenbank. In the spring, beautiful Bullock's orioles nested around the home as they did when Brooks visited the sanctuary. Waxwings nested in the spruce trees in the yard and beyond, around the pools, the green heron, bittern, marsh wren and yellowthroats contributed their rare beauty and song to the pleasant tranquility of the sanctuary. ⚓

in a special exhibit. While the pictures were there, a request came from the Glenbow Foundation, asking to see the paintings again, as a number of their personnel had changed during the period since they had last seen them. Sara and I felt that the time had come to make some concessions and allow the Glenbow Foundation to purchase the pictures, thereby establishing for all time a unique Allan Brooks collection in western Canada. The family at Edenbank retained several pictures of personal interest. Allan Brooks's son also purchased several smaller pictures and one of his father's finest, *Buffleheads Courting,* before the pictures left Edenbank for the last time.

In their place, on the walls at Edenbank, came paintings by Mildred Valley Thornton, who did much

CHAPTER 23

A New Era

During my previous years of dairying, I had worked on an established schedule which left little time for other interests or activity other than what was required to keep the regular work done. Winter was a busy time for a dairy farmer, compared to the winter work hours on the Canadian Prairie farms.

My day began at 5:30 A.M. My first job was to light or stoke up the old gravity furnace, which still used coal and wood to heat the big house. Then on to the cow barn, where I put lights on. All cows were up and ready for their morning meal. I would sweep the barn and feed grain to the cows before starting the milking machines. The three units of the milking machine were assembled and the motor started to create a vacuum for operation. After the machines began milking, the work consisted of washing the udders of the next

cows to be milked, then at four-minute intervals changing the machine from one cow to the next. The milk was weighed in pails with the brass scales that hung on the wall. While the machines pumped away I carried the milk out to the little dairy for cooling. I would then set it into a circulating tank of cold spring water to remain until the milk truck came to pick up the ten-gallon cans from a stand beside the dairy.

With milking over, I put down bales of hay from the mow above and fed the herd. This done, it was time for breakfast at eight, after which I hitched the manure spreader to the tractor and backed into the wide alleyways of the cow barn to clean out the gutters. The spreader was hauled out to the fields, which often meant ploughing out a snowy roadway in winter. A second load was taken from the centre of the

Oliver on a trip up Elk Mountain in the 1960s, overlooking a valley that had changed a great deal since his youth. PHOTO BY BOB YOUNG

This farm scene belies the hard work of a one-man dairy operation in the early 1960s. Oliver backs the tractor down the ramp after a load has been taken into the barn. His grandson Geoff Weeden (the youngest in photo) wears a happy smile, his dad, Dick Weeden (white shirt), is behind.

barn, and that job was finished for the day. Straw or sawdust was put down, giving the cows fresh bedding. By this time it was noon hour.

After a midday dinner, I threw silage out of the silo to feed the cows. Hay, grain and straw were made ready for the next feeding time. It was then time for odd jobs, and at four o'clock I would go in for tea with Sara. The morning chores were repeated in the afternoon. By 6:30 or 7:00 P.M., the day's work was finished, although at about ten at night, I always went down to the barn, just to see that everything was all right, with no animal loose or sick, and all the animals comfortable. For me it was truly the pleasure of the day to open the old barn door, turn on the light and see the long row of cows, their bellies roundly filled, grunting contentedly as they lay and chewed their cuds. Often I would see cows sleeping with their heads swung around to lie against their sides. Occasionally a chain tie would jingle as one got up, but mostly they lay contentedly biding their time until morning came. By early morning their cud-chewing would have digested the last meal and another supply of milk would have been produced and accumulated in their mammary system, waiting the first milking of the new day. I would pass among the cows at night, leaving them undisturbed as I took a casual

stroll through the barn. Then, as for the cows, it was bedtime for me.

I never found work onerous or undesirable, but simply a task that had to be done. I always felt a great sense of accomplishment at the daily renewal of those activities that provided a livelihood and a proud, worthwhile life. Nevertheless, the work represented great physical effort and was usually more than the average dairy farmhand wanted to do for the wages that prevailed in the agricultural industry.

Each winter, by hand, I fed, forked and shovelled one hundred tons of hay, one hundred tons of silage and thirty tons of grain to the cows. About three hundred tons of manure was hand forked into the spreader and hauled out. From the twenty-five or thirty cows I milked, I carried out to the dairy each day an average of one thousand pounds of milk. It kept a man in good condition but was also a gruelling pace to continue. I kept up this routine for several years, normally working alone.

A new day had dawned in the dairy world by the 1960s. The old dairying systems became a thing of the past. As alluded to earlier, to remain in dairy farming on a large scale meant the installation of automatic barn cleaners and the automatic power-feeding of silage. Milk would have to be conveyed by pipeline to bulk tanks instead of filling the old ten-gallon cans. Electric refrigeration would be required to replace the old system of cooling by cold spring water. In 1962, such changes were behind my decision to finally sell the Edenbank Ayrshires. After this a new life opened up for me. For over forty years I had always "watched the clock" and my daily routine had been governed by the slogan "The cows come first," but now an afternoon of pleasure or visiting could be extended until suppertime if I so wished.

I missed my cattle. I had always enjoyed tending them. There seemed an emptiness in the old cow barn, and truly it was the end of an era at Edenbank. Now, with the cows absent, field work became the major concern. Caring for the small Aberdeen Angus herd took very little time. I was thus able to spend pleasant days in the field on the tractor. The speed with which field work could be attended to made this work easy and enjoyable. From the back porch of the old house, Sara would often receive a wide swinging return wave as I raised my arm high in answer to her distant greeting. She understood my great contentment in working the land that I loved.

I had much time to ponder the future of Edenbank. The farm now was almost surrounded by residential areas. The Wells subdivision, which my grandfather had created upon his retirement, established Spruce Drive as the northern boundary of the farm's land. I had sold a few lots facing onto this road. Later, an opportunity came to sell two lots to Air Commodore Earl McLeod (retired), a friend of the family and a son of a pioneer family himself. Other friends such as Doug and Edna Fotheringham were anxious to buy a homesite on a part of Edenbank and said that if I ever considered creating lots along the bank overlooking the sanctuary and park area, they would be interested. This presented an opportunity to pay off a farm loan I had carried for some time.

Eden Drive was therefore established, curving along the bank above the sanctuary and connecting Spruce Drive to Vedder Road. This created an access road for ten residential lots. The road was built after rigid municipal regulations were met, which made it necessary to grade out the new roadbed, put in gravel eighteen inches deep to a width of fourteen feet and place blacktop twelve feet wide. It meant an outlay

Oliver is assembling an exhibit for the Chilliwack Arts Council of fine craftwork down by the Stó:lō men and women. He particularly encouraged and assisted the women in reviving their ancient weaving skills.

Oliver observes John Wallace finishing the interior of a dugout canoe at Edenbank.

of approximately $10,000 to establish Eden Drive and was a far cry from pioneer municipal requirements regarding subdivisions. However, the lots sold at prices ranging from $2,000 to $4,000, prices that seemed most satisfactory at the time.

I retained and farmed about ninety acres after this sale of lands. The big question in my mind was how long Edenbank Farm would hold out as a farming unit against the pressure of encroaching subdivision. With this in mind, I had Tunbridge & Tunbridge, surveyors, make a chart of half of the farm showing contours. I was thinking about the possibility of a deluxe subdivision of good homes on the banks of the two or three old watercourses that formerly crossed the farm. These were the same streams where my father, Edwin, as a boy, had caught trout with a bent pin on a string. To prove water could be found below the present surface, I used a dragline to dig a pond area in a field behind the big barn. The water level proved to be only six feet below the surface and in gravel. There would obviously be no difficulty in re-establishing old water supplies with the aid of pumps. I envisioned a living area as lovely as that on Eden Drive along the Luckakuck.

Then I turned my attention to growing cash crops. Peas and corn were being grown in ever-increasing acreage in the Chilliwack Valley. Both were tried at Edenbank with some success, but there were years

when an average crop would yield little net income. The farm was a great grass farm, and with irrigation I knew there would never be a year of crop failure, so I turned my attention to increased yields from hay and pasture.

Always a livestock breeder at heart, I made one more attempt to obtain a suitable herdsman with the idea of going into Aberdeen Angus cattle breeding in the same style with which I had developed the Ayrshire herd. For years, I had been a fellow exhibitor with Bob Rochard, with the Diamond S Hereford herd at Lytton, B.C. When Victor Spencer, owner of the Diamond S, died, the ranch was sold and for a time Bob was available. I made an offer to him to come to Edenbank. Bob considered it, and came to visit and discuss the idea, which was congenial to both. However, his services were required by the B.C. Hydro and Power Authority, which was establishing an experimental project involving irrigation of benchlands near Lillooet high above the Fraser. Bob went instead to Lillooet to create new records in hay and grass production.

I contented myself with the small herd of Aberdeen Angus, built up mainly from the bloodlines of my two imported cows. In 1965, I took a young bull to the bull sale at Kamloops that was inferior only to the champion, which he in turn outpriced in the sale. The Edenbank bull brought a price of $825, the best price ever for Edenbank Angus. Soon after, an older

Oliver enjoyed rafting with his grandsons in Luckakuck Creek and took them fishing in Liumchen Creek. Left to right: Robert Purkiss, Geoffrey Weeden and friend Bruce Walter. COURTESY OF BETTY PURKISS

Edenbank cow sold for $800 at public auction. I was very pleased with the results of these efforts.

After growing sixteen acres of peas in 1965, I seeded the field to oats, with an under seeding of grass seed, timothy and alsike clover. The following year, the field yielded two tons of oats per acre and two tons of straw. This was the heaviest crop of grain grown on the farm for a period of at least fifty years, and possibly as heavy as was ever grown. Selling at $50 a ton for grain and $25 for the straw, it gave a gross income per acre of $150. The following year, the same field yielded five tons of hay per acre, selling at $32 per ton, giving a gross income of $160 per acre.

In 1965 I decided to specialize in hay growing and purchased machinery with that in mind. From Massey-Ferguson came a 30-horse-power diesel tractor, a plough, a mower and a side-delivery rake. A new centipede hay tedder, an implement which had been imported from West Germany, proved of great value in speeding up the drying process in making hay. Once again, the system of making hay had to be adjusted to changing conditions. With no hired help employed, it was necessary to utilize every advantage gained by the use of machinery. The new machinery called for an investment of $8,500, a large sum at the time.

Sadie Thompson was Sara's partner in S. & S. Company.

CHILLIWACK PROGRESS PHOTO

The basic principle of hay making continued as it had in the days when Old Sam, the Chinese farm-hand, showed the men how to coil hay. But now it had to be cut, cured and baled instead of coiled, in the least possible time to preserve its natural colour and nutrients. Working alone with the new equipment, I could cut, ted and rake ten acres of hay in a long day, making it ready for baling in forty-eight hours if the weather held. A total of five tons per acre was the highest yield ever produced on the farm. During the 1967 growing season I harvested 175 tons of hay from fifty acres, which subsequently yielded the equivalent of another seventy-five tons as grass pasture for the Angus herd in the fall.

The big crop of hay was hardly in the barn when a request came from the B.C. Aberdeen Angus Association, asking Edenbank to join in playing host at a luncheon for a beef cattle trade mission from Japan. Sara and I responded, and in October a most interesting group of Japanese agriculturists visited the farm to see the herd and be entertained at lunch.

Haying became a group project again at Edenbank. Jack Robinson, a neighbour, had for years custom-baled the hay. I continued with his services rather than purchasing a baler. I always had a willing lot of teenaged boys as neighbours who liked to come and help haul in the hay. Other near neighbours readily called up an extra hand or two and they made a "flying" crew. With a low-slung wagon, I only had to drive the tractor and occasionally maintain a degree of order. The boys did the rest, two loading and two building. In fifteen minutes, a load of one and a half tons, seventy bales, was on the wagon. A quick run to the barn, where an elevator, electrically driven, would carry the bales up into the mows, and in only half an hour they had made a round trip. Two loads an hour meant three tons in the mow. In an eight-hour run, four boys and I, with one wagon, could put in twenty-four tons of hay. In the "good old days" of teams and wagons and loose hay, it required three teams, three wagons and eight men to haul an equal weight. That also meant a massive amount of work in the hot farm kitchen!

For two years I worked and continued to ponder the fate of Edenbank. While I worked, Betty and Marie frequently came to the farm with their growing children. Bob Purkiss, Betty's husband, did not mind taking a turn on the tractor, and Dick Weeden always enjoyed any free time he could find on the farm, away from his medical practice. The children just plain loved the farm and being with their grandparents. From the next generation came the suggestion that perhaps a family company could be formed. Sara and I had hoped that Betty and Marie might declare a desire to keep Edenbank as a family farm, and they were happy with the company suggestion. Gordon Pearmain, an accountant and family friend, who as a boy had often come to visit at the farm, was the first to outline a proposal of company ownership. At his advice and guidance, a local legal firm was asked to draw up the necessary documents.

On January 1, 1967, Edenbank Farm entered into an agreement to become Edenbank Farm Ltd., a company composed of myself, as president and managing director, and Sara as secretary. The other co-owners and directors were Betty and her husband, Robert Purkiss, and Marie and her husband, Dr. Richard Weeden. Marie, Dick and their children,

Shelley and Geoffrey, were already living on a residential site beside the old Edenbank home. Provision was made for another residential site for Betty and Bob's family on the other side of the old homesite. They, with their family, Elizabeth, Robbie and Nancy, were then living in Coquitlam, B.C.

Thus a new arrangement came into being for Edenbank. I was able to continue as farm manager and custodian. As well I now had an opportunity to further explore and develop my other wide-ranging interests and hobbies.

For years, I had maintained an interest in church and community affairs. Natural history was a special love. After the sale of the Ayrshire herd, I dedicated many hours to historical research. With others of like interest, I helped organize the Chilliwack Historical Society and became its first president in 1957. For ten years I was chairman of the board. In the B.C. centennial year of 1958, the first small Chilliwack Museum was opened in the RCMP office building on Nowell Street under supervision of the historical society. I contributed several items from the farm, including a handmade leather and wood elevator conveyance that A.C. Wells had made to fill the first upright silo in B.C. A dugout, shovel-nosed cedar canoe made by Chief Sepass and used on the stream at Edenbank by the family I had also preserved and retained for display in an eventual permanent museum.[60]

I was asked to contribute an introduction to the book *Sepass Poems*,[61] published by Eloise Street in 1963. In compiling a brief sketch of the life of Chief Sepass, I became intrigued by the early history of the native people with whom the family had been friendly for three generations. Realizing it would not be long before the older natives, born during the early days of white settlement, would all be dead, I purchased a large reel-to-reel tape recorder and spent considerable time away from the farm on visits to the homes of old native friends. Dan Milo (the same individual who raced on old Molly in the hay field), whose family name was *sloh-kwuh-LAH-luh*, was one of the first I interviewed and recorded. He was totally blind, as he had been for some years. At the age of ninety-seven, when I took him for a drive one day and brought him to Edenbank for a tape-recorded interview, Dan was very much at ease. Over his long lifetime he had known and been friends with three generations of the Wells family. His memory was keen and his natural ability as a storyteller became evident in the successful interview that followed.

During the next three years until his death in Coqualeetza Hospital, Dan contributed much to the history of native people and their early association

Josephine Kelly (shown gathering lichen) was an enthusiastic president of the Salish Weavers, a group formed by the native women to continue production of their craft.

with the white settlers. Mrs. Albert Cooper and Bob Joe, the latter in his ninetieth year in 1967, were also oldtime friends, and I went to them for their stories. I was able to tape-record on frequent occasions the history, language and the legends of the Chilliwack tribes. Mrs. Cooper was the Amy Lorenzetto who had stood by the side of Margaret Smith at the window of Coqualeetza school during the '94 flood. She easily recalled the time when the river steamer brought cattle upstream to Edenbank. In Canada's centennial year only Amy's eyesight had failed; her memory was keen and her mind alert. During her lifetime, she was a much-respected friend of Mrs. Edwin (Margaret) Wells, who often invited her to Edenbank. It was Mrs. Cooper's sister, Agnes, who had regularly worked for my own mother, Gertie. Those were the days when the pioneers depended on the native women to help care for the children and help with the hand washing.

For years, Coqualeetza institute had always supplied Edenbank with extra help during summer months. Among the many native boys who came from Coqualeetza to work on the farm was Peter Kelly, who was mentioned earlier and who later became head of the B.C. Conference of the United Church of Canada.

Sara Wells and some of the Karakul black sheep raised by S. & S. Company for the Salish spinners and knitters.

In 1941 Coqualeetza was refurbished and renovated as a hospital for the treatment of native people with tuberculosis, a disease that had been ravaging many native tribes. In 1948, when Dr. William Barclay was surgeon in charge of Coqualeetza, a fire destroyed a portion of the building. One of the staff, Miss Sadie Thompson, came to Edenbank in search of temporary housing. Sadie became a boarder at the farm for ten years and a dear friend to the whole family. During her stay she showed great interest in all the farm activities. Like Margaret, she assisted with livestock records and became particularly knowledgeable about the sheep breeding program.

The wool of the new Cheviots had been gaining popularity among the natives who were expert sweatermakers. They came to me for several hundred pounds annually and frequently asked for natural black wool, which I did not have. Under normal valuation of wool, a freedom from black colouring was of paramount importance. The native women wished black wool for use in making their designs in Salish sweaters. It was evident that there was also a good local demand for black wool for weaving in general. Because of this demand, a price twice that of regular white wool was established. Sara became interested in this aspect of sheep breeding and after making inquiries learned of others who were specializing in the production of black wool for craft use in homespun fabrics.

Frank Sholty of Fraser Lake in northern B.C. often called at Edenbank on his annual trips to the coast with truckloads of livestock. One day when he came in for a visit, Sara was handing him a cup of tea when she asked, "Mr. Sholty, do you know where we could buy black sheep?" "I just took some beautiful black ewe lambs in to market," he replied. "Do you know of others?" asked Sara. "Yes. There's a neighbour who has a few Karakul ewes, that were originally purebreds. I think he would sell them."

On his next trip down, in November 1962, Sholty called at Edenbank again and brought with him five amazing-looking black ewes. "They might best be described as 'wild and woolly,'" he said, "but they seem healthy." Sara had been talking to Sadie Thompson about the idea of buying black sheep and they agreed to start a project together. So Sara told Sholty, "We'll take them." They were big ewes, grey-black in colour and with more than a year's wool on them hanging in rough matted tangles. When Sadie saw them she, like Sara, was intrigued and amazed by their strange long necks and droopy ears, big soft eyes and slim noses.

Sara and Sadie formed a partnership – the S. & S. Company – and purchased the five ewes. Thus another livestock breeding program was launched at Edenbank. Truly the strangest-appearing animals ever to come to the farm, the sheep had fleeces that were in keen demand and brought $1.25 a pound for the wool.

In the years that followed, it fell to me to manage this flock and keep the records, but the S. & S. Company did the financing of new purchases and reaped the profits from the sale of wool and lamb, which was divided evenly. I was paid for feed and care of the sheep. In 1963, S. & S. purchased seven more black ewes from Mr. Sholty. In 1966 they heard of a fine flock of Karakul sheep for sale and purchased nine good young ewes, a yearling ram known as Napoleon and a ram lamb known as Danny.

The most striking characteristic about Napoleon was his fine set of black horns, which would match the best of those worn by the Rocky Mountain bighorns.

The wool from Sara and Sadie's black flock – a melding of several shades of grey – was highly valued for knitting and weaving.

His most unusual characteristic was his lack of ears, a characteristic which he bred into his offspring. These sheep were beautiful specimens with fine long black wool, long necks and almost invisible drooping ears.

A great culling of older ewes took place in 1967 and in September of that year, Danny became lord of the flock of twenty-four females. They were a half-wild sheep and would carry heads high and leap four feet into the air in any dash for freedom through a gate.

In 1959 Sadie Thompson had previously purchased a residential lot on Eden Drive just north of the big barn, and she continued to make frequent trips to inspect the flock of Karakul sheep maintained at Edenbank by S. & S. Company. She remained a great friend of ours and generously shared with us her Pacific beach cottage on the shores of Gabriola Island.

I entered into another field of specialization with the good white wool of the North Country Cheviots. In my efforts to revive native interest in their own

Coloured wool on the line that has been dyed by Oliver for the Salish weavers. When Oliver discovered there had been many renowned weavers in the area, he began, with Mrs. Amy Cooper's help, to encourage the revival of Salish weaving. He also received support from Mary Peters and her sister Mrs. Emery, who both remembered their mother at her loom.

After Oliver's death the weavers formed a club and eventually opened a retail outlet and headquarters at Coqualeetza. Mrs. Bob Joe.

Mary Peters is weaving in her garden on a loom she constructed herself.

early culture, I began to dye wool with the natural dyes they had used historically on the wool of the mountain goats. Until the turn of the century Salish women had woven beautiful blankets from this wool. With the help of Mrs. Cooper, I was able to encourage some of the native women to re-establish their former weaving skills, using native looms. This created a demand for naturally dyed wool.

Early in 1967, I assisted in the arrangement of a contract between Mary Peters, a local Salish weaver, and the architects responsible for the construction of the new Bonaventure Hotel in Montreal. Mary wove several large tapestries to decorate the hotel lobby. This project required about 150 pounds of fleece wool, part of which was to be natural white and part natural black. The bulk I dyed for Mary by using bark, roots and lichen. During 1967, all the wool produced at Edenbank was sold directly to natives for their weaving and knitting.

With all these projects there was little leisure time at Edenbank, however, in 1967, I took time to locate a suitable large cedar log from which my native friend, John Wallace, carved out an old-style shovel-nosed canoe. John worked in the horse barn at Edenbank and with the skill of an accomplished artist fashioned a beautiful canoe using only a double-bitted axe and some hand-finishing tools. John had been a very large

and strong woodsman in his youth but he now was of quite small stature. Nevertheless, he still had great strength and a skill that he used to advantage. I would pick him up at Soowahlie and bring him to the farm every day so that he might continue his carving.

Having heard about and possibly seen a native canoe and woven native blankets, a Mr. G.H. Poppy, display supervisor at Eaton's Vancouver store, came to the farm. He was then preparing what became one of the finest displays of native craft ever set before the public. For part of his display, he took samples of native weaving, all by-products of the native women's efforts in revitalizing their distinctive native craft.

My interest in cultural advancement for the community had another outlet with my participation in the Chilliwack Arts Council. Mostly I assisted in arranging and displaying works of art, and encouraging local native artists. Initially the arts council had much support from Mary Allen, O.B.E., formerly of Chilliwack and latterly of Vancouver. She was blessed with an indomitable spirit and was a source of inspiration to everyone with whom she worked. I was impressed with her slogan "Make no small plans – they have no magic to stir men's blood!"

On occasion when I was helping to arrange a local arts council display of paintings, Sara and I would host an artist as our guest. One was the late Mildred

John Wallace starting on the mammoth job of creating a cedar dugout canoe. No power tools were used for the carving of these canoes. John carved nine canoes at Edenbank with Oliver's assistance.

Valley Thornton, another Jack McLean, a man famous for his beautiful paintings of B.C.'s western landscapes. McLean came in 1967 for a short visit. Marie, also an artist, and I were both thrilled to meet him and asked him to return sometime to the Chilliwack Valley and paint some of its many beautiful mountain scenes.

As Canada's centennial drew to a close in 1967 in the Christmas season, I wrote these last words to conclude the history of a farm where A.C. Wells's great-great-grandchildren now play.

Christmas 1967 has been another wonderful family reunion at Edenbank. Betty and Bob were home, with Elizabeth, Robbie and Nancy. Robbie has just expressed the wish that it would snow and snow and snow. "Why?" asked his grandpa. "So the roads would be blocked and we couldn't go home tomorrow," came the reply. Marie and Dick, Shelley and Geoffrey are comfortably settled into their home again at Edenbank, where all the children have romped and played together for a week. Tonight, Sara, Betty and Marie have been invited to Sadie's home on Eden Drive, while Grandpa with pleasure babysits the fifth generation at Edenbank. When he kissed Elizabeth goodnight, she said, "I wish tomorrow would never come! Goodnight Grandpa!" December 28, 1967.

Epilogue

My father's story shows the personal hopes and dedication to principles and ideals passed down through several generations of a family over more than one hundred years. It is the story of only one Chilliwack farm family but reflects the farming history of the Fraser Valley and British Columbia as a whole. It is very much a tribute to one person, Oliver Wells, who accomplished so much in his lifetime and became a friend to so many people, both native and white. In addition, the story provides a record of many of the pioneers who worked at the farm and of families who were friends and neighbours in the early days.

Early farming methods used at Edenbank often became a model for others in the province, and the farm's breeding programs were nationally recognized and awarded. Following Oliver's death in 1970, the family continued a more limited farming operation. Our family moved into the old farmhouse both to look after our mother, Sara, and to manage the operations of the Aberdeen Angus herd and the large flock of Cheviot sheep. As time passed, it gradually became obvious that a solution had to be found in which the farm's heritage importance might be preserved.

Many private individuals as well as many representatives of public jurisdictions expressed strong feelings about the final disposition of Edenbank during the 1970s. There were many newspaper articles and letters to the editor published, personal letters received and, in April 1981, even proceedings to do with this issue recorded in Hansard of the B.C. legislature. The following revisits the controversy that raged about what should eventually happen to this unique piece of real estate of such historic significance.

It was apparent as early as the 1960s that the whole Sardis "corridor" between Chilliwack and Vedder Crossing, which contained all the basic services, was destined for development within a few years. Oliver Wells had recognized this fact, noting that the farm was in

A summer scene of the Edenbank home and landscaping, ca. 1930.

the heart and path of this corridor, and he himself began to formulate alternative uses for the property.

The Fraser Valley College was searching for a permanent home for the Chilliwack-area campus in the early 1970s. In 1974, the family at Edenbank, after discussions with the college board, began negotiations with the provincial government to sell part of the land for a permanent college site. The Provincial Agricultural Land Commission finally (after an appeal) determined not to allow this special educational use, even though the land would not have been removed from the agricultural land reserve (ALR). The college proposal indicated the campus would have a need for a certain amount of agricultural use. Both college representatives and the Edenbank family were extremely disappointed with this decision.

Later, the family was approached by Peter Woodward, a local resident who was keenly interested in Edenbank's history. With his encouragement and support, the possibility of heritage designation for the property and possible purchase by the provincial government for an operational heritage farm was entertained. The family was again very excited about this concept. Subsequently, studies were commissioned by the heritage conservation branch of the B.C. Provincial Secretary's office. In 1978, a report was issued by Jack Herbert, a man experienced in national heritage sites, enthusiastically supporting a heritage proposal.

Mr. Herbert had been secretary for the Historic Sites and Monuments Board of Canada for six years. He submitted a very positive report concerning Edenbank after extensive study and consultation. With the backing of the community and district council, and a strong endorsement by the Heritage Advisory Board of the provincial government, his recommendations were (in part, excerpted from Hansard, April 29, 1981):

a. to designate Edenbank Farm as a
   provincial heritage site under part 2
   of the Heritage Conservation Act and

b. that every effort be made to provide for the preservation and conservation of the house and farm buildings together with sufficient land to guarantee their setting . . . ,

c. thirdly, that Edenbank heritage site be used to interpret the evolution of the dairy industry in British Columbia using the life of the Wells family, and reconstructed for the growth in animal husbandry, farming technology . . .

This report was received by Provincial Secretary Evan Wolfe, who then submitted it to the provincial cabinet. The cabinet in closed discussions rejected the proposal. Again a marvellous concept to preserve the property was vetoed, this time by the provincial cabinet. Their reasons have never been made public. Speculation was that the decision was political.[62]

At about this time it appeared to the family and to neighbours that there was no hope of preserving the large cattle barn, now in disrepair and very close to residential homes. In late 1976, the sad decision was made to take down the old barn. Much of the structure, including large timbers, was fortunately saved.

Later on, after a private agreement for sale had been entered into and completion was imminent, the Chilliwack Heritage Advisory Committee made recommendations to district council for municipal heritage designation of the home and property. The recommendations were not acted upon by council. There was controversy because the district council evidently ignored a brief by the advisory committee that was to be brought before council at a public hearing on a development proposal for the property. The recommendations of the Chilliwack Heritage Advisory Committee were as follows.

1. That Edenbank Farm, in its entirety, be designated as a Municipal Heritage site under Part III of the Heritage Conservation Act, and that all possible ways and means be investigated to maintain the complex as a working, heritage farm.

2. That the Edenbank farmhouse, together with sufficient land to guarantee its setting, and sufficient land to maintain the present vista from Vedder Road and the main driveway across Luck-a-kuck Creek, be designated a municipal heritage site under Part III of the Heritage Conservation Act.

3. That in the event of 2 above taking place, the district council of Chilliwack investigate every possible means of returning the property so designated to public ownership.

4. That in the event of 2 above taking place, but failing 3 above, that the private owner(s) of the property so designated be given access to existing municipal incentive schemes for the maintenance and preservation of designated heritage sites.

What has become of Edenbank since that time? In 1981, a sales agreement was completed with Royal International Equities for purchase of the property. The company's intent was to have the front eight acres bordering Luckakuck Creek become a strata-title gated community. The agreement included an assurance that the old farmhouse would be preserved. This in fact did occur. The provincial Agricultural Land Commission later released to this same company, from the ALR, another forty-six acres to the west for residential development. It was amazing to the family that a college within a farming community in which agriculture would be taught was not allowed by the land commission to use part of the land, but then later a private developer's request for housing was accepted. The large remaining hay field of thirty acres farther west is still in the ALR, with both its north and south borders densely populated.

The sanctuary created by Oliver was officially taken over by the Wells Sanctuary Society in about 1990. The society was formed by residents living on the sanctuary's boundary who maintain the wildlife reserve. Recently a restrictive covenant was drawn up and approved by the District of Chilliwack to ensure that the property will continue in perpetuity as a sanctuary.

Today, in July 2003, the old home still stands, a historic monument, well maintained and enjoyed by residents of the housing complex and their friends, who use it as a gathering place and clubhouse. The development of the front acreage was done in tasteful style and design and is a credit to the architects and builders. There have been regrets in many circles that Edenbank did not become a public treasure. Perhaps this annotated story written by Oliver Wells in 1967, in Edenbank's centennial year, will help readers now and in the future to better understand the farm's legacy and some of the events that finally shaped Edenbank as it exists today.

Acknowledgements

A book is not created without the help of many individuals. A special thanks is extended to the following people who knowingly or unknowingly became part of the story of Edenbank.

In 1967 when the original Edenbank manuscript by Oliver Wells was completed and close to publication, Mr. C.M. Rigby assisted Oliver by typing the handwritten script. At that time Colonel R.W.R. Oliver (recommended by Howard Mitchell at Mitchell Press) is credited with early editing of the manuscript, working along with Oliver.

Some years later, after Oliver's death, good friends Bill and the late Rosemary Brown were both an inspiration to the family. Bill, who always had a special interest in the farm, presented a paper to the Osler Society about Oliver Wells and Edenbank.

Peter and Pat Woodward in years past gave us hope and worked extremely hard to convince the heritage branch of the provincial government to designate the farm as a provincial heritage site.

Lloyd Mackey of the *Chilliwack Progress* wrote several excellent articles both locally and in his Victoria column in the '70s supporting the idea of finding a public use for Edenbank.

Larry Blake, president of Fraser Valley College, along with the full college board, made great efforts to have the farm become the permanent new eastern campus for the college.

The Chilliwack Museum and Archives has been a great support. Recently, Kelly Harms, archivist, has been of assistance. Previously, archivist Jim Bowman did a formal edit of the manuscript, which was then retyped by Nancy den Boersterd.

Neil Smith has sent us e-mails, found us photos and researched willingly for us. Mildred (Evans) Hall, historian par excellence, has been a wonderful source and able to answer many questions. She was responsible for completing Casey Wells's research into the Wells family genealogy and also recorded the history of the Evans family (now available at the Chilliwack Museum). Betty Brooks has kindly allowed us to use photos of Allan Brooks's artwork.

Marie's sister, Betty Purkiss, and other family members have been most helpful in reading the manuscript, providing photos and making suggestions. It's been particularly fun to work with Ron Wells, whose great sense of humour put everything into perspective. Nancy Purkiss particularly helped by carefully separating out some family history, enabling us to shorten the text. Marie's cousin in Great Britain, Sarah Reay, and cousin Barbara Nielsen of Surrey helped create the genealogical chart and constantly cheered us on. Both these women are descendants of A.C. Wells's daughter, Lillie. Others we wish to thank are June Mosher and Donna Cook.

We owe much to Margaret (Smith) Wells, who diligently kept records and scrapbooks of farm and valley history. Her four scrapbooks have become a remarkable record and have been donated to the Chilliwack Museum.

Several years ago David Allen of Fraser Valley College read and critiqued the manuscript, as did Shirley Cuthbertson, Tom Leach, Ron Tarves (who also did an early edit), Jim Tallman, Imbert Orchard and Christie Harris. Without exception they gave enthusiastic support for the idea of publication and urged us on.

Recently Fred Bryant and Bill McFaul of Chilliwack name and fame have been of great assistance, as have the McBlain family. By phone or mail we have been able to jog memories to recall names and details of events from fifty years ago.

We wish to especially thank Doug Nicol and Allan Fotheringham for their wonderful recorded memories and insights about the farm. Both have been very supportive, and enthusiastic about this story.

Over the past thirty-three or more years, Professor Ralph Maud has been a support to us in our quest to follow Oliver's footsteps of the past. We owe him much.

A special thanks to Jan Perrier, whose graphic design talents have produced exciting images and whose patience was admirable during a sometimes complicated process.

Finally, to our "editor-in-chief," Naomi Pauls, we give a special thank you. She said to us, "Yes, there is a story there that needs to be told." Naomi has been a wonderful guide with her patient, kindly suggestions and her clear vision for this book.

Richard (Dick) Weeden

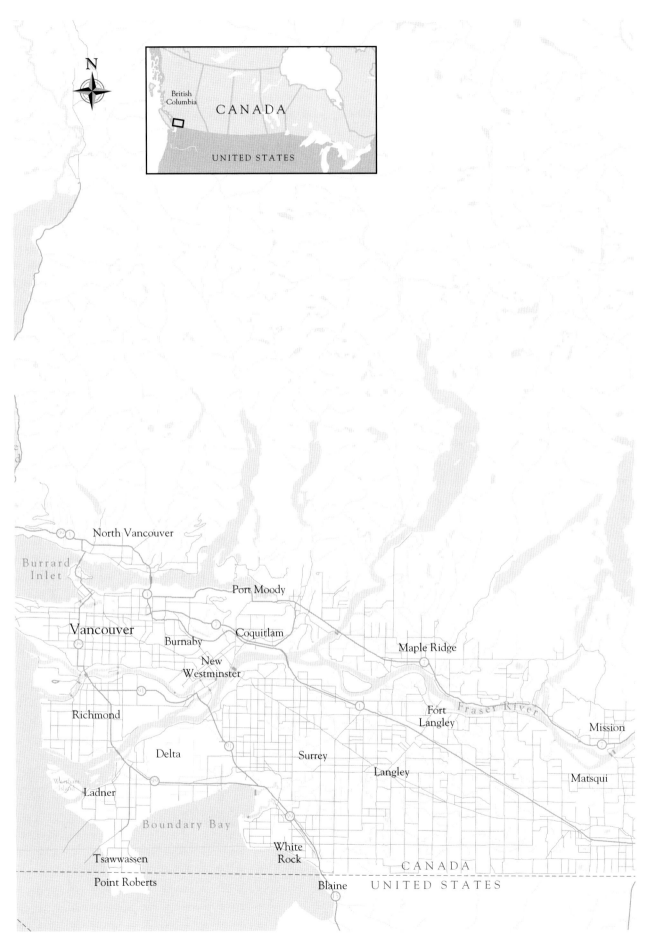

British
Columbia

CANADA

UNITED STATES

North Vancouver

Burrard
Inlet

Port Moody

Vancouver

Burnaby

Coquitlam

Maple Ridge

New
Westminster

Fraser River

Richmond

Fort
Langley

Mission

Delta

Surrey

Langley

Matsqui

Ladner

Boundary Bay

Tsawwassen

White
Rock

CANADA

Point Roberts

Blaine

UNITED STATES

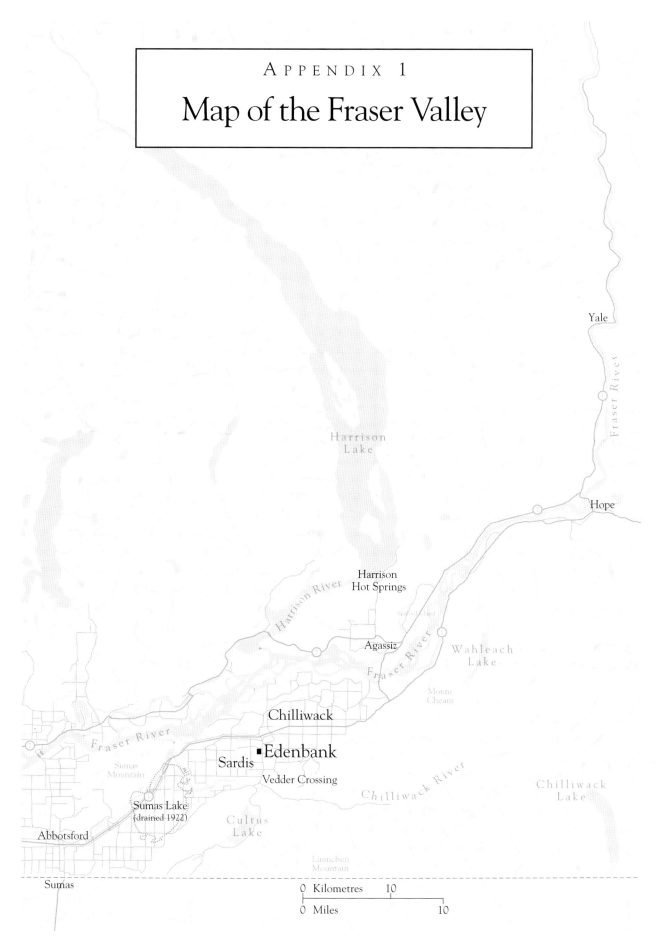

APPENDIX 1
Map of the Fraser Valley

Yale

Fraser River

Hope

Harrison
Lake

Harrison
Hot Springs

Harrison River

Agassiz

Wahleach
Lake

Fraser River

Mount
Cheam

Chilliwack

Edenbank

Sardis

Vedder Crossing

Chilliwack River

Chilliwack
Lake

Fraser River

Sumas
Mountain

Sumas Lake
(drained 1922)

Cultus
Lake

Abbotsford

Linmchen
Mountain

Sumas

| 0 Kilometres | 10 |
| 0 Miles | 10 |

Descendants of Allen Casey Wells

SIX GENERATIONS

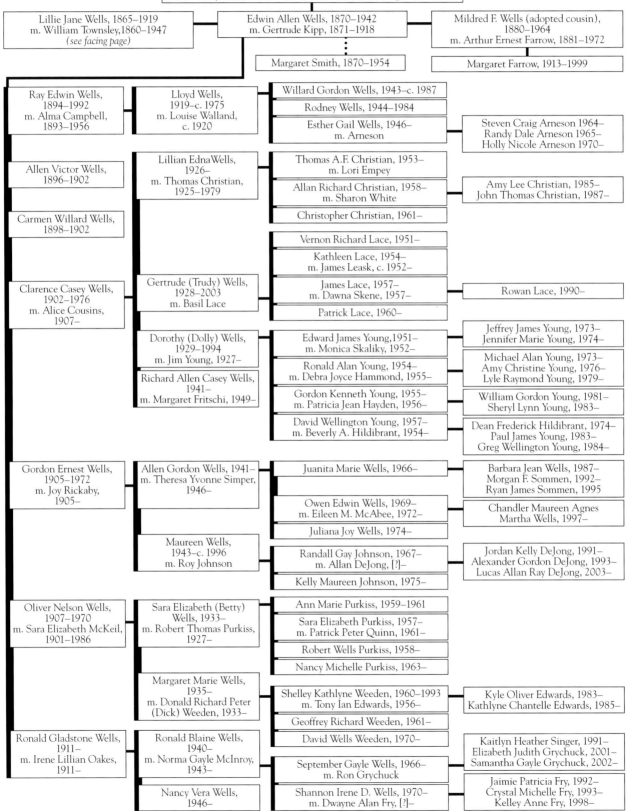

Allen Casey Wells, 1837–1922 m. Sarah Manetta Hodge, 1835–1922

Lillie Jane Wells, 1865–1919 m. William Townsley,1860–1947 (*see facing page*)	Edwin Allen Wells, 1870–1942 m. Gertrude Kipp, 1871–1918	Mildred F. Wells (adopted cousin), 1880–1964 m. Arthur Ernest Farrow, 1881–1972
	Margaret Smith, 1870–1954	Margaret Farrow, 1913–1999

Ray Edwin Wells, 1894–1992 m. Alma Campbell, 1893–1956	Lloyd Wells, 1919–c. 1975 m. Louise Walland, c. 1920	Willard Gordon Wells, 1943–c. 1987	
		Rodney Wells, 1944–1984	
		Esther Gail Wells, 1946– m. Arneson	Steven Craig Arneson 1964– Randy Dale Arneson 1965– Holly Nicole Arneson 1970–
Allen Victor Wells, 1896–1902	Lillian Edna Wells, 1926– m. Thomas Christian, 1925–1979	Thomas A.F. Christian, 1953– m. Lori Empey	
		Allan Richard Christian, 1958– m. Sharon White	Amy Lee Christian, 1985– John Thomas Christian, 1987–
Carmen Willard Wells, 1898–1902		Christopher Christian, 1961–	
	Gertrude (Trudy) Wells, 1928–2003 m. Basil Lace	Vernon Richard Lace, 1951–	
		Kathleen Lace, 1954– m. James Leask, c. 1952–	
Clarence Casey Wells, 1902–1976 m. Alice Cousins, 1907–		James Lace, 1957– m. Dawna Skene, 1957–	Rowan Lace, 1990–
		Patrick Lace, 1960–	
	Dorothy (Dolly) Wells, 1929–1994 m. Jim Young, 1927–	Edward James Young,1951– m. Monica Skaliky, 1952–	Jeffrey James Young, 1973– Jennifer Marie Young, 1974–
		Ronald Alan Young, 1954– m. Debra Joyce Hammond, 1955–	Michael Alan Young, 1973– Amy Christine Young, 1976– Lyle Raymond Young, 1979–
	Richard Allen Casey Wells, 1941– m. Margaret Fritschi, 1949–	Gordon Kenneth Young, 1955– m. Patricia Jean Hayden, 1956–	William Gordon Young, 1981– Sheryl Lynn Young, 1983–
		David Wellington Young, 1957– m. Beverly A. Hildibrant, 1954–	Dean Frederick Hildibrant, 1974– Paul James Young, 1983– Greg Wellington Young, 1984–
Gordon Ernest Wells, 1905–1972 m. Joy Rickaby, 1905–	Allen Gordon Wells, 1941– m. Theresa Yvonne Simper, 1946–	Juanita Marie Wells, 1966–	Barbara Jean Wells, 1987– Morgan F. Sommen, 1992– Ryan James Sommen, 1995
		Owen Edwin Wells, 1969– m. Eileen M. McAbee, 1972–	Chandler Maureen Agnes Martha Wells, 1997–
		Juliana Joy Wells, 1974–	
	Maureen Wells, 1943–c. 1996 m. Roy Johnson	Randall Gay Johnson, 1967– m. Allan DeJong, [?]–	Jordan Kelly DeJong, 1991– Alexander Gordon DeJong, 1993– Lucas Allan Ray DeJong, 2003–
		Kelly Maureen Johnson, 1975–	
Oliver Nelson Wells, 1907–1970 m. Sara Elizabeth McKeil, 1901–1986	Sara Elizabeth (Betty) Wells, 1933– m. Robert Thomas Purkiss, 1927–	Ann Marie Purkiss, 1959–1961	
		Sara Elizabeth Purkiss, 1957– m. Patrick Peter Quinn, 1961–	
		Robert Wells Purkiss, 1958–	
		Nancy Michelle Purkiss, 1963–	
	Margaret Marie Wells, 1935– m. Donald Richard Peter (Dick) Weeden, 1933–	Shelley Kathlyne Weeden, 1960–1993 m. Tony Ian Edwards, 1956–	Kyle Oliver Edwards, 1983– Kathlyne Chantelle Edwards, 1985–
		Geoffrey Richard Weeden, 1961–	
Ronald Gladstone Wells, 1911– m. Irene Lillian Oakes, 1911–	Ronald Blaine Wells, 1940– m. Norma Gayle McInroy, 1943–	David Wells Weeden, 1970–	Kaitlyn Heather Singer, 1991– Elizabeth Judith Grychuck, 2001– Samantha Gayle Grychuck, 2002–
		September Gayle Wells, 1966– m. Ron Grychuck	
	Nancy Vera Wells, 1946–	Shannon Irene D. Wells, 1970– m. Dwayne Alan Fry, [?]–	Jaimie Patricia Fry, 1992– Crystal Michelle Fry, 1993– Kelley Anne Fry, 1998–

Descendants of Lillie Jane Wells

SIX GENERATIONS

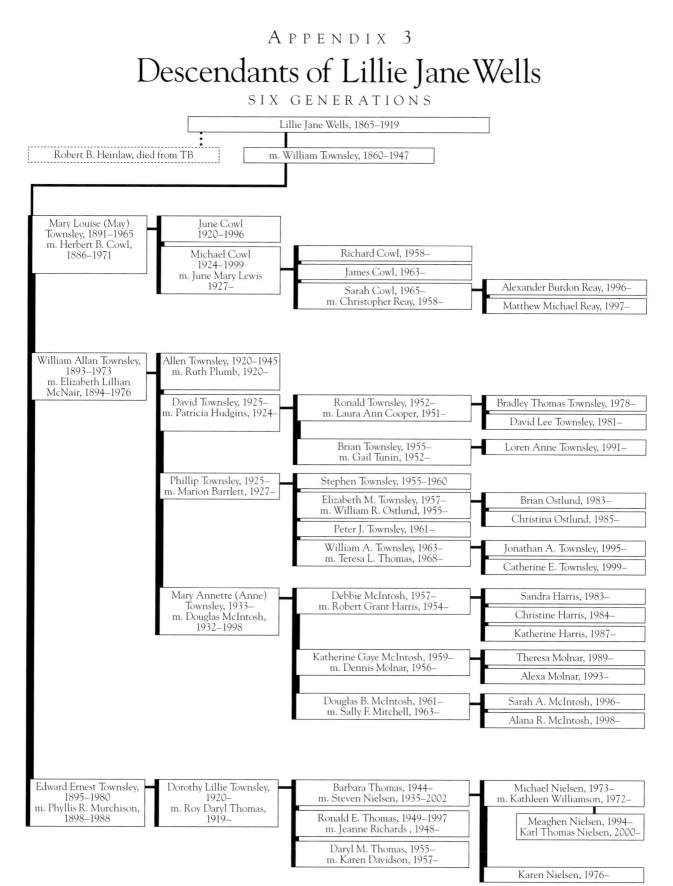

Notes

These endnotes are supplied by the editors, not the author.

1. The author's phonetic system, called the Practical Phonetic System (PPS), was developed by his brother Casey when studying the Halkomelem language. In this transcription system, one accents the capitalized syllables. A period after a syllable separates letters having their own syllable value, for example, Kwa.EE. A colon in PPS indicates a lengthened consonant or vowel. Oliver and Casey tape-recorded and transcribed many lists of words and conversations with native informants and in 1965 published *A Vocabulary of Native Words in the Halkomelem Language.* Subsequently, in the book *The Chilliwacks and Their Neighbors* (pp. 23–27), Brent Galloway described this transliteration system.

2. It took two months to travel from New York via the Panama to Victoria, an extremely arduous trip. On their journey up the Fraser River the miners usually stopped at Fort Langley. This was the head of navigation and the main supply depot for all interior trade of the Hudson's Bay Company until 1858, when the American steamer, the *Surprise,* was guided as far as Hope by Captain John, a native leader whose name was Speel-set. Thereafter, with great respect, he was called Captain John. It's interesting to note that when the first bridge was being built spanning the Fraser Canyon, Captain John was in charge of transporting by canoe the immense cable into place for the Royal Engineers. Keith Thor Carlson, ed., *You Are Asked to Witness: The Stó:lō in Canada's Pacific Coast History* (Chilliwack, B.C.: Sto:lo Heritage Trust, 1997), 116.

3. Agricultural business had become so great at Fort Langley that Puget Sound Agricultural Co. was formed to handle trade. In 1839, there was farming on a large scale there. Denys Nelson, *Fort Langley, 1827–1927: A Century of Settlement in the Valley of the Lower Fraser River* (Vancouver: Art, Historical and Scientific Association of Vancouver, B.C., 1927).

4. At the time Allen passed through, Lillooet had 13 saloons and 25 liquor outlets. Art Downs, *Wagon Road North: The Story of the Cariboo Gold Rush in Historical Photos* (Quesnel, B.C.: Northwest Digest, 1961), 57.

5. Chief Factor James Douglas requested that Alexander Caulfield Anderson lay out in detail plans for the Harrison-Lillooet route and name the large lakes after himself and members of his family. "In keeping with this request, he named the first one out of Lillooet town, *Seton Lake,* in honor of his heroic cousin, Colonel Alexander Seton, commander of the gallant 74th Regiment, that gave to the world an undying example of British courage and devotion to duty, in the troopship *Birkenhead,* when that vessel went down off the African coast in 1852, by standing at attention with unbroken rank as the seas closed over them." This written on an old map, B.C. Archives. B.A. McKelvie, *Fort Langley, Outpost of Empire* (Toronto: Thomas Nelson & Sons, 1957), 94.

6. The same claim, named "Wake-up-Jake," staked by Allen and his partner, apparently produced $80,000 in gold the following year. This information comes from a scrapbook of newspaper clippings kept by Margaret (Smith) Wells, the second wife of Edwin.

7. John Forsyth accompanied Allen to the goldfields and later settled near the land that Allen pre-empted. John's property was District Lot 269, Plan 27099, New Westminster District, noted in the B.C. Land Registry.

8. It was a tragedy that when the women arrived their trunks and possessions were not to be found. Inquiries were made but it was not until many months later that they were discovered where they had been left out on the wharf by the longshoremen and exposed to the elements. All their fine linens and handwork were destroyed.

9. These stages went twice weekly and never missed a trip. The route was from Yale to Barkerville via the Quesnel forks. The first year they carried 1,500 passengers, brought out $4,619,000 of gold and travelled 100,000 miles. The trip took four days and cost $130. Downs, *Wagon,* 51–53.

10. These quotes were taken from *Zoological Notes* by J.K. Lord, a British Columbia naturalist, in his dissertation on "Mosquitoes and Other Winged Pests." Photocopied pages from Casey Wells's files. Possibly from *The Naturalist in Vancouver Island and British Columbia,* 2 vols. (London: R. Bentley, 1866).

11. From Margaret Wells's scrapbook: Isaac Kipp said, "Before going to the Cariboo, Jake, Reece and I and an Indian cut a trail from Yale to Chilliwack. There was nothing in the shape of grain or hay nearer than Frisco and the Cariboo Road was opening."

12. At this time the cabin has been dismantled and moved from its former location at the Canadian Forces Base Chilliwack, Vedder Crossing, the location of a training centre for the Royal Canadian Mounted Police. It has been rebuilt and is located at 1513 Forbes Avenue, North Vancouver, at the Sell Armouries, the headquarters for 6 Field Engineers Squadron.

13. A written report of September 19, 1866, on the operation at the Evans farm when A.C. Wells was the manager read as follows:

    > 500 acres with 50 acres in cultivation
    > 2000 bushels of grain
    > 50 timothy prairie hay
    > 800 bushels spuds
    > 250 bushels carrots
    > 8 cattle
    > 8 hogs
    > 50 cattle are on the way from Oregon

14. The Coqualeetza, a tributary of the Chilliwack River, was later more often referred to as the Luckakuck.

15. Pre-emptions of land were allowed until 1883. According to John Edgar Gibbard, "Methodist influence was dominant in the community. It is said, too that it was prolonged by a sort of voluntary system of land settlement. Whenever a prospective settler appeared in the community he was referred to Mr. Wells. The latter usually invited him to dinner, discovered his religious inclinations and habits and then helped or discouraged him accordingly." "Early History of the Fraser Valley, 1808–1885" (MA thesis, University of British Columbia, 1937), footnote 95.

16. "When the first Protestant church was erected near Chilliwack, we-YOUS-to-lahk, an elderly native woman, wanted to make a donation. She had no money but went to the Hudson's Bay Company post at Fort Langley and worked for sufficient cash to buy wool to make a small mat. On the day of the church opening, she presented it as an offering and said, 'Oh, Great Father, I have no silver dollar. But this mat is myself. I lay it down on the table in Thy house. I am very poor but I give myself.' An Indian chief who witnessed this presentation said, 'This woman's gift made our hearts like fire and our eyes wet.'" Undated *Christian Science Monitor* article from Margaret (Smith) Wells's scrapbook.

17. The Chadsey brothers had settled on the Sumas Prairie by 1863 and were making hay from the natural grasslands. Many islands in the Fraser River, where this natural grass grew three or four feet high, were used to pasture animals for the Cariboo. Chester Chadsey's diary as quoted by Horatio Webb in the *Chilliwack Progress*, "Webb Tells of Pre-Confederation Days in Chilliwack," n.d. Margaret Wells scrapbook #1, p. 29.

18. According to Mildred (Evans) Hall (personal communication, 2002), the falls is where the old picnics were held, on the Luckakuck not too far south of where the Yale-Westminster wagon road ran. The log across the Luckakuck that Oliver refers to in chapter 2 would have been in that area also, as the stream's banks were lower farther south.

19. Sarah would have ridden sidesaddle on her horse trips. There is another story from that time about another young Chilliwack woman, Jessie Lapum, who like many other women helped provide cash by taking eggs to market from their Sardis farm. Jessie's daughter told how one day "Her horse was startled by a pig which ran across her path. The horse reared up, spun about in the other direction and ran for a half-mile before she got it under control and turned back toward town. All this and not an egg was broken!" This story was told by Winifred Manetta Lapum (Mrs. Andrew Atcheson) and is from an article by Andrew Atcheson, "The Family History of the Lapum Family," in Oliver Wells's files.

20. Horatio Webb tells about helping in the 1880s to take the mail by sleigh as far as Silver Creek, near Hope. The trip was hazardous and the heavily loaded sleigh toppled over, dumping all the mail into the snow. From a newspaper article titled "Chilliwack Valley and Its Famous Pioneers," from Margaret Wells's scrapbook.

21. Reverend Robson was hired to be an itinerant preacher in Yale, to minister to the miners and other local people. He came via the Panama by rail, then to Victoria. Victoria's harbour was not deep enough to allow the steamer in at low tide so the younger members of the missionary families were taken ashore in a small boat. In Yale he told how he personally had to haul wood up the bank from the river and with help construct his new little church. Margaret Wells scrapbook.

22. According to farm daybooks, names of other Chinese men who worked at the farm were Sing, Willie, Kwong, Let, Sue, Foo, Tom and Wing.

23. Dan Milo later was to be of great help to Oliver as he told him of the history and language of his people. At the time he talked with Oliver he was one hundred years old and his memory was still vivid and clear. Oliver N. Wells, *The Chilliwacks and their Neighbors* (Vancouver, B.C.: Talonbooks, 1987).

24. Foo was buried in a Chinese graveyard on Little Mountain in Chilliwack. Little evidence of the burial site remains except for a plaque under one of the huge trees lining the north flank of the hillside. Chinese writing can be seen on the slab. Information from Chilliwack Museum and Archives.

25. When Allen's cows arrived from the east, one of his neighbours was quoted as saying, "They shipped the heifers and the horns all right, but they forgot the teats!" Oliver N. Wells, "Edenbank Farm, 1867–1947," unpublished typescript, April 1947.

26. W.L. Macken's speech recorded in the *Chilliwack Progress*, September 23, 1953, on the occasion of the fiftieth anniversary of the Board of Trade, spoke of promissory notes. He mentioned, "The late Isaac Kipp used to say, if you want the winter to go fast, just sign a three month note in the fall. 'I tried it lots of time and it never failed.' As long as the supply of blank forms held out we might do business with notes, usually three months."

27. According to Oliver's original manuscript, a list would probably have included the Coathams, Midgleys, Bellamys and Reids, Frank Canfield and William Atkinson (two young men who came from the east who first blistered their hands on hay forks at Edenbank), the Teskeys, Nicols, Evanses, Stevensons and Knights, Matthew Hall and his brother-in-law, William Hall, William Latta, Andrew Mennel, George Green, the Thorntons, Newbys, Higginsons and Bicknells, Maynards, Baileys, Carters, Pearsons and Irwins.

28. Oliver wrote that by their given names the natives were known as Sepass, Milo, Commodore, Harry John, August Sam, Cooper, Uslick, Big Jim, Short Charlie, Long Charlie, Sick George, Sugar Bill, Billy and Bob Hall.

29. The church building is still standing in Chilliwack, across Yale Road from the Chilliwack Museum and cenotaph towards the east.

30. The Kipp house on Wellington Avenue in Chilliwack was built in 1894 by Mr. Paisley and sold to Isaac Kipp in 1899. He retired there after subdividing most of his original farm. Information from Chilliwack Museum and Archives.

31. Sarah Reay, who lives in Northumberland, England, is the great-granddaughter of Lillie and William Townsley.

32. This Chinatown was west of Yale Road and just south of the present-day Chilliwack campus of the University College of the Fraser Valley.

33. As Fred Zink told the *Chilliwack Progress* in an interview published September 7, 1967, "Reclamation a Big Step in Area's Development": "The Zink homestead consisted of holdings of most of the David Miller and James Chadsey land." Recalling how difficult it was to clear the land he said, "It took four horses or four oxen to pull the large plows that dug 18 inches deep and 20–24 inches wide. There was much cottonwood, willow, buckbrush and hard tack. Like many other families the Zinks leased land to the Chinese workers, gave them powder to blow out the stumps and in return they were allowed to grow potatoes on the land for one or two years."

34. The building situated on the same site, on the northwest corner of Spruce Drive and Vedder Road in Sardis, is a small four-office building owned by Bill Towler of Towler Realty Company and formerly was a store run by the creamery and later by the Chambers family, the Edenbank Trading Company.

35. Allen eventually developed a herd of over one hundred purebred Ayrshires and by 1922 had the largest aggregation of Ayrshires owned by any one man in Canada with the exception of the Ness herd in Howick, Quebec. "The Late A.C. Wells" (obituary), *Canadian Ayrshire Review*, June 1922, 112.

36. Jack Priestman was sent by B.C. Electric to Chilliwack in 1910 to sign up customers for the coming service. From his diary he later recalled how difficult it often was to convince people to wire their home. An interview might get a typical response after he went over the home with the owner and consulted with "Mother." He says: "The best I could often do was – two 16 candlepower lamps, one in the kitchen and one (providing wall paper wasn't damaged) in the parlor. The bedrooms were 'out!' Who would want electric lights in the bedroom? A bedroom is a place for sleeping! Folks would say it was a waste of money to light the hallways or to install wall switches – they'd just want a light hanging from the middle of the ceiling." Quote from Priestman's diary written in 1910, first published in the B.C. Electric Bulletin. Reprinted in "Candle Was Enough in the Bedroom," Farm News, centennial issue, July/August 1971, 8.

37. Fred Bryant on Marie Weeden's request kindly wrote his memories of "knowing at least four generations of Wells" at Edenbank. These excerpts are from his unpublished work "The Wells of Edenbank Story," written in late 1989.

38. Gordon Wells died in 1972 at his own farm home in Sardis. He is now survived by his daughter Maureen's family, Randall Gay Johnson and Kelly Maureen Johnson as well as his son Allen and wife Theresa and three children, Juanita Marie, Owen Edwin and Juliana Joy.

39. The flu pandemic worldwide claimed 20 million lives, twice the number killed in World War I. In Chilliwack, Mayor J.H. Ashwell and Reeve J.A. Evans ordered the closure of schools, churches, theatres, poolrooms and public auctions for a long period of time. Coqualeetza school became a necessary emergency hospital. There were many deaths due to the flu and its complications. Information from Chilliwack Museum and Archives.

40. Gertrude's obituary from the Chilliwack Progress, 1918, from Margaret Wells's scrapbook:

> WELLS – Carman Church, Sardis deplores the loss of one of its most talented and ardent workers in the home-going of Mrs. Edwin A. Wells on Oct 1st. We all expected for her many years of service in the course of God at Sardis, but God saw it fit to remove her at the age of 47. For some months the servant of God has suffered from an incurable disease. A sorrowful husband and five sons are left to mourn her loss and cherish her memory. To all who were in trouble she was a friend, very ready to give her best and spare not herself. Many in Carman can say, "I was sick and in trouble and she visited me." The funeral services were conducted by the pastor, Reverend W.R. Welch, assisted by the Reverend J.F. Dimmick and Reverend T.E. Rowe.

41. The yoke for carrying milk pails is now in the Chilliwack Museum.

42. Angler and Hunter first published this account of Dan and Red written by Oliver Wells in March 1941.

43. In the 1980s, Dick and Marie with Brent and Kate Lister hiked to the top of Liumchen for an overnight camp-out. Brent took a photo of one of the trail blazes done by Edwin and Billy Sepass.

44. Ernest Farrow became a part of the Wells family when he married Allen's adopted daughter, Mildred. He contributed much time to the community of Chilliwack and described in written form what farming and transportation was like when he arrived at Edenbank in the late nineteenth century.

45. In later years Oliver's daughters, Marie and Betty, would help him herd the young stock from Edenbank to this hill-side pasture, heading out across Vedder Road, up School and Higginson Roads and along Chilliwack River Road. One of the girls would ride ahead to guard open gates to the gardens and entries to homes along the way.

46. Ray Wells, in a tape-recorded interview with Jim Tallman ca. 1975, said:

> If you had eight or ten men working you'd hire a cook. At one time in the summer, there used to be so many people working here that they used to ring a bell that was on top of the old root house. Everything was run according to the bell. It was a big bell. (At the present time it is donated to the church up at Cultus Lake... non-denominational church. When they built that, my dad gave them the bell, because we no longer used it here.) It used to be right over there by that maple tree, on about a forty-foot pole. And the Chinaman rung the bell... five o'clock every morning, twelve o'clock every noon, one o'clock, and five o'clock at night. At five in the morning the men would get up and go down to the barn. Cows would be in the barn or coming according to the season, and they'd do the milking and turn the cows out in the summer and come in and have breakfast. There was about two hours work done before breakfast. And then about 7:30 or 8:00 o'clock everybody would go to work in the fields. They worked till noon, come in for dinner an hour at noon. One o'clock they'd go back to work again. At five o'clock they'd come in from the field, go down to the barn and milk. Every man had around ten cows, maybe twelve. And every man milked the same cows every time. (B.C. Department of Agriculture, Film Department, Kelowna)

Jim was researching to produce a film for the B.C. Department of Agriculture on farming at the turn of the century. The completed film, called Earth of Gold, included scenes from Edenbank and the Chilliwack area.

47. Christie Harris later became a well-known Canadian author. She has related that one of her fondest memories was the horse trip she made on this occasion into Liumchen. Mrs. Harris died in early 2002.

48. John Young's sons Drew and Archie recall that there were six children at the time when their family made the journey from Scotland. Archie wrote (personal communication, 2003):

> The adventure began about June 20, 1929, when we sailed down the Clyde from Glasgow on the freighter S.S. Carmia, of the Anchor-Donaldson Line, the only civilians on the ship. Dad, our oldest brother, John, and other men hired for the trip looked after the cattle, when not overcome with seasickness. Of all the family, I, the youngest, was the only one that didn't get sick, and the crew looked after me while everyone else languished in misery. After ten days, we arrived at Quebec City, where the cattle were taken off and placed in quarantine across the river in Lévis, where they stayed for five to six weeks.... Upon completion of the quarantine, Dad and brother John with other staff set off by freight train to Vancouver, arriving in time for the PNE. The cattle [all magnificently horned] were taken off the train just below the PNE grounds, then walked up to the cattle barn, and promptly won most of the prizes at the Ayrshire show – so the story goes....
> I think that Dad's greatest joys in his work were the associations that he had with other Ayrshire breeders – the Red and White field days at Edenbank, at UBC,

at John Paton's, etc. He was president of B.C. Ayrshire Breeders for a time....

Dad was a good cattle judge and he was invited to judge at Chilliwack, Victoria, Calgary and I think Armstrong.... His preparation of cattle for exhibition was meticulous, and I have many memories of helping him with this, and teaching calves to lead with the halter, and learning how to show an animal.

49. Later Sara, in good humour, remarked that she'd taken over many of Wing's chores, such as tending the huge vegetable garden and filling the long shelves in the fruit room in the basement with bottled fruit and vegetables.

50. She told how much the friendship between the families meant to her, and how that friendship remained through the years.

51. The Progeny of Dam class is comprised of one cow's off-spring. The Get of Sire class is the offspring of a sire. These classes allowed breeders to show the success of their breeding programs.

52. On a rainy fall day in 1972, 113 copper beech and green beech trees were planted by the family and friends alongside the B.C. Electric right-of-way on the northern farm border in memory of Oliver. We chose to plant them reasonably close to each other so that as the decades passed their sturdy branches would intertwine as they have done along the rock walls in Scotland where Oliver died.

53. When Marie asked Bill McFaul about his memories of that trip in an interview in 1997, he recalled how bitterly cold it was. "But we were all right, you know. We kept fairly warm because we put a bunch of cattle in there. It was a serious job keeping those cattle in shape. The most difficult thing was to keep the cows fit from one show to another." He recalled with fondness the evening the group including Oliver were presented with canes as recognition of their contribution to the breeding of Ayrshires. On being shown the old photo of the occasion, he said with sadness, "Oh, they're all gone now, those people."

54. At the time it seemed impossible for Oliver to travel to Scotland, however, several years later, in 1970, he and Sara did fly overseas to Britain. It was a sad irony that Oliver met a tragic death in a motor vehicle accident as he travelled towards the Field of Noss to visit the Clynes in October of that year. The Clynes were wonderfully kind to Oliver's family when they heard the dreadful news of the accident.

55. The tribute stated:

His contribution to breed development has known no equal and has included a comprehensive study of the Ayrshire, both on this continent and in Great Britain. The results of his own herd improvement programme have also been beneficial to the herds of many of our number throughout the Pacific North West and the Prairie Provinces. Mr. Wells has earned an enviable reputation in the field of livestock Exhibiting and Judging, and his Edenbank herd has attained Canada-wide honours in both Exhibition and Production fields. Surely his finest contribution has been in the encouragement and help he has given to the young people of the district. Many 4-H Club members and Junior Farmers have benefited from his counsel and assistance. The educational field days and visits at Edenbank Farm will long be remembered.

Signed, on behalf of the Ayrshire Breeders of British Columbia
R.H. Robson – President
Archie Stevenson – Chairman
J.R. Paton

56. Betty remembers that when we were children if we heard the call of approaching geese we knew they were our father's.

57. How falls it, Oriole, thou hast come to fly
In tropic splendor through our northern sky?
At some glad moment was it Nature's choice
Or did some orange tulip flaked with black,
In some forgotten garden, ages back,
Yearning toward heaven until its wish was heard,
Desire unspeakably to be a bird.
– Poem found in an old Edenbank scrapbook

58. The book by Hamilton M. Laing, published in 1979 by the British Columbia Provincial Museum, was entitled *Allan Brooks, Artist-Naturalist*.

59. The painting is now owned by David Weeden, the grandson of Oliver Wells, given to him by his grandmother Sara.

60. This canoe was donated by Oliver to the Chilliwack Museum. Another canoe made by John Wallace was also donated to the museum and is now at the Seabird Island Community School, a native school, where it is on display in the main lobby. A third canoe donated by the family is on loan and is located at Xá:ytem, near Mission, B.C.

61. The *Sepass Poems* were published later under the title *Sepass Tales* and republished in early 2003 as *Sepass Poems: The Ancient Songs of Y-ail-mihth* by Longhouse Publishing, Mission, B.C.

62. Here is an excerpt from a personal letter the Weedens received from Jack Herbert after he had been commissioned by the heritage branch of the B.C. Provincial Secretary's office to report on Edenbank's historical significance:

I have been following the course of Edenbank with more interest than anything I've been involved in as a consultant. It's partly because I felt so strongly, and partly because a consultant doesn't often see his material actually put to the use it was intended. I'm keeping my fingers crossed that between the trust and Peter Woodward's enterprise (I hope he doesn't overlook a new try at Devonian) the farm will take its rightful place as one of our heritage landmarks.

References

Much of the source material for the manuscript and for annotating the text was obtained from the Wells archive that various family members retained and organized over many years. The archive is made up of scrapbooks, daybooks, diaries, building records, inventories, interviews, and many photographs containing notations of persons, events and dates. Oliver made liberal use of these records, although the source is not always mentioned in his original manuscript. The secondary sources listed here include some consulted by Oliver and additional ones that were helpful in editing and annotating the text.

Bryant, Fred. "The Wells of Edenbank Story." Unpublished paper, 1989.

"Candle Was Enough in the Bedroom." *B.C. Electric Bulletin.* Reprinted in *Farm News*, centennial issue, July/August 1971.

Carlson, Keith Thor., ed. *You Are Asked to Witness: The Stó:lō in Canada's Pacific Coast History.* Chilliwack, B.C.: Stó:lō Heritage Trust, 1997.

Chadsey, Louis L. "Chilliwack's Farms." Article of October 13, 1892, reprinted in *Chilliwack Progress*, May 13, 1981.

Chittenden, Newton H. *Travels in British Columbia.* Vancouver: Gordon Soules Book Publishers, 1984.

Cook, Donna H. "Early Settlement in the Chilliwack Valley." Department of Geography thesis, University of British Columbia, July 1979.

Cuthbertson, Shirley. "Mary Ann and Isaac – Chronology." Unpublished paper, ca. 1984.

Downs, Art. *Wagon Road North: The Story of the Cariboo Gold Rush in Historical Photos.* Quesnel, B.C.: Northwest Digest, 1961.

————. *Paddlewheels on the Frontier: The Story of British Columbia and Yukon Sternwheel Steamers.* Sidney, B.C.: Gray's Publishing, 1972.

Duff, Wilson. *The Upper Stalo Indians of the Fraser River of British Columbia.* Anthropology in British Columbia, Memoir no. 1. Victoria: British Columbia Provincial Museum, 1952.

"Early Days in Old Fort Langley." *B.C. History Quarterly* (April 1937): 71–78.

Futcher, Winnifred M., ed. *The Great North Road to the Cariboo.* Roy Wrigley Printing & Publishing, 1938.

Gibbard, John Edgar. "Early History of the Fraser Valley, 1808–1885." MA thesis, University of British Columbia, 1937.

Goodfellow, Florence. *Memories of a Pioneer Life in British Columbia: A Short History of the Agassiz Family.* Agassiz, B.C.: Kent Centennial Committee, 1933. Reprint, 1982.

Hill, Beth. *Sappers: The Royal Engineers in British Columbia.* Ganges, B.C.: Horsdal & Schubart, 1987.

Jeffcott, Percival R. *Nooksack Tales and Trails.* Ferndale, B.C., 1949.

————. *Chechaco and Sourdough.* Bellingham: Pioneer Printing, 1963.

Johnson, Richard Byron. *Very Far West Indeed: A Few Rough Experiences on the North-West Pacific Coast.* London: Low, Marston, Low & Searle, 1872. Reprint, 1985.

Laing, Hamilton M. *Allan Brooks, Artist-Naturalist.* Special publication no. 3. Victoria: British Columbia Provincial Museum, 1979.

Langman, R.C. *Poverty Pockets: A Study of the Limestone Plains of Southern Ontario.* Toronto: McClelland & Stewart, 1975.

"The Late A.C. Wells." Obituary. *Canadian Ayrshire Review*, June 1922, 112.

Lord, J.K. "Mosquitoes and Other Winged Pests." In *Zoological Notes.* Photocopied pages from Casey Wells's files. Possibly from *The Naturalist in Vancouver Island and British Columbia.* 2 vols. London: R. Bentley, 1866.

Macken, W.L. Speech. "Comparison of Early Days with Present Freedom." *Chilliwack Progress*, September 23, 1953.

McKelvie, B.A. *Fort Langley, Outpost of Empire.* Toronto: Thomas Nelson & Sons, 1957.

Nelson, Denys. *Fort Langley, 1827–1927: A Century of Settlement in the Valley of the Lower Fraser River.* Vancouver: Art, Historical and Scientific Association of Vancouver, B.C., 1927.

Ormsby, Margaret A., ed. *A Pioneer Gentlewoman in British Columbia: The Recollections of Susan Allison.* Vancouver: University of British Columbia Press, 1976.

Patriquin, H.F. "Old Timers Recall Valley's Early Days." *Chilliwack Progress*, November 13, 1937. Margaret Wells scrapbook #3, p. 50.

Rendall, Belle. *Healing Waters: History of Harrison Hot Springs and Port Douglas Area.* Hope, B.C.: Harrison Lake Historical Society, 1981. Reprint, Hope, B.C.: Canyon Press, 1981.

Ronayne, Irene., ed. *Beyond Garibaldi.* Lillooet, B.C.: Lillooet Publishing, 1971.

Sinclair, Frederick Nigel. *A History of the Sumas Drainage, Dyking, and Development District.* Chilliwack, B.C.: Chilliwack Historical Society, 1961.

Watson, James Scott, and May Elliott Hobbs. "Cattle and Cattle Breeders." Chap. 6 in *Great Farmers.* London: Faber & Faber, 1937.

Webb, Horatio. "Webb Tells of Pre-Confederation Days in Chilliwack." *Chilliwack Progress*, n.d. Margaret Wells scrapbook #1, p. 29.

Wells, Oliver Nelson. "More Birds for 1940." *Game Trails in Canada*, February–March 1940.

————. "Following B.C. Trout Streams." *Game Trails in Canada*, May 1940.

————. "The Education of Dan the Standard Bred and Red the Bronc." *Angler and Hunter*, March 1941.

————. "Edenbank Farm, 1867–1947." Unpublished typescript, April 1947.

———. *Ayrshire Cattle Breeding at Edenbank Farm, 1892–1958. B.C.'s Centennial Year.* Chilliwack, B.C.: Oliver Wells, 1958.

———. *The North Country Cheviot and Ten Years of Breeding at Edenbank.* Chilliwack, B.C.: Oliver Wells, 1960.

———. *The Ch.ihl-KWAY-uhks and their Neighbours.* Unpublished typescript, 1965.

———. *A Vocabulary of Native Words in the Halkomelem language: As Used by the Native People of the Lower Fraser Valley, B.C.* Sardis, B.C.: Clarence Casey Wells and Oliver N. Wells, 1965. 2d ed., 1969.

———. *Indian Territory, 1858.* Map of the tribal areas of the Chilliwack and neighbouring tribes. Chilliwack, B.C., 1966.

———. "The Chiloweyuck Depot." Unpublished paper read to the Chilliwack Historical Society, November 24, 1967.

———. *Early Times in the Fraser Valley: A History of the Chilliwack Area.* Chilliwack, B.C.: Chillwack Chamber of Commerce, ca. 1960.

———. *Salish Weaving, Primitive and Modern: As Practised by the Salish Indians of South West British Columbia.* Sardis, B.C.: Oliver N. Wells, April 1969. Rev. ed., December 1969. Lithographed by Frank T. Coan, Vancouver.

———. *Myths and Legends of the STAW-loh Indians of South Western British Columbia.* Vancouver: F.T. Coan, 1970.

———. *The Chilliwacks and their Neighbors.* Edited by Ralph Maud, Brent Galloway and Marie Weeden. Vancouver: Talonbooks, 1987.

Wells, Oliver Nelson, ed. *Squamish Legends,* by Chief August Jack Khatsahlano and Dominic Charlie. Vancouver: C. Chamberlain and F.T. Coan, 1966.

Wells, Ray. Interview by Jim Tallman. B.C. Department of Agriculture, Film Department, Kelowna, ca. 1975. Unpublished.

Zink, Fred. "Reclamation a Big Step in Area's Development." *Chilliwack Progress,* September 7, 1967.

Index